Marber on Markets

How to make money from charts

By Brian Marber

HARRIMAN HOUSE LTD

3A Penns Road
Petersfield
Hampshire
GU32 2EW
GREAT BRITAIN

Tel: +44 (0)1730 233870
Fax: +44 (0)1730 233880
Email: enquiries@harriman-house.com
Website: www.harriman-house.com

First published in Great Britain in 2007 by Harriman House.

Copyright © Harriman House Ltd

The right of Brian Marber to be identified as the author has been asserted
in accordance with the Copyright, Design and Patents Act 1988.

ISBN 1-905-64113-3
978-1-905641-13-0

British Library Cataloguing in Publication Data
A CIP catalogue record for this book can be obtained from the British Library.

Printed and bound by Cambridge Printing, University Printing House, Cambridge.

Designated trademarks and brands are the property of their respective owners.

Charts used with permission of CQG, Inc.

CQG, Inc. © 2006 All rights reserved worldwide
www.cqg.com

For

Patrick, Andrew, Debra,

Albie, Fred, Sidney,

&

Shushi

Acknowledgements

I am indebted to the following without whom I would never have become a technical analyst: Bill Citron, a brave speculator, who was always coming up with new ideas on how we were going to make our fortune, and who, in reply to my question "how will we do it this time?" replied, "charts", and introduced me to David Blackwell and Joe Hoare. When they showed me some, it was my epiphany.

Charles Aznavour used to sing a song with the line "I've no one to thank 'cos nobody helped me". Not entirely true in my case, and I do thank William Curran who gave me *Technical Analysis of Stock Trends*, Robert Edwards and John Magee who wrote that wonderful book, William Jiler, Seymour Friedlander, Alec Ellinger, Steve Nison; Patrick Sargeant and Richard Ensor at Euromoney, Ed Miller formerly of Amax who took a chance on me that altered my professional life, Stephen Goodman formerly of the Singer Company whose research revealed that in one year I had the best FX forecasting record in the world, Henry Hely Hutchinson and Bud Schleifer of IOS, Evelyn de Rothschild and Jacob Rothschild who brought me to NMR, David Secker Walker who sacked me from NMR without telling the Rothschilds what he was doing or why, at the BBC Eric Maschwitz who believed in me and Tom Sloane who didn't, Andrea Fryatt who typed all the letters to the Fortune 500 companies, David Cohen who wouldn't give me the salary increase I had asked for (it encouraged me to start my own business, thank goodness), and John Owen the Great Survivor.

George Goodman who inspired me, Patrick Marber who told me to write no more than 600 words a day, Geoffrey Wansell who told me that that was what Graham Greene wrote, and that if it was good enough for him it would do for me as well, also for telling me what I should be paid for my journalism, my editor Stephen Eckett for his light touch and for letting my voice come through, Jonathan Davis for bringing me to Stephen's attention, and all my clients who enabled me to make a living.

Finally, special thanks are due to the multitude of fundamentally-oriented investors whose blindness, while not helping the marketing of what I do, does help in making technical analysis work.

Contents

Charts and Figures

Foreword

In a world that often seems to worship financial markets and to be ruled by their every whim, it is surprising how little attention is paid to what the markets are actually saying. Financial pages and broadcasting airwaves are filled with clashing opinions from the market's self-styled spokesmen – pundits, analysts and rent-a-quote traders. But how often do we hear what the market is saying in its own language and words? The answer is almost never, for two reasons.

Firstly, because the market speaks its own peculiar language. It takes a skilled and experienced translator to turn this esoteric language – expressed in charts of the market's past behaviour – into something that laymen and ordinary investors understand and profitably use. This is what technical analysis is all about. The second reason why we never hear the market's true opinion on any subject is because most of the analysts who claim to interpret and analyse financial markets, are more interested in their own opinions that in what the market is trying to say.

To be able to ignore the conflicting human emotions and events which preoccupy the people who work in markets and yet to follow rigorously all the statistical nuances and tremors that help to reveal the market's real mood, requires a combination of arrogance and humility which is very rare. Brian Marber possesses precisely these qualities, in a combination perhaps unique in the financial world. He has the humility to show an absolute respect for markets, treating their movements as inviolate, objective facts. One of his proudest boasts is that he never allows his intellect to interfere with pure empirical observation: "I am a camera – I do not think, I merely observe."

Yet Marber also has the confidence, some would say arrogance, to devise precise proprietary trading rules which he applies with absolute rigour to produce clearly-defined trading signals and investment advice. These rules are designed to leave investors in no doubt about when they should be buying or selling, cutting losses or taking profits on successful trades. Marber has so much confidence in his rules and trading methods that, unlike most other analysts, he delights in the discipline of exact numbers. He offers methods for calculating exact levels for entering or exiting the markets and insists that these should be rigorously adhered to: "close wins no cigar."

Marber's paradoxical combination of self-confidence and self-effacement explains the financial success of his technical analysis over five decades. But his approach to markets has a third quality which makes him such an attractive interpreter of the market's internal language and guide to its subliminal thoughts. This quality is the sense of humour and acerbic turn of phrase which makes reading his work a delight.

For anyone prepared to take the trouble to understand and learn Brian Marber's methods, this book will offer not only opportunities for profit, but also endless fun.

Anatole Kaletsky
September 2007

The Rules of the Game

- The market will go up and down but not necessarily in that order

- When you're promised the earth; that's what you get

- Advice given for nothing is worth what you pay for it[1]

- Received Wisdom: by the time you receive it, it's too late

- My word is my bond[2]

"All economic movements by their very nature are motivated by crowd psychology. Without due recognition of crowd thinking (which often seems crowd-madness) our theories of economics leave much to be desired. It is a force wholly impalpable – perhaps little amenable to analysis and less to guidance – and yet, knowledge of it is necessary to right judgements on passing events.

Have you ever seen, in some wood, on a sunny quiet day, a cloud of flying midges – thousands of them – hovering, apparently motionless in a sunbeam? Well, did you ever see the whole flight – each mite apparently preserving it's distance from all others – suddenly move, say three feet, to one side or the other? Well, what made them do that? A breeze? I said a quiet day. But try to recall – did you ever see them move directly back again in the same unison? Well, what made them do that?

Great human mass movements are slower of inception but much more effective…The Mississippi and South Sea Bubbles; the Tulip Craze; and the Florida Boom and the 1929 market-madness in America and it's consequences in 1930 and 1931 – all these are phenomena of mass-action and impulsions and controls which no science has explored. They have power unexpectedly to affect any static condition or so-called normal trend. For that reason, they have place in the considerations of thoughtful students of world economic conditions".

Bernard Baruch's Foreword to the 1932 edition of *Extraordinary Popular Delusions and the Madness of Crowds* by Charles Mackay.

---

[1] I just gave that advice for nothing. (On the other hand, you did pay for the book.)

[2] Take the bond.

The game of professional investment is intolerably boring and over-exacting to anyone who is entirely exempt from the gambling instinct; whilst he who has it must pay to this propensity the appropriate toll.

J.M.Keynes

"Game, game! Why did the Master say Game? He could have said business or profession or occupation or what have you. What is a Game? It is "sport, play, frolic, or fun"; "a scheme or art employed in the pursuit of an objective or purpose"; "a contest, conducted according to set rules, for amusement or recreation or winning a stake". Does that sound like Owning a Share of American Industry? Participating in the Long-Term Growth of the American Economy? No, but it sounds like the stock market".

"The Money Game" by George Goodman, aka Adam Smith

There are fundamentals in the market place, but the unexplored area is emotion. All the charts and breadth indicators and technical palaver are the statistician's attempts to describe an emotional state.

Edward Johnson III

We are concerned not with what an investment is really worth but with what the market will value it at under the influence of mass psychology. It is, so to speak, a game of snap, of old maid, of musical chairs, a pastime in which he is victor who says snap neither too soon nor too late, who passes the old maid to his neighbour before the game is over, who secures a chair for himself when the music stops.

JM Keynes

Anyone taken as an individual is tolerably sensible and reasonable. As a member of a crowd, he at once becomes a blockhead.

Friedrich Schiller

There is no opinion, however absurd, which men will not readily embrace as soon as they can be brought to the conviction that it is generally adopted.

Arthur Schopenhauer

The crowd is always wrong

Anon

Preface

I wrote this book because the publishers asked me to.

If they had wanted me to write only about the rules and principles of technical analysis, I would have had no interest in doing so; it's no fun, there's no money in it and it's all been done before. But what Stephen Eckett, my editor, wanted was what I had wanted to do ever since reading George Goodman's superb book *The Money Game* (written under the pseudonym Adam Smith).

What was that? To write about what I do, in a language readers could understand, telling them why I do what I do, and how I came to do it, including market pitfalls and Marber pratfalls. Although when you make money you can learn something about making it, you learn far more by losing it, then finding out how to stop doing so.

This book tells you my methods; when positions have gone wrong, and what you do about it. It makes only passing reference to techniques and indicators I don't use: if I don't use something, it might be because it doesn't work, because I never heard of it (which I doubt), or even because of intellectual or emotional bias.

It's for my clients to say whether I am any good at what I do. But what I can say is that I do have a great deal of experience: fifty-one years in the business gives me that – and I'm not finished yet.

I have read very few books on technical analysis, but those I have read never told the reader when and how a technical signal goes wrong. This book does. In the early days I used to think that the chart would always be right. It wasn't, nor was this author.

Too many long-term investments start life as short-term trades that have gone wrong: in those days I didn't know what a stop was. If the chart, or the reader of the chart, were always right, there would be no need for stops, nor any books.

Technical analysis is about running profits and, by using technically-oriented stops, cutting losses, not when it hurts but, when, from a technical point-of-view, the position you're in becomes untenable.

It was a Rothschild who said that tops and bottoms were for fools. I say, "and for liars". Technical analysis is exactly like huntin', shootin', and fishin': we're hunting for trends, never shooting for a top nor fishing for a bottom. But I am getting ahead of myself. You can't learn about any of that until you have learned about price. At one time I was on the visiting faculty of International Management Institute, Geneva, the oldest business school in Europe. I always began lectures with price, then what price led to: trends, support and resistance, patterns, indicators and ratios. When that had been absorbed, I talked about stops.

This book follows that pattern. It also adds, after indicators, a chapter on candlestick analysis (I hadn't even heard about candlesticks until the 1990s).

What about pitfalls, pratfalls and the experience I've gained in the past fifty-one years? In the middle of the book you'll find the chapter "By the way", and at the end, another called "I remember".

But before "I remember" I show you the nitty-gritty: technical analysis in real time, warts and all, including reports on FTSE, gold, oil and the dollar.

Introduction

During fifty-one years of hard labour since 1955, I have worked for, in or with, fourteen companies: eight were stockbrokers, two were publishers (this book makes that three, and the total, fifteen), two broadcasters; one investment management institution and a foreign exchange consultancy.

One of the broadcasters was Bloomberg, the investment news network. Having been engaged as a market commentator because of my expertise as communicator and technical analyst, my first and last assignment was to comment live on the likely effect on markets of the total eclipse taking place that day.

There was absolutely no effect on markets which, as usual, went up and down, but not necessarily in that order. Accordingly, when asked about my thoughts on the eclipse, I signed off, "It's been so dark, I couldn't see a thing".

I am not a media-clown: I told Bloomberg to remove the free screen they'd installed in my house (it was extremely user-unfriendly anyway), resigning myself to reducing my income by resigning from Bloomberg broadcasting.

CNBC and my lack of experience

About five years ago I replied to a CNBC advertisement for a job as TV broadcaster and commentator on the technical condition of gold, oil, FX and stock markets. At the time, I had been doing this for approximately 39 years (43 now).

For several years I had been on the visiting faculty of IMI, Geneva, teaching technical analysis to many leading executives including the chief investment officer of General Motors (the company became my client), and Bill Sharpe (Nobel prize winner and professor of economics at Stanford).

I also taught my stuff to the Ministry of Finance in Singapore, and to Reuters when they were thinking of launching their technical service several years earlier; as well as writing technical commentaries on FX markets for Euromoney for fourteen years.

Having also been a BBC TV producer, I had the temerity to think that I might be just what CNBC would be looking for. I was wrong, of course; they were looking for someone with more experience.

The trouble with financial broadcasting is that the TV companies aren't really interested in whether their guests get it right or wrong, nor in how well they express themselves; their shtick is nothing more than filling up the time-spaces between adverts (did anyone say newspapers?).

Five of the companies that paid me were known simply by their initials; BBC, IOS, NMR, SKB and BM & Co. I never did very well with initials.

I couldn't be sacked from BM & Co, however, because BM stood for Brian Marber. But with no BM in BBC or NMR (NM Rothschild & Sons, Ltd.), I was less fortunate; the reason for sacking me being the same in both, "no room on the establishment"; NMR and the BBC were the Establishment; as for SKB (one of the remaining seven stockbrokers with which, man and boy, I had been associated), I resigned my partnership because there was no room for that establishment in mine.

IOS

That leaves just one more initials-only establishment, IOS. Not only was IOS no part of any establishment, it was also the most notorious outfit I ever became involved with. Established by Bernie Cornfeld, it initially sold investment plans to members of the U.S. Armed Forces in Germany and France after the war (for my generation, that always means WWII).

After a time, a very profitable one, Bernie Cornfeld decided he would like a piece of the action; the investment management fees action, that is. The trouble was that Bernie had no investment managers of his own. Not one to be daunted by detail, however, he went out and hired some gunslingers.

A gunslinger, or hired gun, Bernie-style, was an investment manager (they weren't known as fund managers then), usually working for an eminently respectable institution. Instead of shooting slugs, the chosen few were given a slug of money to manage by IOS, while remaining with whatever old-established house employing them.

Bernie got his piece of the action because he was then selling not other people's funds but IOS's. And the gunslingers got their piece of the action because they were remunerated according to their performance in the market.

So what? I hear you saying. There's nothing out of the ordinary about being paid according to your investment performance. There isn't now, but there was in the 1960s. In those dear dead days people used to say, "if Schroders or Flemings, Hambros or Rothschild can't make money for me in the market, no one can".

Well, Bernie changed all that: he, and or his colleagues at IOS, invented competitive fund management. But that's not all they invented. They also introduced the fund of funds, and got roundly criticised for doing so. Criticised? There were many who wanted to have Bernie jailed for his impudence in taking two management fees for the price of managing only one fund.

Bernie was jailed, eventually, in Switzerland – not for the fund of funds but for giving bad investment advice. If they jailed everyone in the City for giving bad investment advice, there'd be hardly anyone left; not in the City, anyway.

I had got to IOS by going, initially, to one of their seminars addressed by Henry Buhl III. Buhl I or was it II, I never knew which, had apparently sold Fisher Car Bodies to General Motors; the family was the largest private shareholder.

Buhl III told us at the seminar that his father, Buhl Jr, tended to have the family fortune invested by people with whom he had been to prep school, who wore the same tie, had been elected to the same sorority, went to the same racquet club, dated the same girlfriends etc.

Henry III didn't think very much of this as an investment strategy, and that is why and how performance comparisons began. Henry III asked: why not give the money equally to several managers, monitor their investment performance on a regular basis, throw out the bad performers and give the remaining piece of their funds to the best performing managers, while also bringing in new ones?

It was my epiphany: I had never been so excited in my life, at least, not with my clothes on. Just think of it: no need to have been to Eton; no need to be at Cazenove, Rowe Pitman, de Zoete & Bevan or Sebag; no need to hunt, fish, shoot; game or crap, no need to talk it either!

All you needed was to become a professional; to show *performance* – a word I'd previously heard only in connection with motors and showbiz. www.anker@investbiz.co.uk; here I come, I thought, or would have, but the internet hadn't yet been invented.

Technical analysis had been though, and at the time (1966) I was trying, and still am, to become a chartist. I wrote letters to Geneva (HQ of The League of Nations, Red Cross, ILO and IOS), saying that, given the chance, I could perform, and would do it for them.

That got me a meeting with IOS's London broker, GS Herbert. They certainly weren't herberts; indeed, Henry Hely-Hutchinson, the partner who saw me, was a gent. He wouldn't give me a fund however (IOS didn't give money under management to brokers – they were too shrewd for that).

But I was inspired that day and suggested they give me a dummy fund to run (I would be a dummy gunslinger; no real slugs of money). They did, and although only a tyro technical analyst then, I was soon running IOS's best-performing UK fund (were the other investment managers all dummies or merely fundamental analysts?). Naturally, I went in to see Henry ("triple H", as he became known), and Arthur Lipper III, aka Artur Lipper the t*rd, and demanded some real money. All three said no.

I then wrote more letters to Geneva, telling them that they had inspired me with their revelations about performance; that they should be true to themselves; that although I hadn't been to Eton, Magdalen or even Magdalene, I was nevertheless a performer and that they needed me more than I needed them.

I eventually received a reply, telling me to appear at their London offices, a grand house in Mayfair.

Unlike today, when you can't stop tripping over the doorsteps of a hegemony of hedge fund managers' Mayfair offices, in those days investment institutions didn't hang their brass plates on the doors of grand private houses in that particular area.

If they were Scots, their plates were mostly on the doors of even grander houses, designed by John Adam, in Edinburgh's Charlotte Square. If they were English, the brass plates were on the doors of houses in the Square Mile; equally grand, of course, and filled with people as square as the mile they worked in.

At their lunches the plates weren't brass but silver. And the lunches were very grand, too; Sybaritic, I daresay – hearsay, of course, for at that time I had never been invited to any of them. I had to wait until I joined NM Rothschild to get my feet under those particular, very particular, tables. But although I didn't know it at the time, nor ever dreamed it possible, I wasn't going to have to wait very long.

Wearing my very best suit and a discreet tie, I arrived at the IOS grand Mayfair pad for my meeting with Bud Schleifer, IOS's man in London. Judging from the complete absence of receptionists, secretaries and a cup of tea, Bud (as I soon got to call him) was their only man in London.

"You've been writing rude letters to Geneva, and they don't like it," was his opening thrust. "They deserve it," I replied.

"What do you think of Rank Organisation?" said Bud (Rank, owner of Xerox' UK rights, was a go-go-GO stock at the time).

Not knowing anything about Rank's fundamentals, or indeed any fundamentals about anything, nor ever having looked at the chart, I knew absolutely nothing about Rank. But since when has knowing nothing about a subject ever stopped a broker in his prime? And, at 33, I was in mine.

Never lost for words, indeed, I'd be lost without them, I started waffling. After all, I hadn't been a stand-up comedian for nothing (nor for very much either, but that's another story). Bud soon stopped me. "Do you buy, sell or hold?" he barked.

What a star! I had been in the City eleven years, yet that was the first real lesson about investing I'd ever had.

Soon afterwards I walked out of the meeting, new six-gun in holster and a slug of IOS money under my belt: I'd become an IOS gunslinger. I had often walked down that street before, but the street had always stayed beneath my feet before. Not that day, though. *All at once was I, seven storeys high.*

The high went on. So did my performance, and just over two years later I traded in my IOS six-shooter for a sheriff's badge at NMR, becoming the best-paid (I didn't say the best) investment manager in London.

NM Rothschild

No one at NMR, including Evelyn de Rothschild and his cousin Jacob (now Sir and Lord respectively) who jointly hired me, had the faintest idea what a chartist was or did. But they knew my track record and had checked me out with Leonard Wolfson (now Lord, of Marylebone, not Sunningdale), a golf partner, who told them he'd never done business with me, but from the way I behaved on the golf course, clearly I was straight.

The building that housed the bank was superb. But there were no signs on the doors to mark the lavatories and so, being too embarrassed to ask, for the first fortnight. I used the public toilets at Bank Station.

The food in the lunch room was magnificent; you could see your face in the shine on the apples. The meetings were interminable; the meetings to discuss the agenda for the next one would have been even more interminable if that were possible.

I managed several unit trusts, the house dealing company, and some charities. At a board meeting of one of the unit trusts, which had performed well that quarter, when asked to review the portfolio I said that everything I had bought had been bought because I thought it was undervalued, everything I had sold had been sold because I thought it was overvalued, and everything in the portfolio was there that day, irrespective of the prices I had paid, because I thought it should be there then.

I ended, "time will tell how many, if any, of those decisions are correct. Does anyone want to ask any questions?" There weren't any, of course. What a nonsense reviewing portfolios is.

If the directors or trustees don't like the performance of the managers, what they should do is sack them, not interfere with what they are doing. The board is no more competent to manage investments than fund managers are to interfere in the management of companies in which they have invested; wrongly, of course, otherwise they wouldn't feel they had to interfere.

I know about Higgs of course. I also know that anyone who owns even one share in any company is a part-owner. But how does making what turns out to be a bad investment decision qualify the holder to tell the company's management how to run the company? The owner's sanction is to sell the shares, not pontificate to management.

A reorganisation of the investment department at NMR put a new man in charge. Except in new issues, he had never been in the investment business at all. He instituted a menu, a list of sectors we were allowed to buy, including the permitted percentage holding, to two decimal places. When asked what we were to do if our 4.35% in chemicals, say, rose so that it constituted 4.92% of the portfolio, he answered that we must sell sufficient shares to get back in line with the menu.

That's how I became the highest paid bank clerk in the world.

The sectors were picked by analysts with one or two years experience who had impressed the head of the department with the intellectual validity of their arguments. The net effect: we, the senior managers were dictated to by junior analysts. The investment meetings became a joke. Full of intellectual rigour, and apparently held in the belief that our ruminations would somehow communicate themselves to the market, which would then do what the intellectuals thought it should do.

At one particular meeting, I suggested that we should raise liquidity because the then market level appeared unsustainable. The debate went on for most of the morning; eventually it was decided that we should raise liquidity by 10%. I couldn't wait. But before I could get out of the door and start selling, the chairman added a rider: "we'll give everyone three months to raise cash". Dear, oh dear. The market fell 10% in three weeks.

The new business meetings were the most bizarre of all. Because the chairman set great store by the correct placement of possible new clients on the prospective business spread-sheet. there were interminable discussions on whether this or that contact should be placed in the "excellent", "highly likely", "quite likely", "likely", "unlikely", or not "very likely" column. Does it matter? The only good prospect is the one that has already signed up.

"Placement" was also of great importance when lunching guests, as was the correct way to eat an apple – all of it, hand-to-mouth, with only the stalk left on the plate – and, horror of horrors, god preserve the one who took the nose off the brie. Still, I did learn that the correct way to eat fish is with two forks.

I did like working for the family however, a feeling not shared by many of my colleagues who, not long after I joined, became directors when the bank was incorporated: they resented and spoke disparagingly of "the proprietors", not appearing to understand that they wouldn't even be employed if there had been enough members of the family for the job.

I went to NMR with the fantasy that one day I might become a partner of the Rothschilds. Evelyn, who hadn't been told I'd been sacked, said to me when I went to say goodbye, "I hope it's been a good experience". I replied, "I didn't come here for an experience; I came here for a career."

Writing reports

I did have an experience, but not a good one. Rothschild was a good place to have worked, but not a pleasant one to work in.

Why am I still working? I like writing technical reports, I like trying to get the market right, I like amusing people.

When I started writing regularly in 1973, fresh out of Rothschild where I had been on the receiving end of boring reports from stockbrokers, most of which went straight into the waste-paper basket, unread, I decided reports should be eye-catching: coloured paper (analyses were invariably printed on white), with a joke at the top.

There were three series, "The City's Great Truths", "Great Lies of the City" and "The Thoughts of Chairman Mao Ber" – anything to get them read.

The first great truth was "the new ball game is the oldest ball game in the world", the first great lie, "some of my best friends are brokers", and the first thought of chairman Mao Ber, "man who always put money where mouth is often put foot in it as well".

When I started writing in 1973, I did so out of dire necessity. I was a partner in a Birmingham stockbroker's, running the London office, provincial brokers having just been allowed to open offices in the City. My role was to be largely ceremonial.

To celebrate, in 1972 I had bought a large house, a largish swimming-pool, and had an even larger mortgage. For the first few months without even knowing who he was, I lived Riley's life for him. Then I went on holiday, and while I was away the world changed.

The 1972-74 bear market

Interest rates went up from 5% to 9%, and the Labour government announced that mortgages in excess of £25,000 would no longer be eligible for tax-relief, although in respect of existing ones, you had six years to do something about reducing them to this still very large figure. I know £25,000 is a small sum now, but it was a large one then.

The stock market fell apart. So did the housing market; the interest on my £50,000 mortgage went from the negotiated 9% to 12%, which I had to pay for 25 years. Within six months the house that I'd bought for £95,000 had halved in value (it took eight years to return to the price I'd paid for it), the expression "negative equity", non-existent until then, was born.

Brokers' earnings fell even faster than the stock market; many went broke. My ceremonial role disappeared, as did my income, so I started trying to interest institutional clients in my work, over the telephone. Then it occurred to me that I could reach more clients more quickly if I wrote regular technical reports. I started doing so, but they didn't include charts because, to begin with, there was no way of drawing them.

There was no e-mail, so I was also delivery-boy; delivering by hand was faster than the GPO (it still is).

1972/1974 was a classic bear market: a technical analyst would have to have been seriously stupid not to get it right. By contrast, fundamental analysts couldn't understand it, but then, they seldom can, so they couldn't avoid getting it wrong, constantly looking for value instead of cash.

As prices fall, the extent to which they can and do so is almost invariably under-estimated by fundamentalists: in a long bear market – and 1972-74 was one – with the All-Share Index falling 74%, the good went down with the bad, and many babies got washed out with the bath-water.

The 1972-74 bear market made my reputation. Naturally, when I called its end on 8th January 1975, I wasn't believed – a former Rothschild colleague remarking "Brian Marber always was mad". The index tripled in three months.

In 1979, having discovered technicians were the only analysts who had any sort of decent track record in the foreign exchange market, I became an FX consultant and left the stock exchange, which I'd never liked anyway. But I continued writing about stock markets. I wasn't listened to in bull markets – that's when everyone knows what he's doing – but got my message across, as usual, in bear markets.

Why, if I am so clever and experienced.....and so old, am I still in the business?

Because writing about markets, which started as a way of making a living, has become a hobby. I far prefer staring at an on-line screen in the warm to staring at an off-line putt in the cold. As long as my technical analysis handicap is lower than my golf handicap, I'll carry on carrying on. And maybe I'll achieve my ambition: to become an A.D.O.M.: an Angry, Dirty Old Man.

September 2007

Prologue

From the Book of Sisylana

Source: ©Chatline

The first lesson

In the beginning there was price. Many there were that witnessed it, and marvelled, as at the burning-bush. Yet knew not what they saw, for darkness was over all the market-place. And Reuter said, let there be light: and there was light. And the evening and the morning were the first day.

And there arose in the east a great multitude, come to see price. And they journeyed long, from far and wide. In that deep mid-winter, snow lay round about, deep and crisp and even; even unto evening.

Nick the shepherd blew his nail yet still he watched his flock by night. "God rest ye, merry, gentlemen", cried some old fool. Though the frost was cruel, yet brightly shone the screen that night, and on the morrow, for that matter; despite or perchance because of it, and what with the papers and news items, tips and calls from brokers (oy vey, were there calls from brokers!), there was much casting by swine before pearl, Rachel and Rebecca, too. Verily, did confusion rule in the market place.

And there were some among that multitude that thought that price was good; and these few, these happy few, did buy price; and it did rise; and others there were that saw that price had risen; and they did think that must be good; and they bought price; and when price did not rise as fast as they did hope it might, some there were who washed their hands of it; went on their way and when they did see a poor man, passed by on the other side.

Many, having lost their chips, went mad or hungry. And many there were who thought they had partaken of their last supper.

But some there were who arose, and girding their loins, told wondrous and wondrously untrue tales to others; brought good news from Ghent even unto Aix; yea, publishing it in Gath; and lo and behold, after three days price did rise; as if from the dead; yet still was there confusion over all the earth. And the evening and the morning were the second day.

And there arose profits and false prophets, and pundits and experts and CNBC and BBC and Bloomberg; some, so young they did not know their fork from their forecasting; and much casting of fake pearls by swine there was; and many widows that lost their mites and young virgins that lost other things; yet still did not know what they saw nor whether they would be respected on the morrow. And the evening and the morning were the third day.

Then came others, even from across the seas, and many were the rogues and some were vagabonds, selling bonds; and some there were that were wise men; and many there were that weren't, and some of them were bankers; and there were many fools and many who were fooled by bankers; and many of them were wise men but not necessarily bankers and some that were students from the ell-ess-ee, yea even of the tribe of e-con-o-mists, wise as the ancients in foretelling the past, and pontificators, every one: so all was chaos. And the evening and the morning were the fourth day.

Yet some there were that did think that price was not good and, in due course, after they had sold of course, they did tell it unto others (as you do) that they had sold; yet some there were that said "rubbish" and these did buy the fall; and there arose a great cry, "once more unto the breech", and many there were that lost their breeches; the brokers went broke, the rich became poor; and whether they were bankers or bakers, they did do their dough and having naught with which to buy loaves and fishes withal, did without; wine, even when made out of water, was out too.

There was much wailing and gnashing of teeth; in Gomorrah, town of many women, a lot turned into salt: Sodom; some lost their fortune, others their marbles, and some there were that did unto others what they wouldn't like others to do unto them; there was no forgiveness, not even for those who knew not what they did, especially for those who knew not what they did; for the market doth never forgive; though many are its prisoners, none are taken. And the evening and the morning were the fifth day.

And there came forth a scribe; a man that wrote, a man that could draw; a wise man; a clever man. Not a blind man, he could see very well. Even so, he could not read, not a balance sheet, anyway. He couldn't see why it always balanced. But price he could see. Oh lord, could he see price!

Sojourning, as he did, in a southern-facing tower with no windows, but with thick walls, he neither heard nor needed to close his eyes to the wailing and gnashing of teeth, to the tower of Babel babbling. To all the unseemly goings-on of that great multitude he paid no heed, for when he saw price, he knew what it was doing and what he ought to do about it.

And on each of those five days when he saw price, he marked what he had seen on a palimpsest, and behold and lo, low and high he held a chart. And the evening and the morning were the sixth day.

And on the seventh, whereas there were some that rested, others did not. And the scribe was numbered amongst those who did not rest: for the wicked there is no rest, nor for the chartist.

The scribe read the chart; thought long and hard about it; wrote short and straight about it, then went out into the world to spread the good news thereof.

Many there were who heard, but few there were who listened. But the scribe cared not for he had discovered peace and order where heretofore there had been only chaos and confusion. And many jeered; they knew not the tree of knowledge, nor had they eaten of its fruit: for the scales were before their eyes and they knew not how to find tree or knowledge; they didn't even give a fig-leaf for it.

They just could not see how mere mechanistic extrapolations of the past into the future, as they called them, could possibly be the path to salvation. But he knew that they could, because whereas the old ways relied on theory, theory is theory because it hasn't been or can't be proved. His way, relying on that good old, old-fashioned empirical observation, did.

Yea, did he know that whereas the old way was the triumph of hope over expectation, yet his way was the opposite: the triumph of experience over hope, and that it was better to travel hopelessly than to arrive. And so he went on his way, merrily. And the evening and the morning were the seventh day.

HERE ENDETH THE FIRST LESSON

Glossary

Who ever heard of a glossary at the beginning of a book? That's all right; who ever heard of a book like this, a book about technical analysis that makes sense? At least I hope it will, which is why I am starting with a sort of glossary, glossing over what you don't need to know, to be sure, while letting you know where I'm coming from and what is going to go on before I start going on about it.

The alternative would be like reading Proust or seeing Tom Stoppard's plays: you get to the end without having the faintest idea what's been going on, the only pleasure, the realisation that you'll never have to do it again.

Some of the entries are quite long, but far too short to merit a chapter, some, short but merit inclusion. Others appear again, in one way or another, in other parts of the book.

A

Advance/Decline

The advance/decline line is an indicator that helps assess the strength of an index.

Unlike most equity indices, which are weighted by the market capitalisation of the constituents, the advance/decline line is not, the share with the smallest capitalisation counting equally with the one with the largest. If the A/D line consisted of just two shares, and the smaller went up while the larger went down, the A/D line would remain unchanged: it is the number of advancing issues minus the declining ones that cause the line to advance or decline.

Obviously, if an index is rising and the net total of advances minus declines is doing the same; that is good news because there is then no negative divergence by the latter. The bad news is if the index is rising but the advance/decline line is falling, or not largely mirroring the index's advance.

If so, weak features in the index only become apparent if you look at the A/D line. In other words, the A/D line is an indicator, helping you to understand something about price you wouldn't see if you only looked at price, in this case represented by the index.

What I have described is the cumulative A/D line. There is a variation: instead of adding each day's net advances and declines, it can also be calculated over whatever time-period you think useful – any number from 10 to 100, say – and whatever the chosen period, the oldest number is discarded when the newest is added.

I sometimes look at the weekly A/D line, counting the net weekly total over a 13 week period, watching for large net pluralities. For example, a plurality of 13/0, 12/1 or 11/2 (advances to declines, or the opposite), reveals that the index against which it has been plotted is overbought or oversold.

On Wall Street, if you see a day when 80% of shares fall, you are looking at a market bottom.

I am going to leave the A/D line there, without going into any other variations of the theme for one very simple reason: I don't use the A/D line on its own in any of its guises, not because I don't care if an index is overbought or oversold but because I believe that the other methods I use to assess the conditions are more effective: the A/D line is a second filter, for me, anyway.

B

Back-jobbing

Saying or thinking, "if only I'd done that then, I'd have been this, now". Don't do it; it's a waste of time and very distressing.

Bear market

The interval between two bull markets; it lasts from the high of the preceding bull market to the low on the eve of its successor. For most of the bear market the one year average is falling, but not in the first few months. After the bear market has grounded however, the average keeps falling for the first few months of the succeeding bull.

Beating the Dow

If you want to do that, read the eponymous book by Michael O'Higgins. It's a revelation. The only way you might improve on his extremely successful method is to refine it by using monthly charts.

Brokers

Old brokers never die, they just get fewer calls.

Bottoms

Many years ago, but it was during the 20th century, I wrote a letter to the Financial Times that used the word bottom (in a market context). A sub-editor wrote to tell me off, saying that the newspaper didn't use that sort of language.

It is often said that panic bottoms never hold, i.e. that if the market rallies sharply from a low occasioned by panic selling, sooner or later that low will give way. If anyone ever says that to you, say "rubbish", and remind the expert that after the great crash of 1929-32, the U.S. market turned on a dime – even though many had to borrow one to get into it.

That was no exception. One of the best calls I have made so far was on 8th January 1975. It was also one of my worst. My headline on the London market, "The bear market is over but the bull market hasn't begun" was nonsense: whenever a bear market ends, a bull market begins. My argument was that after a 74% decline the market would need time to recover its nerve, and that while it did so, the low, posted on 13th December 1974, would be tested, frequently.

I was wrong: I'd correctly called the end of the bear market, but not the beginning of the bull market that was to follow. The All-Share Index trebled in three months. My excuse is that I was comparatively inexperienced then: I'd only been in the business eighteen years.

I have since learned that the larger the fall, especially if it has lasted a long time as well, the larger, and swifter the rise that follows.

Bull market

The interval between two bear markets; it lasts from the low of the preceding bear market to the high on the eve of its successor. For most of the bull market the one year average is rising, but not in the first few months. After the bull market has peaked however, the average keeps rising for the first few months of the succeeding bear.

My late partner, Bill Citron, who taught me a great deal about markets, used to say that it took three bull and three bear markets to learn what the business is all about. In your first bull market, he said, you make a lot of money, then lose all of it, and more, in the ensuing bear market. In the second bull market, you make less, the compensation being that you lose less in the succeeding bear market. In the third cycle, you make money in the bull market and hardly lose at all in the bear. Then you're ready.

These days, who's there for three cycles?

Bull trap/bear trap

The chart "says" buy (sell in the case of a bear trap) and almost immediately the signal fails: Technical analysis is an art, not a science. Tough, but true. (see C for charting).

C

Cable

What people in the business call £/$. Most people, that is. I had been in the business for several years before I knew this: I was at a client meeting with Marine Midland, an American bank, and the dealers were all talking about cable; I had to ask them what they were talking about. There was universal derision.

I got my own back. I told the scoffers that they might know the name but needed me to tell them cable's direction. Marine Midland has disappeared; I haven't. Marine Midland didn't disappear as a consequence of my bad advice. After a couple of years they stopped taking it. After a couple of more years they ceased; taken over, I think.

Why cable? In olden days if you wanted to deal in it, you went to a little office at the back of the Royal Exchange and sent the appropriate cable to New York.

Call

When a commentator says buy, sell or hold, he is making a call.

Cassandra

Apollo endowed her with the gift of prophesy, but when she refused his advances, Apollo decreed that no one would believe her. Sometimes I feel technical analysis is like that.

Chart

It's a crossword puzzle, a jig-saw, a mosaic.

Charting

Charting's tough and then you're wrong, according to the old saw. Sore is what you are when it's you that got the chart wrong. But the chart is never wrong: yet chartists often are, including this one. When marketing my services (marketing being an up-market word for selling), the one thing I guarantee is that I'm not always right: if I were, the fees would be prohibitive.

Closing

The closing level, also called the *close* is the last price of a trading session; day, week, month or year etc.

The word is also used to describe the "closing" of an "open" position (the latter being when you move from no position, i.e. you're out of the market, to having one, i.e. you are open). If you close, you are either selling a long position opened earlier or buying back a short one. In either case, by closing it you are going square or flat. You then have no exposure to the market.

Correlations

They are a fundamental concept and therefore have no place in technical analysis. If correlations really worked, there would be no need for technical analysis at all. What do I mean by "really"? "All the time" will do nicely.

One of the most reliable correlations is gold and $: throughout the 1980s, with the exception of one period of six months, when gold went up dollar went down, and vice versa.

The correlation has persisted. Since 1970, gold and dollar have gone in opposite directions 86% of the time. But if you try buying dollar every time gold's PM fix is lower than its predecessor, and taking your profit as soon as a PM fix is higher than its predecessor, there is unlikely to be any profit to take.

Gold and Oil: this correlation works sometimes. Everything works sometimes. But here is the paradox: how many times has something got to work before you start using it, and once you are doing so, how many times has it got to fail before you stop.

Copper: if you want to buy shares in a copper mine because the chart looks attractive, shouldn't you see if the chart of the metal is equally so? It may seem logical; indeed, it is logical, but there's a problem: it doesn't work, except as an inverse correlation.

In 1970, when I was an investment manager, now called a fund manager, at N.M. Rothschild, the chart of Messina was superb. I bought the shares. Then it occurred to me that this might not be considered *haute banque*, so I plotted the chart of copper against the chart of Messina. A horrific picture emerged. There was no way that anyone in his right mind could buy copper after looking at that chart.

Then I realised that I wasn't buying copper; I was buying a copper mine. A little more research soon revealed that the time to buy copper shares was invariably when the chart of copper was a disaster area, i.e. when the warehouses were full of the stuff. The time to sell copper shares was invariably when there was a shortage of the metal. I held on to the shares in Messina until the pattern that had inspired me to make the purchase had reached its objective.

What was copper doing then? Going up. What happened to Messina's shares? They fell.

Cover

If you have bought something or sold short, and you decide to sell your open long position or, in the case of a short position, buy it back, you are covering it. Isn't that the same as closing an open position? Yes, but in foreign exchange markets, covering is the word that's used.

Crowd

In technical lore, the crowd is always wrong.

D

Dealer

Also known as a trader: someone who does nothing but trade intraday. How many times have you met a rich one?

Dealers' remorse

When a short-term pull-back (reversal) in price occurs, frequently but not always, within days of price breaking out from a range or after confirmation of a pattern, it is known as dealers' remorse. If it occurs, price often returns to the breakout or confirmation-point.

When the Singer Company was analysing technical analysts' calls, i.e. their forecasts, in the late 1970s and early 1980s, they found that there was no point in trying to beat the technicians, but if instead of dealing as soon as they received the advice, they waited three days before opening or closing a position, it usually paid them to do so.

Dealers' remorse should not be confused with a false breakout (see F).

Dow

Until 1984, when a group of Japanese technical analysts attended the annual Market Technicians Association annual seminar, Charles Dow, founder and first editor of the Wall

Street Journal, had been credited, together with Edward Jones, as the founder/discoverer of technical analysis.

How Charles Dow "discovered" what is now known worldwide as *technical analysis* is explained in Chapter Two, which deals with price.

In Chapter Seven you will be introduced to Japanese technical analysis, two hundred years older than that "discovered" by Dow & Jones. Yes, it is that Dow and that Jones.

E

Economists

They can tell you everything about the past, but nothing correct about the future. If all the economists in the UK were lined up, head-to-toe, in a line from the Humber to the Wash, many would be underwater, doing nothing to alleviate pollution. But, who knows, it might do wonders for economic forecasting. Economic forecasting? An oxymoron.

Eighty

80%: on Wall Street (and maybe in London too, though I've never checked it) if 80% of shares are down on the day, you've seen the low, at least for the time being.

Elliott

Ralph Elliott was the Poseidon of the Elliott Wave, which is far less fun than the Mexican Wave: no arm-waving. But the Elliott Wave has its disciples, a tsunami of them and, tsunami-like, the unfortunate habit of putting those caught up in it in deep water. Elliott Wave? I advise you to waive it.

Based not only on the Fibonacci series of numbers (see F) but also on the laws of nature, it is far too precise for practical use, although, like economics, it is great for forecasting the past.

Typical example of Elliott Wave thinking-

Many years ago an Elliotician intoned that gold, $320 at the time, would remain in a bear market unless it rose above $500. Having made his *ex-cathedra* prophesy, the priest withdrew in cathedra. He didn't withdraw what he had prophesised however, to the detriment of believers.

The rationale of what he had prophesised derived from the high priest (Elliott) in his teachings on the wave. The Wave Principle, all ten commandments, made any other outcome for gold not only impossible but inconceivable. Obviously the sub-text was that it wasn't going up, and since what doesn't go up usually goes down, gold was probably going to do so.

Having heeded the prophet's prophesy (what else can you heed from a prophet), his followers knew how to profit from it. They certainly mustn't buy gold, but they could sell short; many of the faithful did. And were the poorer for it.

The Elliott Waver, like Tony Blair, is a straight kind of guy, and for these freaks, as is the way with zealots, there is only one way; The Way. Once the Wave has appeared on the beach, it must be obeyed; all must follow, subject to the alternate count, of course. The alternate count (not a count who only appears on alternate weeks) is the If-it-doesn't-do-this-it-will-do-that Syndrome. But this time there was no alternate count.

This time was December 1985 and gold had risen approximately 13% since February 1985's $287.50 low. It was no longer in a bear market at the time, at least, not according to my definition. On the contrary, it was in an already confirmed bull market (see B for bull market).

Chart 0-1: Gold 1985-1988

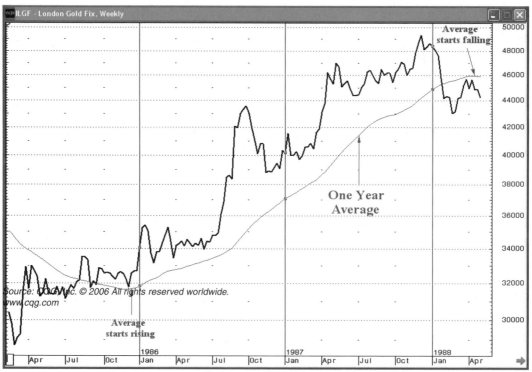

Despite the Wave's pronouncement, and in the face of his acolyte's wailings: "bear market unless $500 is posted," gold did go to $500. True, it took its time, but bull markets do take their time, climbing a wall of worry all the way to the top. Only then do people stop worrying and start extrapolating (see E for extrapolation).

How long did it take gold to get to the top that time?

Almost exactly two years from December 1985, nearly three from the bull market's first day in February that year.

Of course, it was only a bull market as far as your scribe was concerned, together with all other technical analysts, and many who weren't but nevertheless came along for the ride. As for the Elliotticians (not technical analysts, not in my book, anyway), they stayed short or stood aside as the foolish bulls charged on: after all, it was nothing more than a rally in a bear market (see B for bear market).

For goodness' sake, Elliotticians, get a life! And get a chart; a proper one with no 12345s and abcs all over it; a chartist's chart; not an Elliott-rendition of an algebra text-book.

The chart shows gold peaking below $500, but this time, atypically, the chart doesn't show all. The reason the chart doesn't show all is because it is a chart of the PM fix, my criterion for gold: the PM fix was the nearest you could get to know the day's closing level (see C for closing level) when I first started looking at gold's chart in 1969 (see G for Gold or R for Received Wisdom).

But on the morning of 14th December 1987 old yellow fixed at $502.75, allowing it to go into a bull market, at least according to the Wave. Now for the denouement: after that $502.75 AM fix, what you see on the chart is the $493.50 PM fix. Some turn around, eh? You ain't heard nothin' yet! Not only was that a turn around for the day; it was also a turn around for the whole bull market. Those who ride trends got rich; Elliott Wavers got knotted.

At the precise moment the followers were finally in a position to call a bull market in accordance with Elliott Wave principles, technicians saw the end of theirs. The $502.75 AM fix on 14th December 1987 was not seen again until……wait for it………21st November 2005. That is not a misprint.

Everyone is wrong from time to time, but do me a favour. *The technician's job is not to call the market names but its direction.* In 1985 gold's direction was up; it stayed up for another two years, while the followers of the Elliott Wave were denied a place on the golden calf's platform until 1987. They got in then, of course, just as melt-down started. My followers wouldn't be so accommodating if I made mistakes like that, nor would I expect them to be.

Of course, there were bull markets between 1987 and 2006, but only two. The first was 1993-96's (peak: $414.50); the second, 1999-2006's. Most participants are convinced that the latter is still on, going to the moon, or if not, at least to $900. But I have not been a bull since June 2006. That bull market is long past its sell by date.

Although a truism, any day that any price moves one tick off the high might be the birth of the mother of all bear markets. You don't know it at the time, of course. No bear market has yet been confirmed, but breaking my own rules, I called one in June, and may be about to be punished for that hubris (March 2007).

Elliott Wave is all very well, but only if you're waving goodbye.

Experts

The function of an expert is not to be right but, when wrong, to have intellectually sound (fundamental?) reasons for being so.

Extrapolation

A condition that bulls are prone to whenever a trend has been going on for some time. Strange to say, although they ought to be immune, some technical analysts also succumb to it, driven mad by the demented ranting of those already infected, who cannot stop shouting "it's going to the moon". In different circumstances, a related illness affects bears who feel impelled to groan endlessly, "it's the end of capitalism as we know it".

The way to avoid this plague is explained in Chapter Two on trends. The trend is your friend, and no trend ends until the fat lady has not only finished singing but also left the building. Fortunately, having never been infected, and know what steps should be taken to stay healthy and thereby remain wealthy: you need iron. Iron resolve, that is, and a sense of perspective.

F

False

A false breakout occurs when price breaks out of a range or confirms a pattern, giving the signal to act. No sooner have you acted than the technical reason for opening or closing the position goes wrong. "False breakout" is the technician's way of saying that either he or the chart is wrong.

Fibonacci

Leonardo Fibonacci was a thirteenth century mathematician who devised, or discovered, a sequence of numbers, where each is the sum of its two predecessors. The first is 0; the second, 1, the third is 1 (0+1), then comes 2 (1+1), 3 (1+2); then 5 (2+3). 8, 13, 21, 34, 55, 89 and 144 follow, ad infinitum.

How does it help you to know this? I don't know. No, that's not true. I know how it's meant to help you, but it's never helped me. On the contrary, on the odd occasions that I have the feeling that perhaps I ought to use the sequence, trying an 89 or 144 day average, I lie down until the feeling passes; I realise I'm having a bout of elliottitis.

Followers of the Elliott Wave love the Fibonacci series however. They have to because it's the basis of their discipline. For them, the Fibonacci series provides the secret of the universe. It doesn't do it for me. If it works for you however, be my guest.

G

Game, set and match

Do you like eating snails? Of course not. Have you ever eaten one? No, but what's that got to do with it? How do doctors make diagnoses and prognoses? By their experience of the past, I suppose. Isn't that what technical analysts do? Yes. What then is the difference between the doctors' approach and technicians'? Nothing. Is medicine a load of nonsense? Only if you hate technical analysis. Why don't technicians always get it right? Why don't fundamentalists? Q.E.D.

Gann

W.D.Gann. Some players go for Gann's theories and writings, mainly followers of the Elliott Wave q.v. I don't. Going, going, gann.

Gold

There was no gold trading on the US or UK commodity markets in the old days (before the collapse of the Bretton Woods Agreement as far as the UK is concerned, 1975 for Americans). There was one very simple reason: neither US nor UK citizens were allowed to own it. But while the Bretton Woods Agreement was in force, the US Government was obliged to buy all the gold offered to it at $35.00 per ounce.

Received Wisdom had it that the only thing keeping gold up at that level (I did say up, and I meant up) was "the gold window" (the US Government's undertaking to give $35.00 to any poor sap who wanted to sell this out-dated non-commodity as the economists of the time called it).

You already know what I think about Received Wisdom, at least if you read the first few pages of this book, and it was certainly far too early to start skipping then. But just in case you did skip or don't remember, I don't think much about received wisdom because by the time you receive it, it's too late.

It was certainly too late to receive the wisdom that the only thing keeping gold up at $35.00 an ounce in 1969 was the Bretton Woods Agreement: unfortunately, as proved to be the case, it was wrong, by 100%. As soon as the gold window was closed, gold took off. You can bet your bottom $ on it, and your ounce of gold sold, to the US Government for $35.00 (the bottom) when it was open.

Never mind. Mr. Brown sold half of our gold at the bottom in 1999, his American opposite number having made a comparable booboo by not buying gold at $35.00 an ounce in 1970. Why? Because when Bretton Woods broke down, gold didn't fall at all. It went up, and up, and up.........and by the end of 1974 was $200. Received Wisdom strikes again!

And it has repeated the trick more recently. Once the received wisdom merchants had thought they'd gotten away with their stupidity at the bottom, they did the same at or near the top. In 1974, received wisdom had it that when the US administration's ban on their citizens holding gold (due to end at the beginning of January 1975) came into effect, that would be the signal for a further massive increase in its price.

The yellow metal, more than five times higher than it had been in 1970, was going to rocket, ("going to the moon" is invariably the cry in mature bull markets), as soon as Comex started trading gold.

That's not right, of course; Comex trades futures, i.e. paper, not gold. Trading started at the beginning of January 1975, the four year old bull market ending simultaneously. By August 1976 gold had nearly halved. On the way down from end 1974's $195.50 an ounce, gold experts and analysts were bullish to a man, still believing the near 48% fall was a healthy pull-back in a continuing bull market.

But on August 16th 1976, when gold had been falling for 20 months, a Reuters' tape message announced their capitulation:

> *"Senior gold analysts now believe that it will continue to trade between $110 and $90 for the rest of year".*

$112.90 on 16th August, gold had fallen to $102.20 by 30th. That was to be the bear market low. By mid-November it had risen to $139.20 on the way up to an eventual $900.00 at the morning fix on 21st January 1980.

Apart from the first few weeks of the 1976-80 bull market, when it was climbing away from the predicted $110.00-$90.00, the nearest gold has been to $102.20 since August 1976 was at the end of the 1999 bear market, when the lowest fix was $253.00; so much for the considered opinions of experts and senior gold analysts. And it wouldn't be any different if you dropped "gold" from that sentence.

H

Head & Shoulders

You're going to read much more about this in Chapter Four. It is one of the major reversal patterns in technical analysis, also one of the major continuation patterns. Reversal means that the trend in force is reversed when a H/S (head & shoulders) top or bottom has been confirmed, continuation that it resumes when a H/S continuation has been confirmed.

If you are not a technician, and are feeling confused, don't fret: this is only a glossary, explanations come later.

The expression head & shoulders pattern attracts much derision from the ignorant. I've never seen why. When the doctor says you've got flu, you might know what he means, just as you might know what it means when you're told that your big end's gone, but I don't.

I

Indicators

There is a large number of indicators but no group collective noun starting with "I". How about one of these?

> Indigestion, indictment, indulgence, indiscipline,
>
> infestation, indecision, indisposition, inducement

All indicators work some of the time; none of them work all of the time.

J

Janeway

Elliott Janeway: The Prophet of Doom, as he was known. But he wasn't all gloom, and anyone who, when asked "will the market go up or down next year?" replies, "Yes, but not immediately", deserves his place in the hall of fame.

January

The January Rule states that the Dow's direction during the first week of January dictates its direction for the year. If the first week shows an advance, the year ends higher than the previous year.

A second but related rule states that if 31st January's close is higher than the previous year's December close, the close at the end of December will also be higher than at the end of its predecessor.

In the period since December 1944, provided the first week has been up, the odds that the market will also be up on the year are 2/7: if you're not a betting person, that's 7/2 on. If the month has been up, the odds shorten further; 2/11 (11/2 on).

If the first week and the whole of January are both up, the odds of an up-year shorten still further, to 1/6 (6/1 on). I didn't take any expert's word for this; wading through the data myself.

In January 2007 the Dow rose, implying it will end the year above 31st December 2006's close.

Despite these overwhelmingly favourable odds, in this business there are no certainties. Just as well; *pace* Winston Churchill, the potential for loss when gambling on certainties is infinite.

K

Kondratieff

Nikolai Kondratieff discovered a 54-year cycle of economic activity. It didn't find favour with the government of the U.S.S.R apparently, and there are rumours that he was exiled to Siberia.

The last time the cycle was due for a low was in the 1980s; but it got a puncture, failing to appear. If you are a kondratieffnik, provided your career starts soon after a cycle has ended, you will have the good fortune to be retired before the next one is due. You wouldn't be so lucky with Schumpeter however. Another keen cyclist, his cycle was shorter, only 25 years, with mini-cycles, each lasting five years.

> *Kondratieff, Schumpeter and Tandem rode cycles up mountains, down vales.*
> *The first two fell off*
> *in a cyclical trough;*
> *Tandem's, though shorter, prevails.*

L

Long

You go long when, having had no position at all, you buy.

Long run

AKA the long-term, in which, *pace* Keynes, we are all dead. That doesn't mean that the long-term should be ignored, ever. But the long-term never gets to have its day until the short-term's had its say. And if the latter says it loud enough, the long-term's day may not dawn as originally expected.

Lows

As in *New Lows*. Every day, getting the data from the Financial Times, I record on a spreadsheet the number of shares making new lows, and then look at a 10-day average of them on a chart I had to have created.

This indicator is able to spot bear market and other significant lows about one week after they appear.

In September 2001, for example, after the sell-off that followed the terrorist attack on the Twin Towers, FTSE grounded on 21st: the indicator gave a signal at the close of the next trading day.

FTSE made a new low on 24th July 2002: on 25th, the indicator signalled again.

FTSE's last bear market ended on 24th September 2002. The "buy" signal appeared six days later.

The problem with this indicator, for a commentator, is that when it signals, those paying to receive advice find it difficult to accept (see C for Cassandra). I wrote "difficult"? Impossible is the word.

What about new highs signalling the onset of a bear market? That's not how bear markets start. On the contrary, there comes a stage in a bull market when the index keeps making new highs but the peaks in shares making new highs tend to become progressively lower. The same applies at intermediate peaks.

M

Market

The market has no eyes and no ears so it can't see or hear what the experts are saying it ought to do. Having no heart either, it couldn't care less. What the market does have is an extremely eloquent mouth: when the oracle speaks, listen. It always pays to accept what the market says about itself. Never tell the market what to do: do what it tells you to do.

The market is never too high, never too low, except with hindsight. Most people, technicians apart, think markets are cerebral and logical; they're not, they're psychological.

Instead of being just a judge, if the late Lord Denning had been a judge of markets, his *obiter dicta* would have been, "be you ever so high, the market is above you". The market knows far more than any one who is looking at it.

The market was devised to separate the men from the boys and the boys from their money.

Mind

If not prepared to change your mind in this business, be prepared to change your business.

N

Nikkei and Topix

Charles Dow required that movements in the Dow Jones Industrial and Rail Indices confirm each other. I require that these two Japanese indices must do the same.

O

Overbought

The expression doesn't necessarily have anything to do with volume of transactions, but everything to do with inequality between buying and selling pressure.

Overbought means the market has come up too much, too soon. What does "too soon" mean? That depends on the time period of the indicator you're using. In commodity and foreign exchange markets, bonds and equities, indeed everywhere, time periods vary from minutes (seconds, even, but I advise you not to go there) to years.

"Too much"? If the indicator you're using works, when it reaches levels that, in the past, have coincided with reactions in price, price has risen too much, i.e. it is overbought.

Oversold

A price or market is oversold when price has fallen too much, too soon.

P

Paradigm

As in New Paradigm. There comes a stage in every bull market when most participants are extrapolating the trend. Try being bearish, or merely cautious and you find you are fighting "new paradigm" thinking, when "We are experiencing a new paradigm where permanently higher prices are going to be the norm" or similar rubbish, is being spouted by experts (see E for Expert).

The new paradigm is the oldest ball-game in the world.

The new paradigm is less in evidence in the depths of a mature bear market, but the thinking isn't: watch for headlines like "the end of capitalism as we know it", "only the chartists are bullish", or "pension funds are switching substantial percentages of their portfolios from equities to gilts". And look at the number of shares making new lows (see L).

Physics

Technical analysis is a minor branch of physics, being concerned with actions and reactions.

Potential

The glossary excepted, in this book the word will only appear as the *obbligato* to resistance and support, because like charts, resistance and support levels aren't cut into stone, so you never know if either is going to appear. Accordingly, many years ago I devised an indicator to deal with the problem, and as far as I know, no one else has done quite what I have, although the world having gone on for some time, it does seems unlikely that I have discovered anything new, though I might have.

Profit

The word is defined in the OED as the reward for risk-taking (see S for speculation).

Psychological levels

So-called psychological levels, beloved of the media, hardly exist apart from 1.0000 and 2.0000 in FX; 100 and 1000 (but not 10000) in stock markets.

In March 2006 I heard a great deal of nonsense in market news and on financial TV programmes about the psychological importance of FTSE going through 6000. It hadn't even done so, at least not significantly, even though it did so subsequently. But the event was and is without any technical significance, otherwise, once that level had been overcome, it would have stopped FTSE falling beneath it on the return journey.

Surveys carried out in the foreign exchange market reveal that 1.0000 and 2.0000 are psychological barriers, but obviously not permanent ones, otherwise exchange rates would never manage to cross them from either side, except temporarily.

What about 100 and 1000? Both *are* psychological levels: after first hitting 100, and many years later, after hitting 1000, the Dow Jones Industrial Average took seventeen years to overcome these obstacles.

10000? The Nikkei and Hang Seng Indices had little trouble in overcoming that so-called resistance. What's more, once it had been overcome, 10000 was no support when these indices decided it was time to fall beneath it again.

That being so, when the Dow Jones first reached 10000 in 1999, despite the ease with which the Nikkei and Hang Seng Indices had vaulted this particular hurdle several years earlier, the media, bless it, was full of stories about this being the top.

I was one of Bloomberg's favourite commentators then. Accordingly, in the hope and expectation that I would endorse the received wisdom that the Dow couldn't/wouldn't get through, the producer trotted me out. He even gave me a canter in the middle of the trading-day, so that I could be there to make some comment when it finally crossed the line, which it did that day, several times, in both directions.

Closing levels are what matter when support or resistance levels (q.v.) are being considered, and even though I kept on saying this during the broadcast, it fell on deaf ears.

As for my repeated observations about having observed the Nikkei and Hang Seng successfully ignoring the so-called psychological resistance at 10000, and the conclusions to be drawn thereby with regard to the Dow Jones' imminent arrival at it, they didn't want to know.......the noise of the swine in the studio crunching their hooves on my pearls made all informed comment inaudible.

The most notorious example of the myth and mystique surrounding round numbers occurred towards the end of the 10th century. Aided by prophesies and predictions that the world would come to an end on December 31st 999 (it will never be able to go through 1000, don't you know?), the property market was in a terrible state: why build churches when there was going to be no one to worship in them?

On the other hand, the travel business was booming: everyone wanted to get to Jerusalem to see the end of the world, little realising that it would be ending simultaneously in Hertford, Hereford and Hampshire.

How stupid, crass and ignorant they were in the olden days; it couldn't happen now, of course. Or could it? Of course it could; and did. What's more, I predicted it.

Not having been around in the 990s, and not possessing any confidence in most people's ability to learn from experience, but having read Charles Mackay's *Extraordinary Popular Delusions and the Madness of Crowds*, Nostramarbus went around in the 1990s telling anyone who would listen, very few did, that as the millennium approached, nonsense similar to that which had haunted the populace in the 990s would be promulgated.

Did all the computers go from 1999 to 1000, or was it 0000 that they were going to go to? Did everyone's bank balance become zero? Did aeroplanes fall out of the sky, power stations shut down, prime ministers sanction the building of a vast empty space on marshland and fill it with tat?

Only the last, dear reader, only the last. Meanwhile, like travel agencies in the 990s, in the 1990s computer manufacturers had a ball. The only thing man learns from history is that man learns nothing from history, unless, of course, he happens to be a chartist.

PS: The world didn't end on 31st December 999; had it done, it wouldn't have been around to end on 31st December 1999, but you already knew that, and the world didn't end on 31st December 1999, anyway.

What you may not know however is that the early years of the 11th century brought bad times for travel agents but boom-time for property developers: there was a great deal of repair-work to be done on old churches, and those years came to be known as the era of white churches, so many new ones being built to make up for the shortfall during the late years of the 10th century.

Q

Quantitative (as in quantitative analysis)

Don't be fooled: it is technical analysis under a PR-inspired name. It sounds respectable, even posh, and is practised by fundamental analysts when what they are really doing is technical analysis, although they just can't bring themselves to admit it.

R

Received wisdom

Received, it is; wisdom, it isn't. By the time you receive it, it's too late to act. Received wisdom is nothing more than the collegiate judgment of a crowd of experts (see C, also E).

Rules

This book isn't only about rules; the last thing technical analysis needs is yet another book about rules; the last thing I need is to write a book about them. This book is concerned with the rules I use. It's also about why I use some, discard others; about the rules *chez moi*; the ones I've made up, and how and why I came to do so.

S

Shares

To the perpetual amazement of non-technicians, shares frequently lead a life that is almost totally independent of the fortunes of the companies they supposedly represent.

Short

If speculating on a fall, selling or going short means to sell a share, bond, currency etc that you don't own in the expectation of buying it back again at a lower price.

Selling short was considered beyond the pale when I was first in the business, while selling bank shares short was illegal. The theory behind the legislation was that if bank shares suffered significant declines, there might be a run on the banks.

Speculation

Defined in the OED as making an investment with the aim of making a profit, but which carries the risk of loss.

Stops

When you have opened a position, stop is the name given to the level at which you sell. It could be a stop-profit or a stop-loss. The stop is such an important concept that it merits its bold type and its own chapter – which it gets. Although that chapter is certainly the shortest in this book, don't under estimate its relevance.

Support

The level/s where a decline might stop and an advance begin (see Chapter Three). Apart from in this glossary, the word never appears in this book without the adjective "potential" preceding it.

Synchronicity

There are times when the current behaviour of price will imitate price of the same market at an earlier period. Such synchronicity can take place over a period of weeks, months or even years. Synchronicity can also occur when the shape of the chart of one price, say €/$ for example, imitates the behaviour of €/£ several months earlier.

None of this is as strange as it may appear; as you will read in Chapter Two it was Charles Dow's discovery that the shape of Sears, Roebuck's chart might look like Bethlehem Steel's from time to time that started technical analysis in the western hemisphere.

The phenomenon of synchronicity is rather more than a bizarre coincidence: the chart of the earlier period can and does serve as a template for how the chart of the current period might develop.

Chart 0-2: Dow Jones Industrial Average (1924 to 1930)

Source: CQG, Inc. © 2006 All rights reserved worldwide.
www.cqg.com

The chart above is the Dow Jones Industrial Average between 1924 and 1930, the one opposite the same index between 1982 and 1988.

Chart 0-3: Dow Jones Industrial Average (1982 to 1988)

In late 1986, provided you had spotted the similarity since 1982 to the behaviour between 1924 and 1928, you knew what was going to happen in 1929, even to the month (October). As long as the later period continued to imitate the earlier one, you had a template for the future. It did so until April 1988. But the Dow then began to diverge from 1930's behaviour: the game was over; the template had to be torn up. I did so, calling a bull market, but no one believed the call.

At the time, the received wisdom was that 1929-32, the period of the Great Crash, was happening again; that the fall in the market and the contraction in the economy would last until 1990.

The then Chancellor of the Exchequer expanded the money supply (that's what was done in 1929 and after), but this time, from the moment the charts started diverging, the economy did the same, diverging from 1930-32's. The result: the inflation of the early 1990s.

T

Technical Analysis

It's a set of disciplines: you're either for or against them, and it's no good changing your mind in the middle. Everyone who's ever done even the most basic work thinks he's a bit of a chartist. There's no such thing.

Technical analysis is a religion

It must be practised regularly; daily, to be precise, weekends included: there is no Sabbath for chartists; only Mr Market gets any rest at weekends.

The true believer feels that if he sticks with the commandments (he does get to choose which ones: my name's Marber, not Moses, and charts are "written" on palimpsests not tablets of stone), he will be rewarded. When he isn't, he feels let down: his beliefs are challenged, he may cease to believe at all. Many don't stay the course. I won't labour the analogy; I'm sure you've got the picture by now.

But to be a technician, you must believe that provided you stick to the principles, the decision to act will be made for you. Therein lies the discipline: you don't think; you interpret. Thinking is what causes the biggest losses in this business.

Time periods

The periods I use are the ones I use: I do so because they work; for me, that is. For example, I use 21 days (a trading month). I also use 63 trading days (a three month trading period). There is nothing magical about either.

Substituting anything between 14 and 25 days would probably give a similar result to my 21; 55-65 days could substitute for 63. But in the rate-of-change (ROC) the most useful time period is around 63 days. Use anything longer and the indicator doesn't do what it needs to do: indicate the direction of price.

In the rate-of-change, using 21 days is another waste of time. Several years ago I explained the ROC to a particularly arrogant hedge fund manager, explaining why 21 days was less effective than 63 days. He wasn't listening. Because of that, he uses 21 days.

The reason why 21 days is a waste of time is simple. Ten days after a low, provided price has advanced enough, on a 10-day basis it might be overbought (overbought and oversold will be explained in due course). But it is likely to be lower than it was 21 days ago, therefore, on a 21-day basis, it might still be oversold at that time period.

And if price advances for 21 days, it might become overbought at that time period, while remaining oversold at the 63 day period.

None of this would matter, of course, if it weren't the frequent tendency of price to move in trends lasting approximately three months (approximately, not precisely).

My long average is one year, 252 days in some markets, London for example, and anything between 253 and 261 days in others, depending on the number of dealing days in the year in the market concerned.

Using time periods of less than 15 days, say, is largely a waste of time, although I have recently started looking at the 9-day Relative Strength Indicator and at 5-day stochastics, but only as second filters: so far, I am impressed by what I see.

Tops

In the section on bottoms, I wrote that the faster the fall, the faster the rise: bear markets frequently end with a V. Bull markets behave differently: it usually takes time, sometimes as much as several months, for a top to be formed.

Trader

Calling someone a "trader" is about as insulting as you can get. I have already asked the question, how many times have you met a rich dealer? (which is what traders used to be called). Dealer/trader, they're the same. By rich, I mean one who (a) works for and by himself; not for a rich institution; (b) who makes profits, keeping most of them rather than frequently going broke.

U

Up trend

You are going to read quite a lot about up trends, but not here.

> *When in a major advance,*
> *You're still led a merry old dance*
> *If that trend's in no hurry,*
> *You'll climb walls of worry,*
> *But must give the up trend a chance*

V

V bottom

The market goes straight down with no rally; it then goes straight up again. The reason, especially if the downside reaction occurs after an extended decline, as in a bear market, say, is that the sellers are exhausted and when the buyers appear there is a vacuum that has to be filled.

Volume

Volume doesn't matter as far as I'm concerned, and my concerns or lack of them is what this book is concerned with.

W

W

Another name for a double bottom.

When

When you make money, you also got lucky. When you lose it, it's your own fault.

Whipping-boy

The market is the whipping-boy of industrialists and politicians. Both are happy to lavish praise when the market's rising, since "it is clearly reflecting the well-justified faith of investors in the soundness of the economy", they have nothing but scorn whenever it falls.

The cry then is: "Why is the market falling? It isn't reflecting the true state of the economy". Of course it isn't; the market is neither mirror nor thermometer; it's a barometer.

Whipsaw

Acting on a buy (or sell) signal that doesn't carry the market very far, and is followed by a sell (or buy) signal. You take your loss on the first trade, initiate the second one, take the loss on that one, and then the whole process happens again, and again and………..etc.

X

Marks the spot.

Y

Why go into the investment business? It's indoor work and no heavy lifting.

Z

Zantac

The *obbligato* to being involved in markets (it's a drug for people with ulcers).

Zig-zag

It is loved by Elliott Wavers, therefore not for serious discussion.

1

Price and Chart

Oscar Wilde defined the cynic as a man who knows the price of everything and the value of nothing. So is a chartist. That makes the man who knows the value of everything and the price of nothing a fundamental analyst.

Who would you prefer to look after your investments?

My first pick for the job would be a really first class stock-picker; not any old fundamental analyst, and certainly not a young one. And I said stock-picker; not necessarily the same thing as a fundamental analyst; a good stock-picker is a totally different animal.

Old fundamental analysts never die, they say, they just make fewer calls. Young ones? Investment genius is a short memory and a rising market, whereas investment intelligence is gained only through a long memory of falling markets.

If fundamental analysis really were the name of the game, all practitioners would be multi-millionaires, and technical analysis would never have become the force it is.

If you really are a gifted stock-picker, and there are few of them, you may feel you do not need to learn the rules that follow. Nevertheless, you really ought to know them, as well as the glossary, and certainly the Chapters "By the way" and "I Remember".

Although you can have price without a chart, and a chart without price (a pie-chart), in a book about technical analysis you can't have one without the other. At least, you can't in this book. So this chapter is about chart as well as price.

Below is a chart of price.

Chart 1-1: FTSE100 Index (2003-2006)

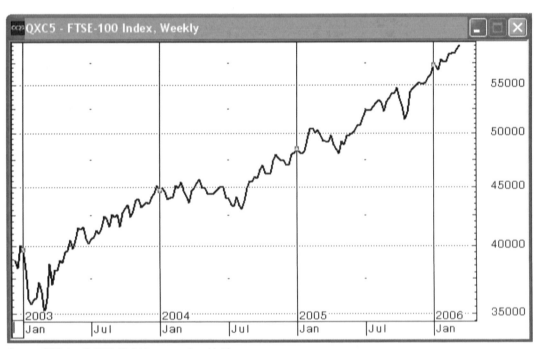

Source: CQG, Inc. © 2006 All rights reserved worldwide.
www.cqg.com

What is the first thing you do before deciding whether to buy or sell?

No cigar if your answer is: look at the price.

That's what everybody does.

What next?

Unless you are already a technical analyst, you then have a look at the fundamentals you consider relevant not only to the share itself but also to the company it represents: the relationship to it's sector, the index, economic conditions in general, domestic and international, interest rates both current and future, the outlook for foreign exchange rates, etc, etc, etc, *ad nauseam.*

Finally, having made your decision, what is the last thing you do before giving your order?

Look at the price.

Once again, no cigar!

Since you start by looking at price and finish by looking at price, just like everybody else, isn't it possible that price itself contains the sum of all existing fundamentals as well as the consensus of all perceptions about the future? Possible? There's no argument about it.

> **NOTE**   Price contains everything you need to know about everything.

A chart is the daily, weekly, monthly, yearly (or intraday if you must, but I wouldn't) record of price, and reading what it says is what technical analysis is all about. A chart is nothing more than a constantly updated record of investors' recognition of the fundamentals and their willingness to try and discount the future.

Price, and therefore the chart of price, contains in its movements not only all the facts but also all the fantasies, plus hopes, greed and fear. When you look at a chart of price what you see is a graphic representation of a psychological state; you are not looking at real value because there is no such thing. It isn't real value that drives markets up and down but people's perception of future value.

Faced with the same information, one person says buy; meanwhile, another probably says sell.

Price is the balance between supply and demand. Stock and bond markets, foreign exchange markets even more so, are the nearest approximation in real life to the classical economists' definition of the "Perfect Market", a place where buyers and sellers can meet freely;

where price is determined purely in accordance with the Law of Supply and Demand: if there are more buyers than sellers, price goes up; more sellers than buyers it falls.[3]

How do I know? Because, when I was at university, I read economics and law. I also got a degree in economics and law. Correction: I hold an honours degree in economics and law. Correction: I hold an honours degree in economics and law from the University of Cambridge. Sounds impressive, doesn't it? But since in economics I was grade II and in law, grade III, there were no honours in either.

And if "third class honours degree" isn't the finest example of oxymoron since "economic intelligence", what is? Fundamental analyst.

NOTE	Price is the most important technical indicator, not only because of its obedience to the law of supply and demand but also because it contains the sum of all knowledge about any market you're looking at.

In April 2006, stock markets had been rising since 2002-03 for two reasons. The first reason was there had been more buyers than sellers. The second reason? That *was* the second reason.

The reason why there are more buyers than sellers is irrelevant, except when forecasting the past. Do that, you're an economist. Paradoxically, forecasting the past is up-market but if you are forecasting the future, that's down-market, especially if forecasting a down-market.

NOTE	When forecasting the future, all you need do is recognise that there is about to be an inequality in supply and demand.

On the one hand I'm writing like an economist, on the other, like a chartist. And on the third hand, as we economists are won't to say....on the third hand?

"There are two types of economist; those who don't know and those who don't know they don't know."

JM Galbraith

---

[3] Being an economist I do know that there can never be more buyers than sellers, and that only inequality between buying pressure and selling pressure, or some such nonsense, moves price.

The first tenet of Dow Theory, which was the first technical study outside Japan, is that price and indices discount everything, except acts of God. Reflecting the influence that market pundits' media-expressed views exert, plus the market actions of thousands of investors, amateur and professional, day traders and long-term holders, technicians and fundamentalists, the clever and the stupid, the well-informed and ignorant, both individual share prices and indices know everything that can be known.

But how can they possibly cope with the unknown, with what's unknowable? Even unpredictable calamities, natural or otherwise, are quickly appraised and soon absorbed into market consciousness, their possible effect on future price movements being discounted almost immediately.

A prime example occurred on 11th September 2001. Wall Street closed for a week but, like the Windmill Theatre, in London we never closed. FTSE did fall heavily on 11th, but seven further sessions passed before that day's close was broken. Two days later however, the index made a low that was to hold for another nine months.

What about Wall Street? It had been closed on 11th, the received wisdom being that markets were about to fall apart. The trouble with received wisdom however is that by the time you receive it, it's usually too late. When Wall Street opened again on 17th September, the market did fall, and continued falling for four more days. But that's all, folks! Like London, Wall Street hit ground zero on 21st.

Didn't investors care about the tragedy? Yes, but the market didn't because as soon as the news broke, every potential buyer and seller started taking into account what further terrorist atrocities might follow, and the new situation was soon factored in.

When reading economics at Cambridge in 1952, in addition to learning the law of supply and demand, there was something else that stuck in my mind: the law of diminishing returns. George Malthus observed that successive applications of equal amounts of fertiliser to a plot of land yielded an increasing crop at a diminishing rate until the nth[4] application. Then, while the fertiliser still enabled that plot to produce a larger crop, it sold at no more than the cost of the fertiliser applied to produce it.

What's all this got to do with price? Everything. The law of diminishing returns applying just as well as it does to land: keep feeding the market the same piece of news, or crap, and after the nth time it reacts in the opposite way to the first.

---

[4] Don't ask me why economists use letters, not numbers; I was absent from the first algebra lesson, and since then have never been able to understand the subject. I know $(a+b)^2$ is $a^2+2ab+b^2$, but why, and why, in any case, are the numbers in lower case when in geometry they're in upper case...?

Why do people buy shares? Because they think prices are going to rise. And why do people sell? Because they think they're going to fall. No one ever buys because they think prices are going to fall; nor sells because they think they're going to rise. Accordingly, to forecast markets, you need to know what people think. Not what they ought to think – but what they are actually thinking.

The best way to do that is by looking at a chart of price, showing as it does not only the balance between supply and demand but also all knowledge, hope and expectation about indices, individual issues, the economy, politics, FX, interest rates and whatever else may be motivating investors and traders. By investors and traders, I mean people.

What people think, they do in the market, buying, selling, or writing about it. And what they do affects price, and that affects other people's thinking.

You and I go racing. We back a 100/1 outsider down to 2/1; we tell the jockey that he is now the favourite. We also tell the horse. Does that affect how the race is run? No way, but the shortened odds certainly affect the way other punters think, and maybe how they bet.

The stock market works the same way: buying enough shares to move the price dramatically doesn't affect the company at all, but certainly affects the attitude of other market-players, whether investors, traders, or commentators.

Perhaps you are now thinking, suppose he's right about price, but does that make reading the chart worthwhile? Of course it does. Price is what people are thinking, now, about the future. Price yesterday was what they were thinking about the future yesterday, price the day before yesterday what they were thinking about price the day before yesterday etc.....etc.

As a child, I remember "pictures" consisting of dots, numbered, apparently, at random: you could see them yet couldn't understand a thing. But if you joined the numbered dots up, 2 to 1, 3 to 2 etc, eventually you got the complete picture. Price charts go one better. Look at the one overleaf.

Chart 1-2: Brent crude

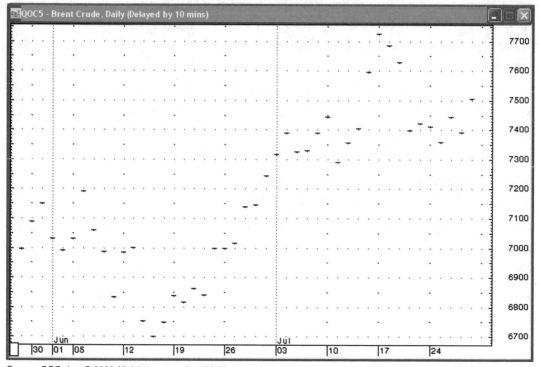

Source: CQG, Inc. © 2006 All rights reserved worldwide.
www.cqg.com

I know what you're thinking: it isn't clear at all. You're right, of course. But look what happens when you join up the dots...

Chart 1-3: Brent crude

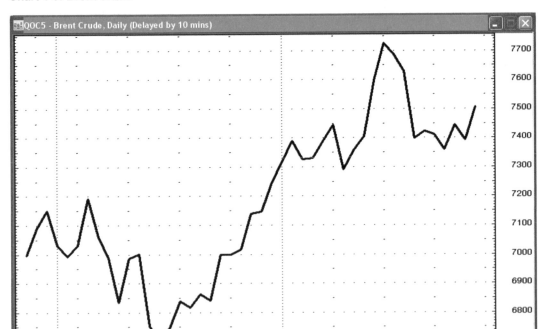

Now it's clear, and you have a chart. The picture that's emerged not only tells the past but also what the future may look like; and if I do my job correctly in this book, you'll be able to do the same.

How do I tell the future from the past?

Empirical observation. Technical analysis is short on theory but long on empirical observation. Contrast fundamental analysis: long where it should be short, and short where it should be long, the triumph of hope over experience. Technical analysis is the opposite, of course; the triumph of experience over hope.

Would you go to sea without a chart?

If you did, you'd be in grave danger of running aground, overturned by adverse currents and likely to founder on the rocks. With a chart, however, you'd have a very good chance of avoiding them. So when you go to market, go with a chart, and even if you encounter one or more of the hazards mentioned in the preceding sentence, you'll still have a good chance of escaping a watery grave.

In case you're not yet totally committed to technical analysis, and think that markets move according to news and fundamentals, think again, and ask yourself: "What news and which fundamentals?" To say nothing of in what order they might affect it?

It isn't news or information that moves price in markets, it's the market's reaction to them that counts; the only thing that counts. That depends entirely on its technical condition when news or information hits. The technical condition is therefore the only fundamental that matters.

To understand the technical condition you don't need a fundamentalist; what you need is a chartist. Accordingly, fundamental analysis is a fundamental waste of time.

Price can be displayed in several different ways, in addition to the line/closing level above.

Point-and-figure

Here is a point-and-figure chart of FTSE for the period since 1st October 2005 to 31st March 2006.

Chart 1-4: FTSE100 Index – point-and-figure chart

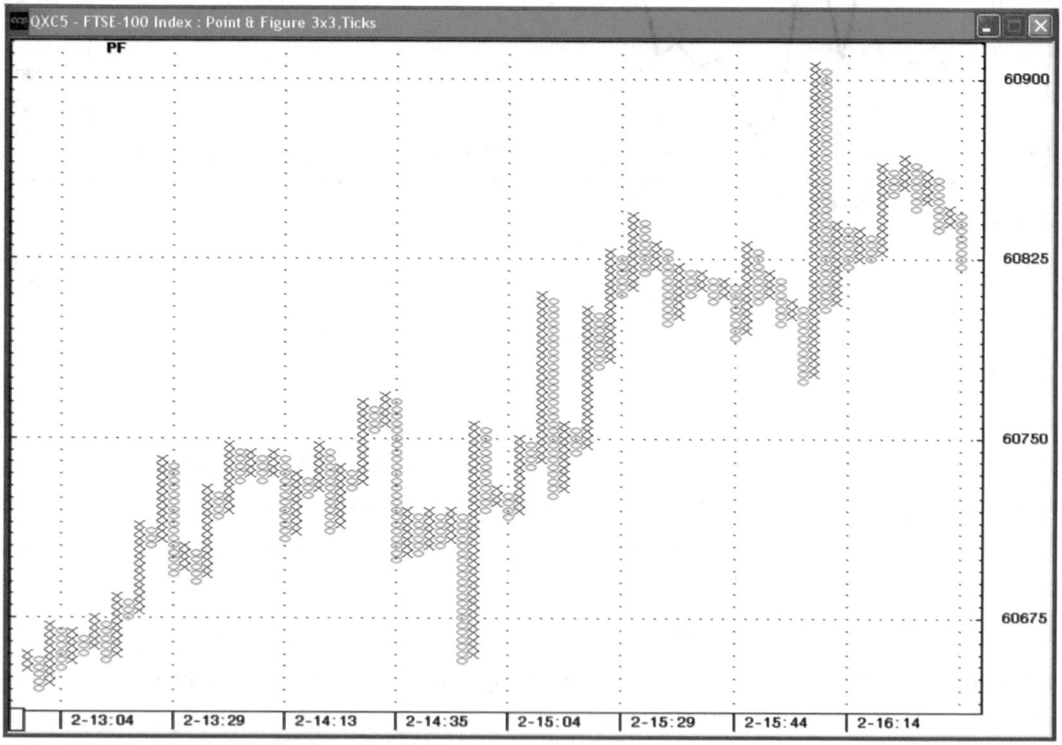

Source: CQG, Inc. © 2006 All rights reserved worldwide. www.cqg.com

What you see looks like a crazy mixed-up game of noughts and crosses. But that's not why I don't use point-and-figure. I don't because point-and-figure charts usually have no time scale, at least on a daily basis, although this one does, being updated at every tick (it is the only one I could get hold of).

Although technical analysis is about probability and timing, and more about the former than the latter, there are certain techniques that can help you assess market-timing, which involve the use of indicators, especially momentum (to be discussed in a later chapter), which expresses the latest close as a percentage of the close x days previously.

Without a daily time scale, you can't have momentum. Without momentum, you can't have timing.

Do you need timing if you're an investor?

Indeed you do: even if (especially if) you have chosen a share purely on fundamental grounds (there are some investors who do, apparently), you don't want to buy when a fall is about to start, or sell if your chosen indicator/s suggest (they don't dictate) that a bear market rally is about to start, do you?

But point-and-figure analysis has no time-scale, so indicators that do can't be applied. Although price is the single most important element, it isn't the only one in technical analysis.

And what about analysis of foreign exchange markets where there are few investors: practically everyone's a trader, most working on extremely short time-scales, with, for example, some taking positions only during everyone else's lunch-break, and closing them when the lunch-wimps return. Players such as these have to employ techniques that help with timing; so point-and-figure is a no-no.

For the past 27 years I have been largely involved in analysing foreign exchange markets without neglecting equity, bond, gold, oil, and commodity markets however.

I am glad to say that I don't forecast FX or any other market on an intraday basis, believing, as I do, that such analysis is rubbish. Moreover, while I work mainly with daily charts I don't make day-to-day forecasts because they're rubbish as well.

Apart from stating the obvious, that price can go up, down or stay the same, charts can't tell you today what the market will do tomorrow.

How do I know? Because in the early 1980s the Bank of England carried out a survey designed to assess whether technical analysis worked in FX markets. The bank's chosen method was to call a number of technicians once a week and ask them where £/$, $/DM, $/Yen would be one week out.

They called to invite me to take part (at the time, the bank's pension fund was one of my clients). I refused because when they told me their chosen method I told them it wouldn't work; there was no way the chart could tell anyone consistently where any market would be one week out.

The survey was carried out, the result was as I had predicted, yet I came out smelling of roses because to spare the participants' blushes, all were known only by an initial letter, and one anonymous chartist, known only as M, was the single successful guesser.

Readers of the survey thought M must stand for Marber, and I never disabused them, until now.

If you want to trade intra-day or day-to-day, why not try using this chart…….

Start at 12 o'clock, read like a clock

                    Then   Prices   Fall
                Up here   A point
            Shares   Or two
        Back   In a
      And buys   Day or
      Bullish   Two and
    Turns   Every
    Trader   Dealer's   Trader
    Every   Clock   Turns
      Two and   Bearish
      In a day or   On the
        Or two   Market
        A point   And
          They rise   Sells
              Then   Shares
                    Down here

I'm sure you now understand my aversion to intraday and day-to-day forecasting.

Nevertheless, having been involved with FX markets for more than thirty years (with stocks, bonds and interest rates, more than fifty, with gold since 1970 and oil since 1973), naturally, to a very great extent my work includes market-timing, so point-and-figure analysis, lacking a time-scale, is not for me. Since I don't employ it, I won't tell you about it. Why waste my time, and yours?

Important point about forecasting: time

It is vital that adviser and client understand each other on the question of how long the former is talking about when making any forecast that includes time. What is the short-term, what, the long? Everyone has a different answer. Remember JM Keynes? "In the long run we are all dead"

Price can be displayed in various different ways

Here is a bar chart

Chart 1-5: Example of a bar chart

The top of the bar is the high trade of the day, the bottom, the low one. The cross-bars show the close. I don't use bar charts, so I'm telling you nothing more about them.

Chart 1-6: Example of a candlestick chart

This chart is a variation of a bar chart called a candlestick chart. The top and bottom of every candle's wide part (the real body) show the opening and close (the candle is black if the former is higher than the latter, white if it is lower than the latter) while the long thin bits, known as shadows or whiskers, show the high and low trades of the session (day, week, month).

Candles are extremely useful, much more informative than either point-and-figure or bar charts, but sometimes too informative, too complicated; therefore, especially when looking at long histories, less useful than closing level ones. I do use candle charts extensively however, in conjunction with line or closing level ones, and will tell you about them in Chapter Seven. Not in Japanese, although some of the terminology is.

Candlestick analysis was devised in Japan where it began more than 200 years before Charles Dow did his work. But what the Japanese were doing was completely unknown in the West until a group of Japanese technicians turned up at the Market Technicians' annual seminar in the 1970s. Candlestick analysis had been used in Japan, in the rice market, since the seventeenth century.

Technical analysis in the western world

In America, the economist, Charles Dow, who founded The Wall Street Journal, started by recording prices (together with Edward Jones, I presume) in the newspaper numerically…84, 84¼, 84½ etc.

Subsequently he decided it would be easier to visualise changes in price if they were recorded as graphs. If changes in price were anything other than random, it wouldn't be unreasonable if Bethlehem Steel's graph sometimes looked like the graph of U.S. Steel, as, no doubt, from time to time it did.

But at other times it would resemble the graph of Sears, Roebuck. Why? Unless all charts covering the same time period are similar to each other, irrespective of the companies they represent, which they aren't, it doesn't appear to make sense that some do. But does it matter? If you can learn something to your advantage from these phenomena why not employ that knowledge?

Dow noted not only that charts of different companies sometimes resembled each other, but also that when certain patterns appeared, certain price changes tended to follow; not always, but sufficiently often for predictions of future price movements to be made.

Of even greater importance, it was also discovered that the magnitude of the move that tended to follow the formation of a pattern was directly related to its size.

While I feel certain there must have been many statistical studies of patterns since Dow's work turned graphs into charts in the closing years of the nineteenth century, it isn't the business of this book to go into them all.

But I do note one of them on the efficacy of the head & shoulders, the iconic reversal pattern much derided by the lunatic fringe. This study, carried out by D.C.Damant and Dr. D.H.Girmes, concluded,

> "A significant degree of success for the pattern is noted…
> A confirmation of the use of head & shoulders tops seems to have been achieved"

The Investment Analyst, May 1975

Dow-Jones averages

Like Spencer of the eponymous Marks and..., Edward Jones seems to have been largely forgotten, but both appear here. In 1897 two Dow Jones averages, one comprising 20 railroad companies, the other, twelve industrials, appeared.

They weren't devised to please chartists: I don't even know, or need to, if there were any then. The theory behind the averages was economic. The shares of twelve industrial companies were considered by Charles Dow (an economist, remember) to represent the wealth of American industry. Since there wouldn't be any industrial wealth unless there was demand for the goods being produced, the railroads were needed to get them to the consumers provided those companies were producing the goods

Accordingly, one of the tenets of Dow Theory was that if the movement of these two averages, railroad and industry, failed to confirm each other (a new high or low in one, unaccompanied by a new high or low in the other), the move was suspect. Maybe the goods were being produced for example, but weren't being sent round the country because they weren't being ordered.

A spanner in the works?

In the penultimate paragraph I told you that Charles Dow's selection of the shares of twelve companies represented the wealth of American industry. Without wishing to belittle Dow's work, I beg to differ. Actually, I don't beg at all; I disagree. And I won't use the clichéd prefix, "with respect" because what usually follows the use of that expression involves no respect whatsoever, but not in this case.

Charles Dow was an economist, and as I have already written, the theory behind the creation of the averages was economic, not technical.

The shares of a company represent not it's wealth but people's opinion of its future wealth; and that's something very different. People express that opinion by buying or selling the shares of that company, and it is an eternal truth that shares frequently lead a life that is totally different to the fortunes of the companies they supposedly represent.

When we buy shares we are dealing in the future, and were doing so long before the arrival of the futures market. How many times have analysts heard an entrepreneur saying that the market doesn't understand what's going on in his company?

Shares are always too low or too high in the opinion of the directors. But that's not surprising; they're not in the investment business, which has different time-frames from industry. Beware the CEO or anyone else on the board who says his shares are the right price.

In the 1970s, I knew a technical analyst who worked for the brokers to Rotork Controls. He told the partners the chart was a disaster: the shares were about to fall apart. His forecast was greeted with derision, it being pointed out to him that the CEO was the one who was buying the shares, no one knew more than he, he saw the orders daily.

The shares did fall apart. I am not saying the sellers knew more than the buyer, merely that one day the orders stopped coming in. Perhaps the sellers believed that a full order book was already in the price.

We have come full circle: I started this chapter by saying that the chartist is a man who knows the price of everything and the value of nothing. Price is everything he needs to know: in the end, price takes care of everything, including the emperor's new clothes.

2

Trends

The Trend is your Friend

A trend is a trend; all are friends.
If you buck one you must make amends.
If the old one reverses,
Shout hooray, never curses.
Ride the new one. Up, down; mind the bends!

The technician is no more adept than anyone else at spotting a trend before it starts. That isn't his business. His skill lies in almost invariably identifying trends after they have started, and then, relying on well-tried rules, riding those trends until soon after they have reversed.

Trend lines, trends, and trend channels

To have a trend, you have to have a trend line

A trend line is drawn between two points. Which ones? That's where the trouble begins. The books say between any two. I say that's rubbish. Although there are some exceptions, which I will tell you about in Chapter Four, which deals with patterns, to draw a trend, you need to obey the rules.

1. You must start at the bottom when drawing an up-trend; at the top when it's a down-trend

I mean the absolute bottom (or top), not some point near to it, just because it suits what you are trying to prove: you shouldn't be trying to prove anything when reading a chart, just observing what the market is saying about itself rather than imposing on it any preconceptions you may have acquired.

> **NOTE**   The market is cleverer than all of us.

2. Never cheat when drawing a trend line

Never look at the right-hand side of the chart; when you draw, never draw the first line straight from the absolute low to the last low before the absolute high (when drawing a down trend line, from the absolute high to the last high before the low). Why not? Because that's where you're hoping it will be.

> **NOTE**   Technical analysis is not about hoping but observing. Trend lines are only likely to be where you hope they'll be if you choose to ignore where they've been cut on the way up or down.

Why?

Because if that's what you've done, go back to the point where the trend line was cut and then re-draw it from the original starting-point through the point or points you chose to ignore, and you'll find it will be rather lower than your "hope-it-will-be-line" by the time it gets to the right-hand side of the chart.

> **NOTE**   It is better to travel hopelessly and arrive at the right place on the chart than travel hopefully and arrive at the wrong one.

Chart 2-1: FTSE100 Index – drawing trend lines

Trend lines 1-4 were all right until cut or broken (I'll explain the difference), but only 5 is right, now.

3. Supposing the trend line breaks?

If the first up or down-trend line breaks (see rule 1), draw a new trend line in accordance with the rule. What rule? Rule 4.

4. The Rule of Four

When drawing an up trend line, it cannot be drawn before you have seen–

1. **the absolute low**;

2. **the first high thereafter**: you'll know it's the high because, by then, price will have backed off from it and you'll see a peak;

3. **a higher low** than the one at the bottom;

4. **a higher high**, higher than the first one you saw.

In a down trend, or – to be precise, when you're looking for one – reverse the process.

> **NOTE**   Whenever you draw a trend line, pay attention to *The Rule of Four*. If you ignore that rule, you're dead in the water and you haven't even got to the starting-line.

Chart 2-2: FTSE100 Index – The Rule Of Four

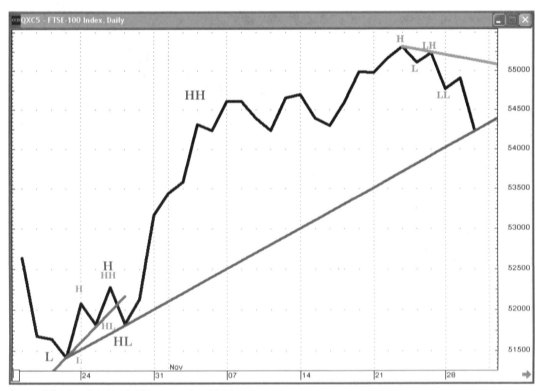

L=Low; H=High; HL=Higher low; HH=Higher high

The pink letters enabled the first up trend line to be drawn.

The green letters, the second up trend line (it only became possible to draw it once the sequence of pink L, H, HL, HH had ended).

The red letters enabled the drawing of the (red) down-trend line.

Trend line becomes trend channel

As soon as you have a trend line, you have a trend channel

Note: By employing the Rule of Four, I could have drawn more trend lines and channels on the next four charts than I have done. Don't let it worry you. I did it to make the charts easier to understand.

Chart 2-3: FTSE100 Index – trend channels

Source: CQG, Inc. © 2006 All rights reserved worldwide.
www.cqg.com

The presumption is that all trend channels are parallel

The blue down trend channel on the left hand side of the chart on page 52, is a parallel one.

The red up trend channel has an up trend line, of course, and, above it, two more lines, called the upper return lines. The thin one, having been the first one that could be drawn, is parallel to the up trend line, but there has been no other contact with it, hence the second return line, drawn (as it had to be) on the early and late November highs: it converges on the up trend line, as the chart shows.

> **NOTE**   The chart almost invariably shows everything there is to see.

When the red upper return line was contacted again in January 2006, it acted as resistance, stopping, and eventually reversing the advance.

> **Upper return lines are always potential resistances, just as lower return lines – drawn parallel to a down trend line – are always potential supports: when contacted they tend to reverse a decline.**

The dark green lines, and the pale blue ones below and above them, like the thick red ones, are three converging trend channels.

Don't concern yourself now with parallel or converging trend channels, along with all the other types of channel, they will be fully explained later in this chapter. As for the word "potential" in relation to support and resistance, a later chapter will explain it.

Give the trend line, and the trend, a chance

While the light at the end of the tunnel might be a trend going in the opposite direction to the one you're riding, sometimes it really is the light at the end of tunnel: always give the trend a chance.

Fortunately, there's a rule that allows you, no, *commands you,* to give that chance:

> **Rule governing when a trend line has been broken**: with shares, an up trend line breaks when it has been cut by 3%. *Not* 2¾%, *nor* 2.999% recurring, but **3.00%, at the close**.

Why only at the close?

Because that is what Edwards & Magee wrote that you should use, and you don't re-write the psalms. In any case, the close is what people read in the newspapers every morning: it is likely to influence the reader more than any evanescent intraday one.

I also use 3% in gold, oil and all other commodities. Others may use different percentages, but what others do, apart from Edwards & Magee of course, doesn't bother me.

Pace Edwards & Magee–

> **A share index trend line breaks on a close 2.00% above or beneath it. I also use 2.00% in all other indices apart from currencies.**

Exceptions to the 3.00% and 2.00% rules

There was no 3.00% rule however when I first became involved in the FX market. And there was no way any client would wait for a 3.00% or 2.00% break of any rate's up or down trend line to confirm that it had been broken.

"Confirmation" is when the line has been broken by the required percentage.

Way back in the 1970s, when looking for a point where a currency's trend line would be broken, I decided to try 1%; it seemed to work. Technical analysis, being all about empirical observation rather than unreliable theories, I started using 1.00%, and still do. I also use 1.00% in bonds.

With bond or currency indices, the break is a close 0.50% above or below the line.

How did I know about 3.00% in shares and 2.00% in indices?

I read it in *Technical Analysis of Stock Trends*, the granddaddy of all books on technical analysis, indeed, the Chartist's Bible.

Written by Robert D. Edwards and John Magee, it was the first book on technical analysis I ever heard about; indeed, it was one of the very few books on technical analysis I ever read or do read now, and I never even finished it, or any of the others: too excited, I just couldn't wait to start drawing my own charts.

Drawing?

Yes. It was in the 1960s and there were no computers that could display charts; no calculators either. So when I found out about moving averages (a treat in store for you in a later chapter), I had to calculate and draw them by hand, and head; and pencil – an extremely sharp one to get the trend lines in the right place.

Trend reversal

Once a trend line is cut or broken you can draw a new one, apply the Rule of Four.

When does a trend reverse?

An **up trend** reverses only when–

1. the up trend line has been broken, at a close, by the 3.00%, 2.00%, 1.00% or 0.50% required;

2. a down trend line has been drawn according to the Rule of Four;

3. the last significant low on the way up has been broken at three successive closes.

For a **down trend** to reverse–

1. the down trend line must be broken by the appropriate margin at a close;

2. an up trend line has to be drawn in accordance with the Rule of Four;

3. the last significant high on the way down must be exceeded at three successive closes; the last significant low on the way up, broken at three successive closes;

4. the relationship of the price to one or more averages may also have to be taken into consideration (averages will be dealt with in a later chapter).

Chart 2-4: S&P500 – up-trend reversal

The chart is the S&P: the 2% rule applies–

- Red line: broken trend line.

- Blue line: trend line not broken by the required 2.00%.

Up trend line 1 became red when the index fell to point A, 2.00% below it; if it had closed for three successive days below point Z, the last significant low on the way up, the trend would have reversed.

Up trend line 2 is blue because it hasn't been broken by 2.00% (point X was less than 2.00% below the line); if/when line 2 has been broken by 2.00%, point O will become the last significant low.

With a down trend line, the reverse applies. The grey line on the chart opposite wasn't broken by 2.00% until a close at point B had been posted. Point H, the last significant high on the way down wasn't exceeded until two days after point B had been reached (the third successive close above it).

Chart 2-5: Nasdaq Composite – down-trend reversal

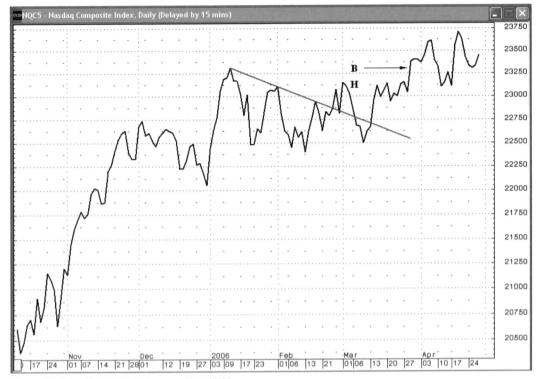

Source: CQG, Inc. © 2006 All rights reserved worldwide.
www.cqg.com

Why is the line grey? I didn't want you to be confused. It was actually red for resistance until point B had been reached, and would then have become blue, signifying support (and if that has confused you, it won't do so once you have read the chapter on potential support and resistance).

Do intraday levels matter?

They do if you are taking a profit and have set a target that has been reached. And if you are an intraday trader cutting a loss, intraday levels might also have some merit.

But this book isn't aimed at intraday traders, or day-to-day ones either, because, and I've said it before, and won't say sorry however many times I have to say it again in this book, and elsewhere, *charts cannot tell you whether any market will be up or down tomorrow, or one week from now.*

Intraday charts however (say an hourly or half-hourly candlestick) might tell you where the market could be in an hour or half-an-hour. But if that's what you want to do, this book is not for you.

However, as you're reading the book, and have paid for it as well (I hope), having got this far, you might as well carry on. After all, as your local, friendly lawyer is bound or bound over to say, you might learn something to your advantage.

Day trading

Not only is this book not for day-traders, it isn't for day-trading either; neither am I. Once upon a time, and once was enough, for one whole day I tried using a half-hour candlestick chart, together with the appropriate time-adjusted indicators – I'll get to them in a later chapter – purely as an experiment. There I sat, not glued to the screen (you can't see anything that way), and trust me, it's no way to make a living.

At five minutes before the end of your pre-set time-frame, you must be in front of the screen in order to have sufficient time to read and analyse the chart. And as the session ends, if you are required to act, you have to do it then, not thirty seconds later.

No lunch, except at your screen; no calls of nature, or any other calls for that matter as your witching-hour, half-hour, fifteen minute period (get the picture?) looms. No time to look at more than one chart, unless of course you stagger your time-periods, thereby, at the least, doubling your work-load, not to mention your stress ditto.

You *can* make a living day-trading, or so I am told, but you'll probably do it better using your guts rather than a chart. Personally, however, I've never met a rich trader (see Glossary). Have you?

Is intraday trading a way to make a living?

No way. No way to lead a life, either. Normally, I hate dumbing-down expressions, but in this context they might be appropriate. Do me a favour, get a life!

I have never read any books on technical analysis of the foreign exchange or bond markets. I didn't have to. A chart is a chart, is a chart, and you don't need to know the name at the top in order to read and analyse one. Indeed, it's better for your *sang froid*[5] if you don't; if you do, the sang gets chaud, and hot blood makes for bad chart-reading.

---

[5] George Orwell would not have approved my using French, but I've never heard of cold blood in English, or hot blood for that matter, except with reference to crime.

And whatever fundamentalists may say to the contrary, technical analysis is not a crime, although it certainly involves a criminal amount of hard work. There are compensations however: no need to examine balance sheets, analyse reports or read the opinions of others in newspapers. Indeed, you don't even need to *read* newspapers.

Do you need to read other chartists?

I don't. It's a waste of time. I don't mean that other chartists are a waste of time (there are good ones and bad ones, just as there are good fundamental analysts; Warren Buffet, for example, and plenty of bad ones too).

But if I do read other chartists, what's in it for me? If you lose money because you were influenced by Mr. X or Mr .Y, or even Mr. Z, are any of them going to give you back what you lost when following their advice? Of course not. When you make money, never forget, you got lucky. And if you lose it, it's your own fault.

I never want to put myself in the position of trying to put the blame on anyone but myself: when you lose money, you can't get it back. You *can* make some more, but you can't get your money back.

Why not?

Because it's no longer your money, that's why; it's somebody else's.

And it doesn't matter what market you are operating in, shares, bonds, oil, gold, commodities, FX, or any other thing you think might make you money; shares, bonds etc don't know you own them. So you can't get back at the market, either.

When looking at anything on a chart, you don't need to understand the so-called intellectual rationale; the name of the game is:

>   *If you can't beat 'em, join 'em.*

Correct me if I'm wrong, but markets are for making money in; they are not an intellectual exercise.

If what you're using works (for you, that is), use it. But therein is a great big problem: how many times has something got to work before you start relying on it, how many times has it got to stop working before you stop relying on it? There is no answer to that one.

Even so, if you buy or sell something, I think you should have a reason. If you do, then, according to some commentators, you're investing. If you have no reason for buying or selling, they say you're speculating. But, as we shall soon discover, that might be too narrow a definition.

> **NOTE** This chapter being about trends, trend lines and trend channels (extrapolation of the trend will be rubbished in a later chapter), if you have found a share with a trend or trend channel, i.e. a low, a high, a higher low and a higher high, and you think that trend or trend channel might continue, and therefore decide to buy, try to bear in mind that those are the reasons for your action.

If, subsequently, in accordance with the rules I hope you've already absorbed by now, the trend or trend channel subsequently breaks, you no longer have any reason to be holding the position. If you continue doing so however, you are no longer an investor; you're a speculator, trading on hope.

Don't get me wrong; although the word may have pejorative connotations, there is nothing wrong with speculation, defined in the OED as

> *"the practice of investing in stocks, property, etc., in the hope of profit from a rise or fall in market value* **but with the possibility of loss***"*

As for "profit" the classical economists defined it as "the reward for risk-taking".

I take the view that if the reason for taking the position has gone, the position should go, too. In my example, you bought for the trend, so if it breaks, you're out. But do you get out at the close on the day the trend breaks? The answer is complicated and must wait for a later chapter.

> **NOTE** Even so, at the close on the day the trend line breaks you have been put on notice that the position has gone wrong, and from that moment on, market conditions could move further against you.

When opening the hypothesised position for the reasons suggested, it is logical to place a *stop*. It is called a stop because you use it to stop or cover your position, i.e. to sell it out if long, or buy it in if short. A stop is placed to stop you out of an open position in any market if the technical condition causing you to open the position no longer exists. Stops have a chapter to themselves.

Charts can have up-trend lines

Chart 2-6: FTSE100 Index – up-trend lines

Charts can have down-trend lines

Chart 2-7: FTSE100 Index – down-trend lines

Charts can have both up and down trends

Chart 2-8: FTSE100 Index – up-trend and down-trend lines

Source: CQG, Inc. © 2006 All rights reserved worldwide.
www.cqg.com

Although the trend lines drawn so far have been multi-coloured, normally I use red when showing down-lines, blue for up-lines, and grey for speculative ones. The last-named will be explained in the chapter on support and resistance.

Accelerating trend channels

Trend channels require two trend lines.

How do you get two trend lines?

You draw them, of course. Where you draw them is another object-lesson in empirical observation. As already pointed out, there is a tendency for markets to travel in parallel channels; a tendency, not a commandment carved in stone.

Here is a *rising parallel trend channel*.

Chart 2-9: Weekly chart of gold (1970-1981) – with rising parallel trend channel

Source: CQG, Inc. © 2006 All rights reserved worldwide.
www.cqg.com

Line 1 is the original trend line drawn as already demonstrated at the beginning of the chapter; line 2 is the first accelerated trend line, line 3, the third. Lines 2 & 4 show the parallel trend channel drawn on the late 1971 and 1976 lows, while line 4, the parallel to it (also known as the upper return line), has been drawn from the 1974 high.

Terminal blow-off

That upper parallel of the chart on the previosu page was penetrated at $588.00 in December 1979, gold reaching $850.00 at 21st January 1980's PM fix (the AM fixes, and 21st January's was $900.00, are not shown: in those days, the PM fix was the nearest you could get to the daily close). The upside penetration of line 4 was a spike, the advance above the upper return line being reversed immediately. A *terminal blow-off* followed. Gold's stay above $500 was short-lived; despite 21st January's $900.00 AM fix (or was it because of it?), price was well below $500 by the end of March.

When price breaks out above a long-lasting upper parallel line (in gold, that means a PM fix at least 3.00% above it), that breakout is usually followed by a terminal blow-off; "usually" because in this business the word "always" has no place.

When a parallel trend channel has lasted months rather than years, different outcomes tend to follow.

Here is a parallel rising trend channel that lasted only a little more than 19 months.

Chart 2-10: Daily chart of Royal Dutch Shell – with a parallel rising trend channel

The 19-month long parallel trend channel was succeeded by an upside break of 3.00% that looked like a spike at first, but January 1996's fall was reversed above the upper parallel (contrast gold's spike or terminal blow-off when the initial fall went below that line and no lasting recovery was to follow).

Eventually a new rising parallel trend line appeared: I haven't shown it because, like the too many cooks and the pudding, too many lines spoil the chart. But you can visualise that channel anyway: two lows in Q1 1996, and three highs, two in Q1 and one in Q2 1996.

That parallel channel was resolved by an upside break in mid-May, when the new channel became not another parallel one but a rising wedge, the upper line converging on the lower one.

The chart of *a falling parallel trend channel* follows, and, as with gold's rising parallel trend channel, once again there was a terminal blow-off.

But this one was on the downside. The lower parallel line (aka. the lower return line) was penetrated in Q4 1973, and the terminal blow-off was not reversed until Q4 1974.

Chart 2-11: Monthly chart of 2½% Consols 1945-1980

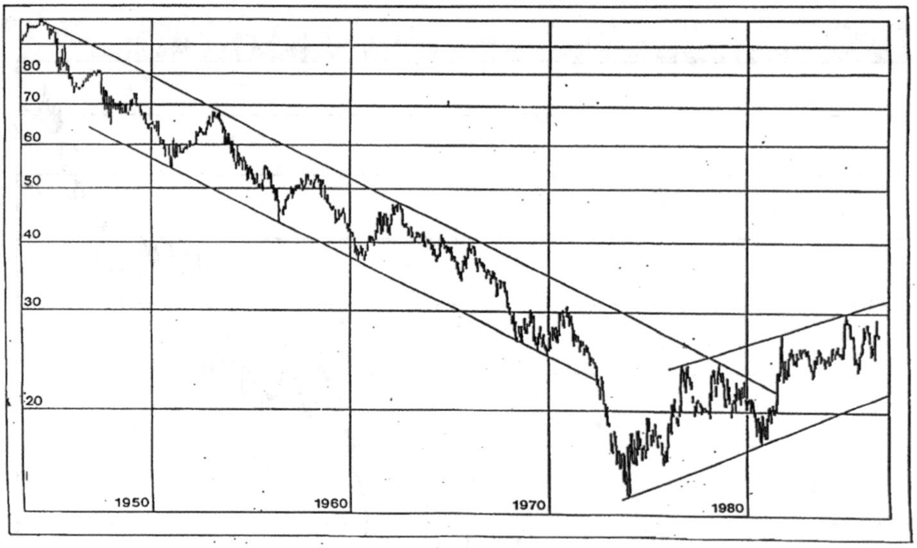

Isn't that something?

The parallel trend channel in 2½% Consols, the oldest of all British Government Securities, lasted 27 years. The breakdown from that channel in Q3 1973 was not reversed until Q4 1974.

| NOTE | The longer the channel lasts, the longer lasting the blow-off tends to be. |

That 27 year trend channel in 2½% Consols did not make an appearance then because the world and his adviser were chartists: in those days, there were none, at least, not in the U.K. Government Securities market.

The chart was "formed" not by chartists and their followers but by the uncoordinated actions of thousands of investors. Most of them, if not all, had never even seen a chart, let alone acted on one. And if you think that's weird, even mystical, you could be right. What does that demonstrate? Although they may not know it, people think in parallel lines. Why? who cares? If that's how people think, accept it; if you can't beat 'em, join 'em.

In a later chapter ("I remember"), there is an account of a long parallel trend channel even more remarkable than Consols'. It is so because the chart doesn't even exist.

So far, the trend channels I have shown you have been rising or falling ones, and nearly all of them (the exception was Shell, where there was a wedge) were parallel.

But trend channels can travel east, when they are called sideways channels or trading ranges.

Chart 2-12: £/$ (1977) – sideways channel

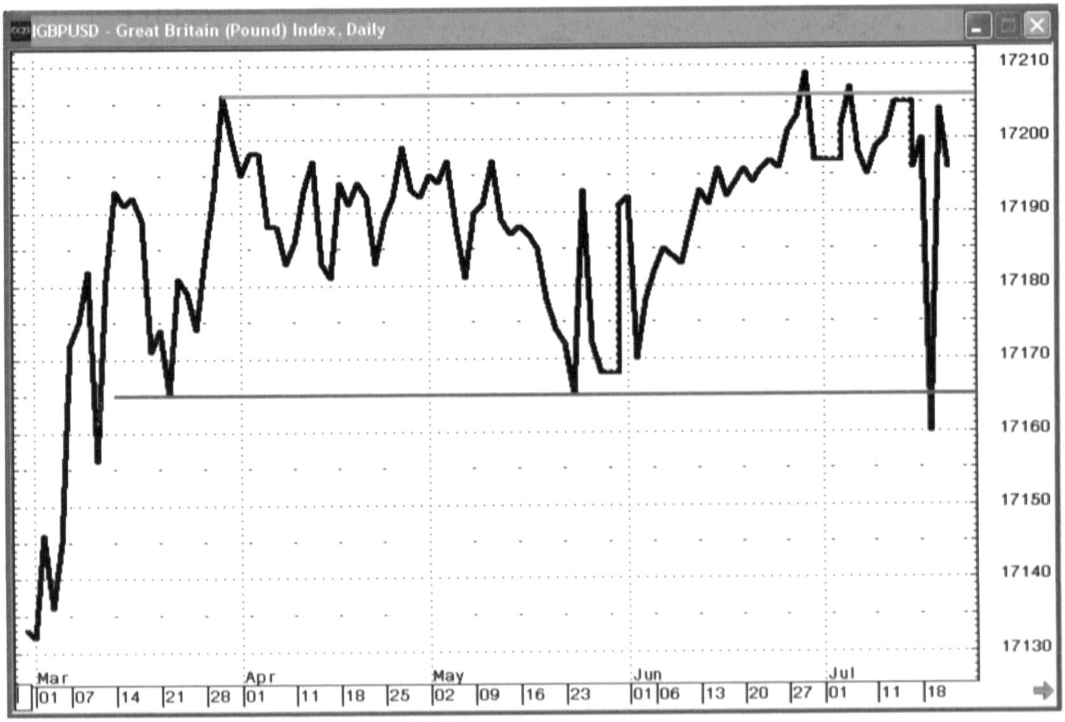

Source: CQG, Inc. © 2006 All rights reserved worldwide.
www.cqg.com

Chart 2-13: Vodafone (2000) – falling trend channel

Eventually all trend channels come to an end, terminated either by an advance above the upper return line or down trend line, or by a decline beneath the lower return line or up trend line.

You have seen two examples of parallel trend channels breaks: the weekly charts of gold (upper return line) and 2½% Consols (lower return line). In both cases, a spike or terminal blow-off followed.

I also showed you the chart of Royal Dutch Shell where a rather shorter parallel rising trend channel was broken; a spike appeared that was succeeded not by a sharp decline but by a reaction that became another trend channel whose upper return line converged on the up trend line. On many occasions, breakouts from trend channels become patterns, described in the next chapter.

Re-cap

- Rising parallel trend channels

- Falling parallel trend channels

- Sideways parallel trend channels

- Rising trend channels with converging sides

- Falling trend channels with converging sides

What about trend channels whose up trend and upper return lines diverge from each other?

You can bet the chart book they exist. But you needn't bet at all, because between 1988 and 1990 the weekly chart below has a rising trend channel whose upper return line diverges from its up trend line.

Chart 2-14: Barclays (1988-1990) – divergence

And here's one where the lower return line diverges from its down trend line, something that frequently happens in a bear market: the downswings become progressively deeper.

Chart 2-15: BSkyB (1996-1998) – divergence

Source: CQG, Inc. © 2006 All rights reserved worldwide.
www.cqg.com

Frequently, an upside breakout occurs from a rising parallel trend channel. When it does, the return line switches roles from resistance to support, reactions thereafter tending to reverse when price falls to it. But I don't want to get ahead of myself by discussing support and resistance now. These important concepts must wait their turn in their own chapter and in that on patterns.

It is important to bear in mind that a falling trend channel can be broken either by an advance above the down trend line or by a decline beneath the lower (return) line. In the former case, the trend might reverse from down to up; in the latter, the down trend accelerates.

In a sideways channel, if the break is on the upside, that channel becomes a double bottom, which can be either a reversal or a continuation pattern, but if the break is to the downside, the channel becomes a double top; sometimes a reversal, at others a continuation pattern (patterns have their own chapter).

A rising trend channel can also be broken, either by a decline beneath the up trend line or by an advance above the upper return line, the former frequently leading to a reversal of the trend, the latter to an acceleration of the existing up trend.

Royal Bank of Scotland (1996-1998)

Blue lines A & B mark the original rising parallel trend channel. At X that channel was resolved by an upside break. The reaction from X then found support at line B, which, by then, had become the up trend line of a second rising parallel trend channel whose upper return line is marked C.

It became legitimate to draw line C as soon as X had been exceeded at end-1997. The shares were below 780 then and line C was 920. But it became possible to forecast that RBOS, already at a bull market high, would achieve the further 18.00% advance needed to reach the upper return line. The advance was rather more than that, of course, because when line C was reached, it had risen to 930.

Chart 2-16: Royal Bank of Scotland (1996-98) – upside break

Source: CQG, Inc. © 2006 All rights reserved worldwide.
www.cqg.com

The chart also shows lines D & E, marking a second trend channel that came into being when end-September's peak exceeded May's.

It became legitimate to draw the third channel (the green one) when point X was exceeded (see the rules for drawing trend lines at the start of this chapter).

We have now come to the end of trend lines, the trend and trend channels, but not to the end of the story about trends.

NOTE	The trend doesn't end until it has reversed.

Extrapolation of the trend

A trend is a trend is a trend;
It's the line that you've got to defend.
But extrapolation,
The devil's creation,
Signals it's going to end.

While there are certainly many traders, shorters and hedge fund managers, for example, who have every reason to love bear markets, the majority involved in the investment business, including unit trust management groups, newspaper commentators and TV broadcasting pundits, prefer bull markets.

But let any phase go on long enough, even a bear market, and people become so accustomed to it, and so reluctant to change their minds (they become more and more reluctant, the longer any bear market lasts) that it becomes increasingly hard for them to accept the possibility of the trend being reversed.

Technicians, blessed, like Cassandra, with the gift of prophecy, are, like her, also cursed: no one believes them. And this is never more true than at major turning-points because, by then, all the non-technicians (and some of the technicians, as well) have fallen so much in love with the trend, even if it's a bear market, that they cannot possibly see any end to it. If the phase has been an extended bull market, the love affair becomes even more ardent. Extrapolation, like the experts' opinion of the market's direction, goes to the moon.

Although trees don't grow to the sky, nor do their roots extend to Australia, try telling that to the majority after an extended bull or bear market: you'll find there are no takers. I have often been asked what my best calls have been. Simple: all of those that no one can remember.

In this business, when you're right, no one remembers; when you're wrong, no one forgets. It is often said that you're only as good as your last call; if only that were true. You're only as good as your next one. Unless, of course, that call is about a major turning-point. If it is, no one is going to believe it.

The lesson

Fund managers, analysts, clients, indeed, everyone, should use his technician not to confirm his own fundamental view but as a valid counter-argument to it, asking himself whether the chart might not know something he doesn't. The market certainly does: it knows more than the sum total of all those involved in trying to work it out. At major turning-points the chart takes over from the (extrapolated) trend as your friend.

The recently retired chairman of Vodafone, Sir Christopher Gent, is credited with identifying, at a very early stage, the trend towards mobile telephony. Apparently another chief investment officer of Standard Life leaned across the table at their first meeting, "Sonny," he said, "this'll never catch on".

Many years ago, the then chief investment officer of Standard Life, in answer to my question, "Being committed, as you are, to fundamental analysis, why do you take my chart service?" replied it was because I sometimes wrote things so manifestly different from their fundamental opinions that, knowing I had form, they then went back to the drawing-board to see if they had missed something.

He was extrapolating the old trend, a common human failing; failing completely to spot the new one and give it a chance. Of course, that didn't necessarily mean Standard Life didn't know the arts of investment from its elbow.

Extrapolation of the current bull market in gold: April 2006

It is easy to see the current bull market, which started at Q3 1999's low: it is already the longest by far since these records began in 1975, including the great bull market of 1976/1980.

Chart 2-17: Gold (in CHF) – multiple trend channels

Source: CQG, Inc. © 2006 All rights reserved worldwide.
www.cqg.com

The weekly chart of this bull market, gold in SF for a change, shows, in addition to the original trend channel (blue), three more, in grey, pink and green. There is no rule governing the number of trend channels in a bull market, but if gold breaks out above the upper green line, the next trend cannot avoid being virtually perpendicular. If so, it will be the final trend channel of this already mature bull market.

But what is a bull market?

Everyone has his own ideas, and mine appear in this book's glossary, but I am going to repeat them. They haven't changed since I became a technician in 1963.

Bull and Bear Markets

Although a bull market begins as soon as a bear market ends (see glossary), it takes time for the one year average to stop falling and start rising. Indeed, you don't know you are in a new bull market until that average has reversed direction from down to up. The average's new direction usually provides final confirmation that a bull market has begun, even though, with hindsight, it did so at the absolute low.

When the bull market has made its peak, the bear market starts the next day, although you don't know it at the time. The one year average is rising and you only know you are in a new bear market once it has started falling. Reversal from up to down usually provides final confirmation that the bear market has begun, even though, with hindsight, it did so at the absolute high.

According to this definition, because the one year average has both risen and fallen since July 1999, there have been several bull and several bear markets. However, a bull market is also marked by a succession of higher highs and higher lows, otherwise there couldn't be an up trend line, the sine qua non of an uptrend, and a bull market is one.

Bull market/bear market – does it matter?

The technician's job is not to call the market names but its direction. I don't care what the market does, as long as it does what I've said it would do. My only interest is in getting the market right.

Some people argue that my definition is wrong, especially regarding the present gold bull market, in CHF. The *gravamen* of their case is that no one made any money until 2005. Having lived through bull and bear markets, not by reading about but by suffering them for 51 years, I refute this argument.

Don't concern yourself with the red line below the price chart (it will appear several times). It's an indicator, a very important one that will be explained in a later chapter.

In the early months, sometimes early years, of bull markets, having endured falling prices for a very long time, i.e. a bear market, many market participants don't believe there has been any change from bear to bull or that there ever will be.

What follows is a report written in April 2006.

Chart 2-18: Gold (in CHF)

The most egregious human failing is extrapolation of the trend: let any trend go on long enough and everyone except the odd chartist (and I do mean "odd") refuses to believe it will ever change. Accordingly, after, often long after the bear market has actually grounded, they all carry on as before, standing aside or selling short.

I am certain you've all heard of a dead cat bounce; what the early months of a major upswing are inevitably called by the "experts" pontificating in newspapers, brokers' offices and on TV. Experts don't have to be right, of course, merely to have sound, usually fundamental and invariably intellectual reasons when they have been getting it wrong.

As for the bouncing dead cat, eventually those same experts who have been pronouncing its repeated death realise that this particular pussy isn't bouncing but pouncing: moggy transmogrified into bull. Dead cats don't bounce; they lie on the floor getting smelly. Sometimes, indeed, oft times, I wish the experts would lie down with them. If you lie down with dogs you get fleas, that's for sure, but with dead cats, experts have an advantage: most already have fleas.

Traders can't believe their bad luck when seeing prices rise for a change. They just keep selling short. Finally however, when they have cut their last losses on short positions and graduated to long ones, a trading mentality prevails; short-term long positions are the order of the day/week/month.

cont...

...cont

That is the main reason why the market keeps on going up: a profit is snatched; "I'll buy on the fall" is the cry. Do you think the market doesn't know that's what they're trying to do? Of course it does; the market knows everything, despite having no eyes, ears or brain.

What the market does have is an eloquent mouth and it pays to listen to what it is saying, not tell it what it ought to do. The market can't hear what experts are saying is right for it to do: it doesn't have morals; and it doesn't care. It does what it wants; and when it wants to do it.

The scalpers and day-traders eventually realise that if only they'd stayed with their original positions taken at the start of the bull market instead of hoping to make a franc or two, get out and in again, they'd be better off, and certainly have slept more soundly.

Of course, that way they would have missed the feelings of machismo so loved by traders; to say nothing of the bottles of bubbly. Or should that be Champoo? Either way, eventually, they get the message: it's a bull market, so let's be in for the long-term.

They are then joined, rather later, by the short-sellers for the Dead Cats Bounce Parade: yes, even they decide this kitty is pretty, and go for a bull-shot. The man-in-the-street, then comes to the same opinion and, trying to avoid being run over by the man on the Clapham omnibus, climbs aboard.

Then the worrying starts. Bull markets climb a wall of worry. Why? That's human nature. Eventually, however, that good ole boy, Ext-rap-o-lation, joins the party, which, he says, will last for ever.

Chart 2-19: Gold (in SWF)

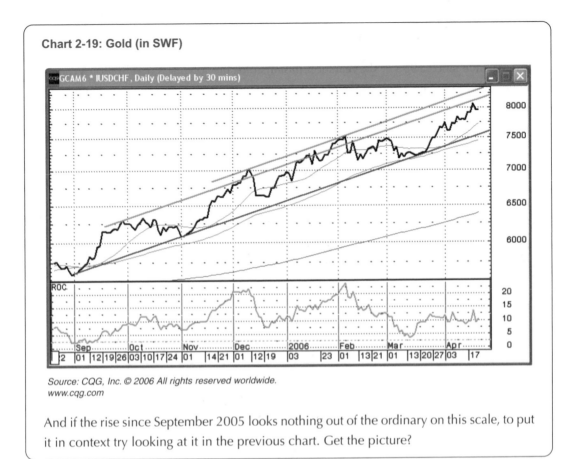

Source: CQG, Inc. © 2006 All rights reserved worldwide.
www.cqg.com

And if the rise since September 2005 looks nothing out of the ordinary on this scale, to put it in context try looking at it in the previous chart. Get the picture?

The report, sent on 20th April 2006, ends there. I wasn't calling the peak then because the technician's job is not to anticipate the reversal of a trend, but to identify at a comparatively early stage when one has reversed or if it may be about to. Gold peaked in May and is lower now (August 2006) than in April.

However, the problem in April, in whatever currency you held gold, was that the bull market had been going on a very long time showing all the characteristics of a terminal blow-off or spike top, as described at the beginning of this section and displayed in the previous weekly chart.

When the party ends with a spike top, the hangover is immediate and long-lasting: selling one month after the top gets you out of the market no worse-off than selling one month before would have done.

Of course, I could be wrong, but nothing goes on for ever, even the opera, and (some might say) my musings. But musings can be amusing, which is more than you can say for the opera.

What follows is a companion-piece on extrapolation, written the same day as the one above.

GOLD $625.00 PM fix 20th April, 2006

The advance since 1999 is six years ten months old, the longest since Bretton Woods' failure. Having gained 147% at 20th's high, posted today, it is already the third largest bull market.

All five bear markets since the high of the first post-Bretton Woods' bull market started between 14th December and 16th February, which doesn't necessarily imply however that all future bear markets must start in those months.

Chart 2-20: London gold fix, weekly chart (1999-2006)

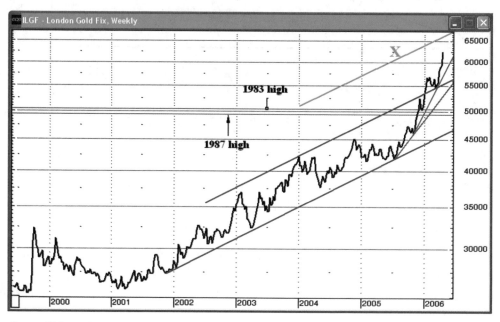

Chart 2-21: London gold fix, daily chart (Apr 2003 – Apr 2006)

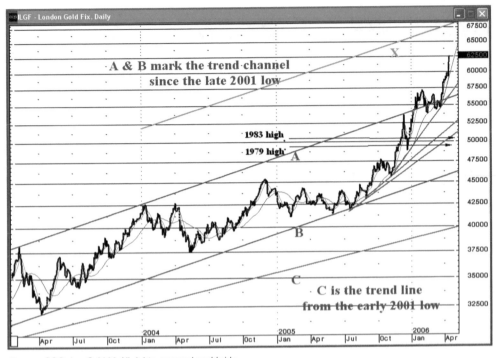

Source: CQG, Inc. © 2006 All rights reserved worldwide.
www.cqg.com

The first up trend line from 1999's $253.00 low, is now at $255.00, below the chart's limits.

Daily or weekly, it doesn't matter: both show the appearance of terminal blow-offs, although dyed-in-the-wool bulls might draw solace from line X at $675.00.

Line X is parallel to lines A & B, and the same distance from A as A is from B. Sometimes, but not always, breakout from a long-established parallel trend channel is eventually followed by an extension of the advance to that third line, although its equivalent remained beyond gold's reach at the apogee of the 1980 blow-off.

Now look at the rate-of-change (the red chart on page 82): its highest levels are usually reached in the opening stages of a bull market, the eventual bull market high in price being posted after the first overbought, as measured by the ROC (the three month rate-of-change), has been approached (as 1999's was this January) but not exceeded. 1980 was the exception: the final overbought was greater than the initial one.

[*Note*: The ROC, also overbought and oversold will be fully explained in the chapter on indicators.]

Chart 2-22: London gold fix, weekly chart with ROC (1999-2006)

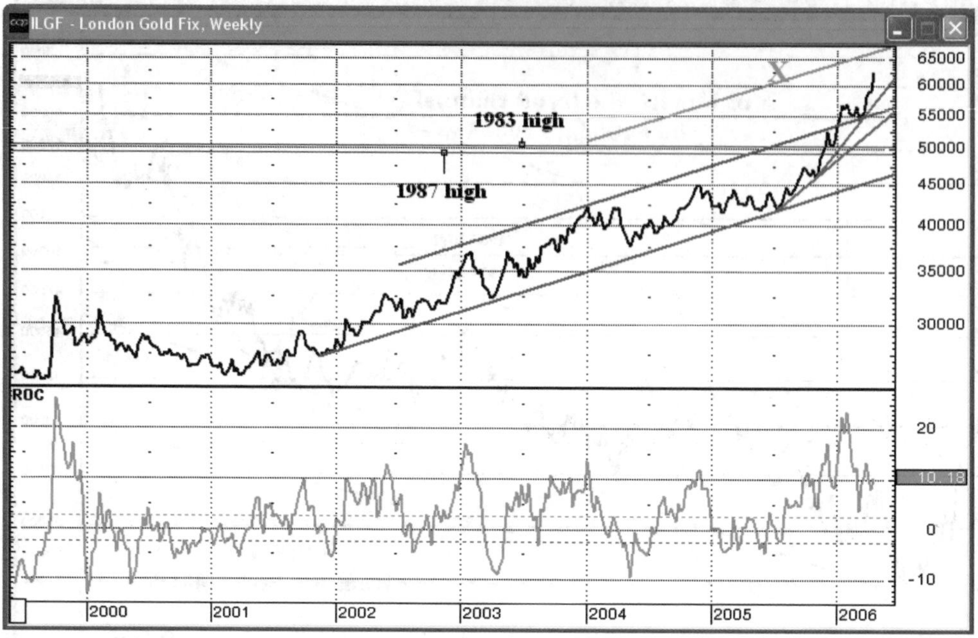

ILGF - London Gold Fix, Weekly

1983 high

1987 high

ROC

The nitty-gritty is: what is the ROC's state now? Good. At 19th's PM fix, without showing any overbought condition, it reached its highest level since mid-February; its average (blue) started rising.

Chart 2-23: London gold fix, daily chart qith ROC (Nov 2005 – Apr 2006)

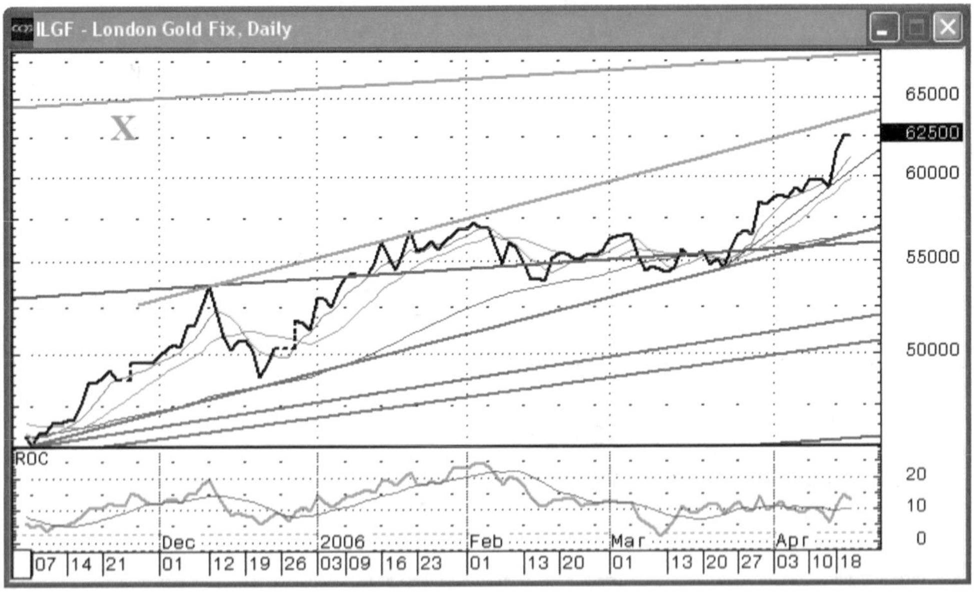

Where the ROC points, price tends to follow: gold could rise further.

But look at the potential resistance offered by the two red lines on the chart of price.

Then look at the differential between today's AM & PM fixes.

On the following chart, vertical blocks show the AM & PM fixes: a black one means that the PM fix was lower than the AM's; a white one, the opposite.

Chart 2-24: London gold fix, AM and PM fixes

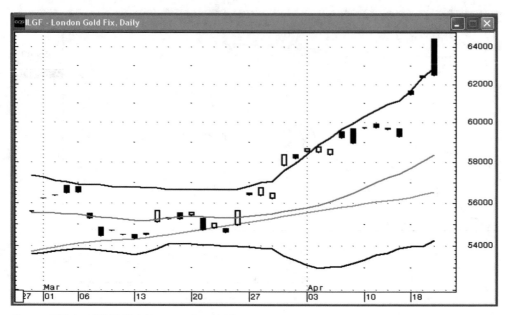

ILGF - London Gold Fix, Daily

Source: CQG, Inc. © 2006 All rights reserved worldwide.
www.cqg.com

Today's differential between the AM & PM fixes rang a bell: I examined the differential between all AM & PM fixes when the latter was below the former, going back to the 1970s. The objective: to discover if large differentials were associated with high levels in gold. This is what I found.

Between today's AM & PM fixes, the differential was 3.03%

29th September 1999

The AM fix was $317.25, the PM, $307.00: the differential was **3.23%.**

Four trading days later, on 5th October, the AM fix was $325.50. The PM fix was lower; another black candle, but the differential between AM & PM was minimal; 0.23%. 5th October's $325.50 wasn't to be posted again for 2½ years. In the interim, gold fell 21.37%, fixing at $255.95 on 2nd April 2001.   cont...

...cont

20th October 1987

The AM fix was $481.60, the PM, $464.30; the differential was **3.60%**.

39 trading days later, the AM fix was $502.75, the bull market peak. The PM fix that day was, $499.75. The AM fix was 4.39% higher than 20th October's $481.60 (differential, 0.60%). Two years later, the PM fix was $355.75; gold had fallen 29.24% from the peak.

Gold was even lower at the end of the 1990-93 bear market, and much lower still ($253.00) at the end of 1996-99's. $502.75 (the AM fix on 14th December 1987) wasn't seen again until December 2005.

The largest differential of all was 21st January 1980's 5.56% (the AM fix was $900, the PM fix, $850).

Conclusion

The four largest differentials between AM & PM fixes over the past 35 years have been listed. All have been associated with major peaks in gold; in 1980 there was no gap between the day the differential took place and the market's peak; in 1987 the gap was 39 days, in 1999, four days. In 1987 the peak was 4.39% above the differential day; in 1999, 2.44% higher.

I am not saying gold's bull market peak was today, but bearing 1980 in mind, it's possible. But if it wasn't today, 39 days from now the red lines on the chart two pages back will be at $685.00 and $691.00. What goes around comes around; otherwise there'd be no technical analysis.

I have been in this business since 1955 and seen many bull markets that were going to last forever, Canadian Natural Gas (1953-56); Gold (1970-74); Gold (1976-80); Nickel (two, Western Mining's and Poseidon's); electronics; dot.com; the industrial holding companies; Oil (the 1970s); commodities (the 1980s); conglomerates (revival of industrial holding companies); technology etc.

Greyhounds (post-WWII); bakelite gramophone records (pre-WWII) were both before I went into the City, as was Wall Street (1929). So was the Dutch Tulip Mania (C17). Tokyo (1982-90) wasn't.

cont...

...cont

Most of those listed, I've experienced. The ones before my time, I've read about.

None of the booms listed on this page, or anywhere else, were ever going to end. All of them did.

Lemmings go over cliffs.

That's all, folks!

Leave it out.

Byeee.

"There is no opinion, however absurd, which men will not readily embrace as soon as they can be brought to the conviction that it is generally adopted."

Arthur Schopenhauer

"Anyone taken as an individual is tolerably sensible and reasonable. As a member of a crowd, he at once becomes a blockhead."

Friedrich von Schiller

Investment genius is a short memory and a rising market. Investment intelligence is a long memory of falling ones.

Modesty forbids

As I wrote that report, Jim Rogers, a justly celebrated fund manager, was talking gold to $1,000. Eleven days after my report went out the bull market peaked at $725.75, apparently; "apparently" because, according to my normal definition, we won't know that gold is in a bear market until the one year average starts falling.

In 1980, this didn't happen until eleven months after the peak was posted.

In NYC in the 1870s the city elders, worried about the possible effects on the environment of the growing number of horses, commissioned a study. Many months passed as the economists on the one hand, the environmentalists on the other, and stable-owners, farriers and grain merchants on the third, fourth and fifth hands, argued their respective cases. Eventually however a report was published, the conclusion being that if the horse population of New York City were to increase in the following 100 years at the same rate as it had in the previous 100, by 1970 NYC would be three storeys deep in horse-s***.

An eminent banker (bankers were eminent in those days) was overheard whispering to his partner, "if they're talking about Wall Street, it's already three storeys deep in horse-s***".

The point I'm making is this: the motor-car was not invented to deal with the manure problem in New York City.

NOTE	When the name of the game is extrapolation, something always happens to spoil the party.

And since in this story illustrating the dangers of extrapolation I have mentioned motor-cars, do you know how many motor-car manufacturers there were in the USA in the early years of the 20th century? More than 700. They were going to need them, of course, to cope with the expected demand.

General Motors does survive….just. But do you remember when the Americans used to deride the fledgling Japanese motor industry? Today, they're not deriding Japanese cars, they're driving them. And General Motors is no longer the largest automobile manufacturer in the world; Toyota is.

But before this account of extrapolation becomes an extrapolation too far, and having dealt with trends and what follows the extrapolation of trends, it is time to find out what happens to trends when they look like ending, and when they have ended.

Support and Resistance

The potential for loss when gambling on certainties is infinite.

Winston Churchill

There is no such thing as support and resistance

Why write about it then?

I'm doing so because support and resistance are two of technical analysis' most important concepts. The trouble with the words "support" and "resistance" however is the word that's missing. That word is...

> *potential*

I've often read, usually in brokers' reports, but also in newspapers, that there is key, crucial, important, long-standing, strong, weak, historical, psychological, critical, good, major, minor, enormous (Minnie Mouse, too, no doubt) support or resistance at such and such a level. There isn't. All those words are used only by wannabe, unprofessional semi-chartists, TV or newspaper commentators and brokers, trying to get an order to buy or sell something.

The latest example of "psychological" appeared in today's (29th April's) Daily Telegraph: "a psychological barrier was jumped when the FTSE250 broke through the 10000 level".

As already explained elsewhere, other markets have had no difficulty whatsoever in breaking this non-existent resistance. Support and resistance are none of the above; they are nothing other than potential because you never know whether they are going to work. So the proper name for this chapter is

Potential support & potential resistance

Once it has been tested, provided it works, potential support is what stops price from falling, while potential resistance is what stops price from rising, provided it works. Once potential support has been broken, it becomes potential resistance; once resistance has been overcome, it becomes potential support; it never becomes resistance or support.

Provided it works?

Many years ago, I used to write treatises on support and resistance, explaining, perfectly logically, that whether support or resistance would materialise depended on how overbought price might be when the former was tested, how oversold when the latter was. Logical, it was, but correct? No.

Through bitter experience I discovered that oversold or overbought conditions had no influence whatsoever on whether support or resistance would actually appear. Technical analysis being based entirely on empirical observation, I went back to the drawing-board. Literally: there were no computers for displaying charts then; you had to do your own drawing.

In Chapter One I told you about Edwards & Magee's rules regarding the breaking of trend lines in shares and indices, and the amendments I use when analysing FX and bond charts.

I reasoned that if support and resistance were broken by 3%, 2%, 1% or 0.5%, surely it must be logical (dangerous word) that if they were tested, and price not only failed to overcome resistance or find support but also reversed by the appropriate percentages, then, on the face of it, support/resistance had appeared, or worked. And that's how the prefix "potential" got into my lexicon.

The concept of potential support or resistance working, or becoming actual, is mine; I have never read about it in any book, and have never seen any reference to it in any TV broadcast or newspaper article. Until now, I have never told anyone about it except clients.

Then why am I telling you now?

Because I'm 72. Given my views on extrapolation of a trend, I won't extrapolate my own trend *ad absurdum*, and would like to leave something totally original behind me.

Of course, the world having been going on a long time during which a vast number of books on technical analysis has been written, it is certainly possible that other technicians have worked out for themselves the methods I think are mine. Indeed, it would be very surprising if they hadn't. After all, I am not that clever. But I have never seen any mention of "my" rules anywhere but in my work.

And I've never seen the prefix "potential" either: key, crucial, major etc, yes; but "potential", never.

Of course, if everyone who reads this book starts using my rules, markets being what they are, the exercise might become self-defeating. If so, the person who would suffer most would be your far from humble scribe. And what a laugh that would be.

The meaning of "provided it works"

When potential support or potential resistance has been tested, and price reverses by the same percentage as that required to "break" the support or "overcome" the resistance, the potential support/resistance has worked or become actual. It does *not* then become strong, key, crucial, major etc.

A test is

- a close in a **share** at/within 1.50% of potential support or potential resistance,

- in a **currency** at/within 0.50% of it,

- in a **currency or bond index**, at/within 0.25%.

In other words, I halve the percentages required to break a trend line.

Supposing potential support or resistance is broken, but not by the amount required?

If potential support/resistance isn't broken by the amount required, it isn't broken at all, merely cut. Accordingly, to calculate a reversal at that potential support/resistance, when price re-enters the trend channel it is still valid, so you measure 0.5%, 1%, 2% or 3%, as appropriate, from the re-entry point.

What happens once a reversal at potential support/resistance has taken place?

Price is likely to continue its new direction. For how long it does so depends largely but not entirely on the proximity of the nearest potential support or resistance, which might be a trend line within the trend channel or an average; the one month is likely to be the nearest.

Averages can be potential supports or potential resistances: it all depends on whether they are rising or falling, but detailed discussion of their propensities must wait for a later chapter.

Of course, if support and resistance always worked there would be no up or down markets: clearly there are, so, equally clearly, they don't always work. Frequently, following reversal at the potential support or resistance proffered by a trend line, having encountered no new support or support (potential, of course), price reverses again, and re-tests the original potential support or resistance.

If a trend line is horizontal, it will naturally be re-tested at the same level as that at which the initial test took place. But if that line is rising or falling, it will be tested at a higher/lower level than that at which price failed the original test.

This has been dry stuff; it has also been necessary. But there is no point in describing what's happening on a chart unless you can see one, so here is the chart of what I've just described.

Chart 3-1: London gold fix – potential support and resistance

The original up trend line is green, and couldn't be drawn until the high at A had appeared, above point 4, creating the necessary sequence: low, high, higher low, higher high.

When the green line had been broken, on the downside, there was no up trend line until point 3 (higher than A) had been posted, and the sequence: 1, A, 2, 3 (low, high, higher low, higher high) appeared.

At that moment, the supposition being that all trend channels are parallel until proved otherwise, it became legitimate to draw line 4-5, parallel to 1-2. Why wasn't 4-A the line? Because, with some notable exceptions which I will explain in the chapter on patterns, and have already alluded to in the one on trends, you can't draw downtrend lines at all when there is no high, low, lower high, lower low sequence, or the reverse if drawing an up trend line.

Points 1 & 2 show the current up trend line, 4 & 5 its parallel upper return line. The thin lines marked -3% & +3% have been drawn 3% below line 4-5, and 3% above line 1-2.

Look at line 4-5. Potential resistance, it had worked (become actual resistance, but only on that occasion) when price reversed at point X, which was less than 3% above it. At the end of June it worked again; and again at point 5.

Why are highs potential resistances?

Because some people bought at them and are waiting for a chance to get out once they have been put in a position to do so without loss, i.e. they are potential sellers if their buying price is regained, i.e. when it is tested.

Accordingly, point X was potential resistance when it was tested at Z, less than 1.5% beneath it. X became actual resistance, i.e. it had worked, when price then fell more than 3%.

Where did price fall to?

Ignoring the potential support at just above 315 (September's lows[6]), price fell to the blue up trend line 6-7, a potential support. Indeed, that line was cut, but a cut is just that; it only becomes a break if it is 3% deep. And potential support has only worked if is tested, and price then rises 3% at a close, which why as soon as price had risen 3% above line 6-7-8, it had provided support.

Red line P-Q on the chart below is an accelerated trend line [see below] drawn from point 2 on the previous chart. It became legitimate to draw line 2-P-Q when that chart's line 4-5 was exceeded by more than 3% on the way to point R on the extreme left-hand side of this one.

The thin red line is drawn parallel to and 3% above line 2-P-Q. The thin red line drawn parallel to the lower one is 3% below line R-S-T, the upper return line drawn parallel to 2-P-Q.

---

[6] Lows are potential supports because some people bought there, making others think that that must be a good level at which to buy when they have been revisited after the decline from a rally high.

Chart 3-2: London gold fix – potential support and resistance

Accelerated trend lines

If price rises 3% above any parallel trend channel's upper trend line, as it did on the way to point R on the preceding chart, as soon as the Rule of Four can be applied again (in this case, as soon as point R was exceeded in September 2003), it becomes legitimate to draw a new trend channel starting at the take-off point from the first trend channel (point 2 on previous chart) through the low (point P) posted following the ending of the rally that breaks out above it.

If you look, not at the preceding chart, but at its predecessor, you will see that you might have drawn a number of accelerated parallel trend channels from point 2, but the only one that could be drawn after line 4-5 had been exceeded, at the peak of the rally to point R on the chart above, is the red one.

Line R-S-T was overcome by 3% at point C. When the latter was exceeded at the end of January it became legitimate to draw line B-D, also upper parallel return line C-W. Recently (it is 6th May 2006 as I write), point W was also exceeded by 3%, permitting line X, the eighth up trend line since the bull market began in 1999, to be drawn.

You can only see five up trend lines on the preceding chart, but there is a sixth, lower than any of these, on the preceding one. Before that, there is a line from August 1999's low through April 2000's, and another from July 1999's $253.00 through August's of the same year.

Chart 3-3; London gold fix

The chart above is weekly (the two preceding ones were daily), and avid trend line counters will already have noticed that it only has seven trend lines, and that the lowest only has one point-of-contact, with August 1999's low (it was beneath 2001's low).

The explanation is simple: on the daily chart the absolute low was July 1999's $253.00, not far below where Gordon Brown managed to sell vast quantities of our gold, and that point doesn't show on a weekly chart. And whereas the chart with all the red lines shows five trend lines since July 2005, the weekly only shows four. Once again, that's because the weekly doesn't show the lows in the same place as the daily.

Why not show the daily for the period being examined?

You can't get all that data on a daily chart.

There has been no other time when gold has had eight up trend lines, the original one plus seven accelerating ones. In 1976/1980, the largest bull market of all, at least since the failure of the Bretton Woods Agreement, there was one, plus six, making seven in all.

What does this mean for gold today?

Some would say a new ball-game. I believe we are seeing the final blow-off of the current bull market, already the oldest (nearly seven years) and third largest of all.

By the time you read this, we shall know for sure whether it's new ball-game time or if there is no such thing as a new ball-game. Since I am a technician, I don't believe in new ball-games, but in what goes round comes round ones.

What you think depends on how you answer this, which is not a trick: if you go into a casino and hear that black has come up seventeen times in a row on the nearest roulette table, which do you back, black or red? The law of large numbers tells you that, subject to zero not appearing, the chances are even every time the wheel spins. So whether you back black or red will depend entirely on how you feel: chartists must be entirely devoid of feeling however because they're unreliable.

PS: the market is not a roulette wheel: whereas the latter has no memory, and critics, notably the perfect market theorists and random walkers say the former doesn't either, people do. And it is people who buy and sell in markets.

We are not finished with potential support and resistance.

Averages have powers of both. Originally they were placed in their own chapter, but could have been placed in the chapter on indicators just as easily (everything used in technical analysis is an indicator), or in that on trends.

Some books call averages an indicator, or a *confirming* as opposed to a *leading* indicator. I don't. "Indicator" surely implies that it tells you something is going to happen, not that it has already done so. I call that an economist.

Averages

Averages, at least in technical analysis, usually have the adjective "moving" in front of them. But not in this book: averages will do.

In case you think I was being pedantic about the difference between leading and confirming indicators, and therefore my reluctance to applying the word to them, averages can and do tell you something about the nature of the market, but can never put you in at the bottom or out at the top. What they do is put you in after the former, out after the latter: in that sense they confirm rather than lead. But that's all right; tops and bottoms are for fools (Rothschild), and liars (Marber).

Come to think of it, technical analysis is the opposite: it's not for fools, or liars: it's all about not picking tops and bottoms; not being clever; not having gut feelings, or, at least, not indulging them; not acting unless the evidence is clear.

Averages don't have a chapter to themselves, because although they are important enough to merit one, frequently telling you something that price can't do by itself, I have placed them with support and resistance, one of the major qualities possessed by them.

If Investment Research had heard of averages, they evidently didn't think they had any useful application. You'll read how and where I discovered averages in Chapter Seven (the averages' chapter).

When I first saw a stock market chart in 1955, it had no averages on it, and I didn't even know what an average was until several years later. When I first became aware, Investment Research of Cambridge (then trading as Cambridge Investment Research, a clever marketing ploy to associate the firm with academe until the University cottoned on,) weren't using them.

NOTE   I now use three averages in my work; one month, three month and one year.

These three are plotted as–

- **21 days** (the approximate number of *dealing* days in a month – 100% accuracy isn't necessary, even for pedants, and I am one;

- **63 days** (a *dealing* 3-month period); and

- **252 days** (a *dealing* year, at least in the London market, and near enough the same on Wall Street).

In Tokyo I use 20, 60 and 240 days. What about the foreign exchange market? Like the old Windmill Theatre's proud boast "we never closed", nor does the FX market, so I use 21, 65 and 261 days.

When looking at weekly charts, I use four, thirteen and fifty-two weeks, dealing weeks that is: weekends don't count, although some Elliott Wavers do. Count weekends, that is. But Elliott Wavers don't count. Not with your far from humble scribe, that is, anyway.

> Why do I use the word "dealing" when you're probably more used to its successor, "trading"? Because I'm frightfully old, set in my ways, traditional, conservative with both c and C, and "dealing" is what I grew up with in this business.

I also pay a great deal of attention to history, something that the young – anyone under 45, say – don't seem to know about, or care about, any more. But if you're a technician, I've been trying to be one for 43 years, while the most important thing to read is what the charts are saying today, it isn't enough.

To have any chance of making further out calls you need to look, for example, at how long bull and bear markets tend to last. When you read Chapter Two on extrapolation of the trend, which goes into detail on this, you'll see exactly what I mean.

Why do I use the averages I use?

The answer, which is the same as the answer to many questions in technical analysis, is, because they work. The first ones I ever saw were 10, 20 & 60 days. That was in the offices of a firm of jobbers (nowadays called market makers).

They used 10 days because that was the length of a stock exchange account in those days, and they felt therefore that that was as good a number as any to use for starters. 20 days was as near a month as made no difference, and also twice 10; very useful in pre-calculator days (if you wrote down two columns, each of 10 days, you could read across both of them to get a 20 day average; read across three columns of 20 and you got 60. *Voila tout!*) I started with their numbers.

I went to a seminar conducted by a U.S. technician who told the audience that my numbers were useless. In USA, he told me that the averages used were based on the different tax rates applicable in respect of short and long term capital gains.

He mentioned 200 days, and then, in the same sentence, used 30 weeks as a synonym. When I queried this, his reply was that 200 days was the same as 30 weeks. I pointed out that 30 weeks was only 150 dealing days, and that if you counted weekends, it became 210; also 60 of those days were ones when the market was closed. He didn't seem to care.

After starting with 10, 20 & 60 days, I decided 10 was too short for me; also that I needed a longer average than 60 days (for a jobber, anything longer than 60 days was a nonsense). So I graduated to 20, 60 and 240 (4x60).

Most technicians have never heard of 21, 63 & 252 days, which I was only able to employ once I had a computer to do the work: and one month, three months and a year sounded sensible to me. But I have heard of 5, 10, 20, 30, 40, 50, 100, 200 days being used. The last-named has no logic for me, and is too volatile, anyway. With a long-term average I want to know when it changes direction that it is unlikely to reverse again soon afterwards. Even here, I have had my disappointments.

Some people use numbers in the Fibonacci series: 8, 13, 21, 343, 55, 89, 144, 237, etc. I have a colleague I tried to teach, who misheard me when programming his computer. Instead of 252 he input 273 days. He is obstinate, and wouldn't correct his mistake. I then discovered that 273 days was 13 lunar months. Problem solved, at least as far as he's concerned.

If the foregoing is leading you to the conclusion that technical analysis is an art, not a science that is precisely what I have been trying to lead you to. Anyone who tells you it's a science is a charlatan, or con-artist, not a chartist.

If it works for you, it works for you. If you can't beat 'em, join 'em may not be the name of the game, but it's not a bad sub-title.

I also know of two notorious sisters who swore that in gold the only period that mattered was 63 weeks (approximately 1¼ years). At least, 63 weeks is what they swore it was all about until, using this period, gold went horribly wrong for them in the 1980s, when they chose to ignore 63 weeks altogether, without really admitting it.

How do you create an average?

For the sake of simplicity, let's take a ten-day average: you add the most recent ten days' close together and divide by ten. Voila! A ten day average.

Mathematicians tell me that the most recent plot of a ten-day average should be five days back from the current price, a 20-day average, 10 days back etc. As far as I am concerned you can plot it in Australia if you want to, but it's easier to see what an average is saying if you plot it in line with price.

What I have described is an *arithmetic* average, and that's the only one I am going to describe. Some technicians use *exponential* averages, others, *geometric* ones. I've tried them all and I prefer arithmetic ones.

The proponents of the averages I don't use argue that they are more sensitive than arithmetical ones. Indeed they are, but that isn't necessarily an advantage: sensitivity creates whipsaws more easily.

The trouble with the averages I don't use is that it is impossible to work out what price has to do in order to get them to change direction, which is why I don't use them.

What do averages do?

1. Rise,
2. fall,
3. move sideways,
4. cross each other,
5. change direction,
6. bunch.

Chart 3-4: FTSE250 Index – averages

Source: CQG, Inc. © 2006 All rights reserved worldwide.
www.cqg.com

The chart (the FTSE250 Index since late 2002) shows three averages, 21-day (green), 63-day (red) and 252-day (blue). Why I use these particular time periods is explained in the Glossary.

If you've looked at the chart and its averages, no doubt your appetite has been whetted by seeing that when price falls to or beneath a rising average, its tendency is to start rising again. If it hasn't been whetted, you are never likely to become a technical analyst.

When I first saw coloured lines on a chart, I hadn't the faintest idea what they were, but to say that my appetite was whetted would be a gross under-statement because I immediately saw their tendency to behave as described above. I have seldom been so excited, at least not by markets.

I was a lunch guest at Blackwell & Co, at that time (1963) the leading London jobbers in oil shares. I asked David Blackwell what these strange lines were, and why did price reverse soon after it had hit them. "Averages of price", was the answer to the first question, "because they do", to the second.

I could hardly wait for lunch to finish: I rushed back to my office and using the lists of prices I had been recording in linear form for some considerable time, started drawing charts by hand. Yes, by hand; there were no computers. What about calculators? There weren't any of those, either, so I started calculating them..........slowly and very laboriously.

Averages: rising and falling

Averages (arithmetic ones, anyway), start rising if price closes above where it was 22 days previously in the case of a 21-day average (64 days previously if it's 63-day, 253 days previously if it's 252-day) and continues doing so until price closes beneath the close posted 22,64 or 253 days previously. As soon as it has done so, the average starts falling.

> **NOTE** A rising average is potential support. A falling average is potential resistance.

The potential support offered by a rising average does not work in the same way as a trend line. In other words, a 3%, 2%, 1% etc close beneath a rising average does not mean that support has failed to appear. Nor do similar closes above a falling average mean that resistance has failed to appear.

When does potential support/resistance from an average appear?

Ideally, as far as I am concerned, and what concerns other technicians doesn't concern me at all, potential support appears (has become *actual* support, or has *worked* if you prefer) when a renewed close above a rising average follows one or more closes beneath it. It doesn't matter how many closes there are below a rising average, or how far below it price falls, as long as the average is still rising when price closes above it again.

And it doesn't matter how many closes there are above a falling average or how far above it price rises thereafter, as long as the average is still falling on the day price closes beneath it again. At that close, the potential resistance provided by a falling average has worked etc.

Once support/resistance has appeared, what happens next?

That depends on which average has provided it. I use three: short, medium and long (21, 63 & 252) if the averages are daily ones. Provided all three averages are in correct bull market order (shortest above medium, medium above longest), the shortest is going to be the first to be tested if price decides to fall. If support appears following the test (see previous section), price should return to the previous high.

Chart 3-5: FTSE100 Index – averages

So far, so good, but supposing that high is reached but not overcome or not reached at all, and price starts falling again, what happens then? Support becomes less likely to appear the second time. If it doesn't, and the average starts falling, thereby becoming potential resistance. Accordingly, unless the most recent low beneath the average provides support, price is likely to fall to the next potential support.

That might be a trend line or another average, but sometimes it will be neither, yet price still stops falling: charts can't always tell you everything, though they often tell most of what you need to know.

In the following chart, support was found in December 2003, and again in January 2004 following declines below the rising 21 day average (green). In early February, the index fell again, and that support would have failed if end-January's low had been broken at any close, as described previously. There was no such close. On the contrary, the 21 day average, still rising, supported price once again.

Chart 3-6: FTSE250 Index

At A, in March, although the 21 day average did fail to provide support, the three month (B) didn't. The inference was a test of the high, and it was tested (a close within 1% of it), but price couldn't overcome the potential resistance. The one and three month averages, having turned down at (C), were no longer potential supports.

The potential supports at March and January's lows didn't work either (previous lows are potential supports because some investors will remember price had risen from those levels the last time). But the rising one year average – another support – did work at D (close above it following one beneath it).

During the advance that ensued, the one month average, potential resistance because it was falling, failed to halt the rise. On the contrary, it turned up, becoming potential support. But look at the three month: although price went on up after crossing above it, that average remained potential resistance because it never stopped falling.

Price reversed direction at E, and the one month average was tested this time, it was falling again, therefore not potential support but potential resistance. The three month, which had never stopped falling, was no support either. As for D, a previous low? Same story.

What about the one year? It was potential support. As I told you in the explanation of averages, it doesn't matter how long price stays below an average, the latter remains support as long as it keeps rising. And when F was reached on the rebound from Z, the index was above the average again: the support had worked.

When a rising (falling) average starts heading east, what does it tell you?

Nothing. It isn't working. The only thing that's always working in technical analysis is the chartist.

What can averages do?

I told you they can do six things. Three of them, rise, fall and move sideways, have been explained. All that is left for them to do, and for me to explain, is that they can–

1. cross each other.

2. change direction.

3. bunch.

Sometimes the averages cross before both are rising or falling, at others the change in the direction of the averages precedes the crossing. Finally, the averages sometimes cross, but the longer one doesn't change direction.

In January, at the bottom left-hand corner of the following chart, the one month average (green) changed direction, starting to rise, thereby becoming potential support for a falling price rather than potential resistance to a rising one. Shortly afterwards, at 1, it crossed above the three month average (red), the event being followed by the latter changing direction from down to up, i.e. a golden cross.

Golden Cross

The expression used whenever a shorter average crosses above a longer one, and the latter starts rising. Following the appearance of a golden cross, a significant advance frequently follows: Z, 3, 5 & 7.

Chart 3-7: FTSE250 Index – Golden Cross

Source: CQG, Inc. © 2006 All rights reserved worldwide.
www.cqg.com

Dead Cross

The expression used when a shorter average crosses beneath a longer one, and the latter starts falling.

Following a dead cross, a significant decline frequently follows: 2 & 4, but not Y & 6.

Why not?

Two reasons–

1. In a bull market downside reactions tend to be smaller than they are in bear markets. In June/July 2003 there had been a golden cross of the three month and one year averages, final

confirmation that a bull market was underway, therefore there was always the possibility that the dead crosses at Y & 6 were likely to be small.

2. Technical analysis is about probabilities, not certainties.

Dealers' remorse

In the week following a golden or dead cross, and sometimes for longer, a rally to/towards the crossing-point frequently but not invariably follows: see between 2 & 3, and at X8.

Averages in trading ranges

As I told you in Chapter Two, trading ranges are misleading: apart from riding the range (also explained elsewhere) you might as well stay home on it. Averages don't help when price is ranging. On the contrary, although the signals they can give in a trend are helpful, in a range, provided it lasts long enough, they tend to give buy signals when they start falling, sell signals when they start rising.

Chart 3-8: EUR/GBP – trading ranges

Source: CQG, Inc. © 2006 All rights reserved worldwide.
www.cqg.com

Since May 2003 €/£ has been in a triangular trading range. When price is trending and the one year average starts rising, it confirms that the major trend has turned up; when the average starts falling in a trending market, it confirms that the major trend has turned down. But during the life of the current range this average has done the opposite.

Three months after January 2004's one year average downturn, €/£ grounded. January 2005's upturn by the average occurred at the top; August's downturn, near the bottom; March 2006's near the top.

Bunching

When all three averages bunch together, and all are falling in correct sequence: green, lowest, then red, then blue (one month, three month and one year), with price below all three, a significant and long-lasting decline almost invariably follows, i.e. 1999, 2000 and 2005.

Chart 3-9: USD/GBP – bunching

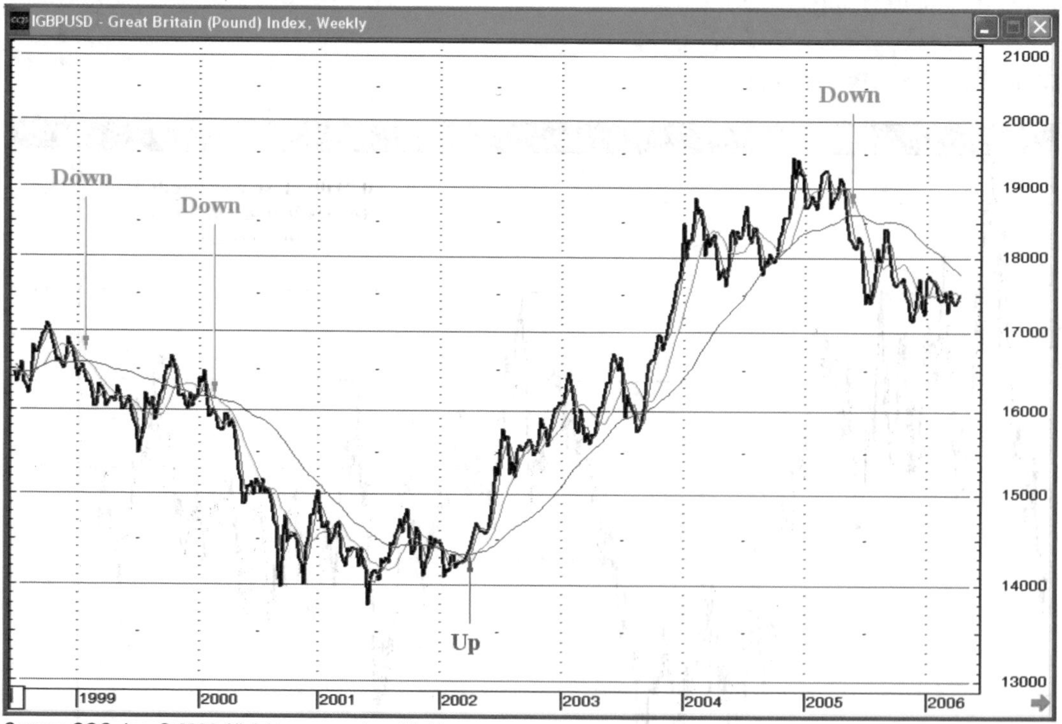

When all three averages bunch in correct sequence and price is above them, a significant and long-lasting advance almost invariably follows, 2002's bunching and 2003's providing shining examples.

The chart is 3-9. Accordingly, the averages are 4, 13 & 52 weeks, the approximate equivalent of 21, 63 & 261 days (261 for a currency, not 252).

Tailpiece

The nature of averages means that they can never precede or herald a change in the direction of price. Accordingly, they are confirming rather than leading indicators. In this sense, there is no difference between them and most other indicators. But there is one indicator, the rate-of-change (ROC), which can and often does lead price, causing consternation to the uninitiated, and to some of the initiated as well, by which I mean the BOAC (bit of a chartist) fraternity.

4

Patterns

Reversal patterns, continuation patterns, short-term patterns

Volume

Broker: "I have bad news and good news"
Client: "What's the bad news?"
Broker: "The stock we bought at 50 is trading at 3"
Client: "What's the good news?"
Broker: "It fell on low volume"

Some of you, no doubt, are thinking, why on earth does the word *volume* appear in a chapter on patterns? The reason is simple. In Edwards & Magee's classic work, *Technical Analysis of Stock Trends*, the authors consider volume to be the *obbligato* to pattern formation and confirmation.

When I became a technician in the 1960s, the volume of any individual trade was never disclosed because no jobber wanted his peers to know the size of his book: how many shares he had bought or sold in any particular bargain (the then current word for trade).

Technicians had to do without volume; yet we managed, by which I mean that we did without volume and still had our fair share of correct forecasts.

But that's not the only reason I am suspicious of volume. Point-and-figure analysis works, but the charts, having no time-scale, can't record volume even when it is available.

And what about the foreign exchange market, where, like the old jobbing system, but not for the same reason, though recorded, volume is not immediately available for chartists to work with? Technical analysts in general have a better record in FX forecasting than we do in any other markets.

We also have a better record than fundamentalists in FX forecasting, but I am not about to fight the battle of Agincourt all over again on the question of technical analysis versus the fundamental variety.

Chart 4-1: S&P500 – volume analysis

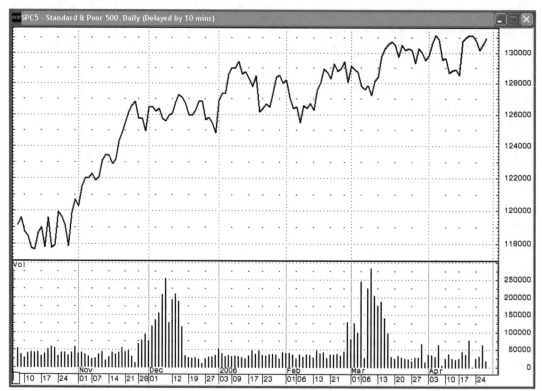

Source: CQG, Inc. © 2006 All rights reserved worldwide.
www.cqg.com

The chart of the Standard & Poor's 500 Index, chosen at random on the day I was writing this section, shows some of the anomalies in volume analysis.

In December volume was high but the index was trading sideways; in March, volume rose as the market fell, considered bearish by volume-readers; at the month's low however, volume peaked: sellers getting out or buyers getting in? Finally, the market rose on falling volume; bearish, once again, according to those who take volume into account.

Maybe, although it would appear that no one told the market it was bearish. Or if the market was told, it didn't care. But the point is that the market went up. High volume, low volume; price doesn't care.

I've said it before, and I'll say it again: price takes care of everything. That's hardly surprising: more people look at price than at price & volume together. Prices can fall on low volume; volume can peak on the low day; prices can rise on low volume; peaks are often attended by high volume.

That being so, you've just read all you can about volume, at least in this book. Having never read a book devoted to volume, I can't recommend any.

Reversal Patterns

A reversal pattern is a reversal pattern because it reverses the preceding trend. But before getting down to the nitty-gritty of head & shoulders, double bottoms and tops, broadening formations etc., I must remind you that you don't have to have a pattern to reverse a trend.

In Chapter Two I wrote that an up trend reverses when the up trend line has been broken at a close by the relevant percentage; a down trend line has been correctly drawn, i.e. according to the Rule of Four, and the last significant low on the way up has been broken at three successive closes.

As for a down trend, it reverses when the down trend line has been broken at a close by the relevant percentage, an up trend line has been drawn according to the Rule of Four, and the last significant high on the way down has been exceeded at three successive closes.

Frequently, but not always, a reversal pattern appears, and is confirmed either just before or soon after the trend line has been broken. (Don't worry; "confirmed" will be explained).

Head & Shoulders

The king of all reversal patterns; it stands head & shoulders above all others.

When Charles Dow, an economist who founded The Wall Street Journal and was its first editor, started recording share prices, they were listed only as numbers. Subsequently, and purely as a mnemonic, Dow started recording prices in graphic form: *he thought it would be easier to visualise price changes that way.*

Before you see one, however, when looking at the graphs of various shares' prices, Dow was astounded to see not necessarily that Bethlehem Steel's might resemble U.S. Steel's for example, as might have been expected, but Sears Roebuck's.

Even more astounding to Dow and his colleagues, was that share prices frequently made patterns, and when they did, certain price changes tended to follow, not always, but with sufficient frequency to make possible the prediction not only of changes in direction but also of the size of future price movements.

What was the reason?

I don't know if Dow & Jones ever gave one, nor do I care. If it works, use it; if you can't beat 'em, join 'em are the names of this particular game.

The most widely known chart pattern the head & shoulders, appears frequently when an advance is topping out and, inverted, when a decline is coming to an end.

The time has come to look at a head & shoulders.

The chart happens to be Vodafone in 1993-94, but forget the name above the chart; we're all chartists now, so it doesn't matter what it is.

Chart 4-2: Vodafone – head & shoulders

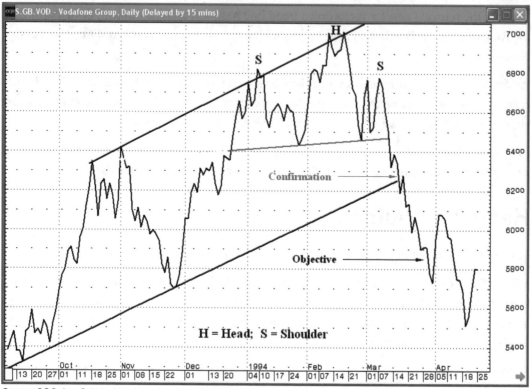

1. The pattern starts with an up trend channel. In this case it happens to be a parallel one, as many of them are, but it could just have easily been any of the others described in chapters two and three.

2. Price rallies. In this case, in January 1994 it hit the upper return line, a potential resistance.

3. Following an initial back-off of 3% to 67, failure at the resistance was confirmed. But the fall didn't stop there, and although it could have been extended to the potential support from the up trend line, just as its predecessor's had, it decided not to do so.

4. On this occasion after hitting the channel's mid-point, price decided to rally. The starting-point of this rally completed the formation of a left shoulder.

5. The rally extended more than 3% above January's peak, hitting potential resistance from the return line as it did so. Price then made two attempts to overcome it, failing at the second

when it fell 3% to 67. But it wouldn't have mattered to the formation of a head & shoulders if there had been no potential resistance at that level or any other: price goes up, and down.

6. The fall reversed following a test of the potential support at January's low (previous lows are potential supports). When price started rising again, the head of a potential head & shoulders top had appeared.

7. Another rally took price up to just below the point of what had now become the potential pattern's left shoulder. It would have made no difference however if price had reversed somewhat lower than it did or if the rally had been extended above the point of the left shoulder, as long as it wasn't within 1.50% of February's peak.

8. The subsequent fall might have stopped at the grey line, a potential support, but didn't. When price hit the line at 64.69 however, the range between February's low and that point became the right shoulder of what was nevertheless nothing more than a potential head & shoulders top.

9. When the fall was extended to a close 3% beneath that line however, it confirmed that a head & shoulders top had been formed.

If I explained myself correctly in Chapter Two, as you read the chart of the head & shoulders top, you were saying that when drawing the grey line referred to in point 8 I broke the Rule of Four, which states that to draw an up trend line, which the grey line is, you needed a low, a high, a higher low and, finally, a higher high.

But I also wrote that there were exceptions to the rule which I would explain in this chapter. The neckline (that is what the grey line is called) is the first: I use grey when the line is speculative, by which I mean that it defies the Rule of Four by having no higher high (lower low when it is a down trend line).

Otherwise, when drawing potential support lines according to the Rule of Four in my regular reports, I colour them blue; for potential resistance lines, I use red.

Red and blue have also been used in various places in this book to differentiate one trend channel from another. Black, too, as, for example in the chart you've been looking at.

Once a head & shoulders top has been confirmed, the neckline is coloured red, signifying potential resistance (it is a broken trend line).

The measurement factor following confirmation of a head & shoulders

Once a head & shoulders has been confirmed, the normal expectation (based on your other dependable friend, empirical observation – the trend being the best friend of all) is a decline equal to the distance between the head and the neckline, measured from the point where the latter is cut. Broken is a cut of at least 3% beneath the neckline at a close, if the head & shoulders is a top, 3% above if it's a bottom (aka an inverted head & shoulders).

If the head is at 100, and the neckline is cut at 80 (20% below the head), the objective becomes 64, 20% below the neckline.

Semi-log scale

It is time to tell you what I use: it makes more sense to me to use semi-log rather than arithmetic scale. Apart from making it easier to compare percentage movement visually, It tells you the truth: 125:100 as 100:80. With the arithmetic scale however, 100:80 as 120: 100.

Something else appeals to me about log-scale; it's slower, therefore, in my view, safer than arithmetic scale: up trend lines break sooner; down trend lines, later.

Inverted head & shoulders

Being a reversal pattern, when a head & shoulders pattern has been confirmed, it can reverse not only up trends but also down trends. Naturally, the pattern has to be a top to reverse the former, inverted to reverse the latter.

Chart 4-3: Standard & Poor's 500 Index – inverted head & shoulders

The inverted head & shoulders that reversed the Standard & Poor's 500 Index bear market in 2002-03, confirmed where shown, 2% above the neckline (it's an index). The objective (an advance equal to the distance between the point of the head and the neckline) then became 1117.

Whereas the neckline of the first head & shoulders, Vodafone's top, sloped upwards, this one slopes down. But the slope doesn't depend on whether the pattern is a top or bottom; it can be either up, down or flat. What it mustn't do is slope too much.

Chart 4-4: Glaxo Smithkline – not an inverted head & shoulders

Source: CQG, Inc. © 2006 All rights reserved worldwide.
www.cqg.com

This isn't an inverted head & shoulders: the blue line slopes too much.

What is too much?

Point 2, which would have completed the head and started the right shoulder of a valid pattern, was below point 1, which would have been the point of the left shoulder if the blue line's slope had been flatter.

There is no rule governing the permissible angle of the slope, but in an inverted head & shoulders, point 2 must be above point 1, say at least half-way between it and the neckline. In a head & shoulders top, point 2 must be below point 1 by the same amount.

Traders' remorse

Following confirmation of a head & shoulders (either top or inverted), a return to the neckline frequently follows. If it always followed, how simple life would be, but it doesn't. The neckline becomes a valid trend line (remember, when I first showed you, it was grey, signifying that it was a speculative line) as soon as the pattern has been confirmed: if it's a top, the line is red, signifying potential resistance, if a bottom (inverted) the line is blue, signifying potential support.

What happens if a return to the neckline doesn't stop there?

The books say a head & shoulders only aborts, if the point of the right shoulder is exceeded at a close.

This means that unless you anticipate the confirmation of a pattern, something that I never advise (I'm an adviser, not a fund manager), in the case of an inverted head & shoulders you are put into the market 3% above the neckline – you don't have to buy there, of course – but confirmation puts you on notice about what may eventually happen.

Let's say that you wait for trader's remorse to provide you with a more attractive entry-point, and that you get lucky: price returns to the neckline. You buy there, but won't know that the reason you bought has disappeared until the market is several, maybe many, percentage points lower than your entry-point, dependent on the size of the right shoulder.

I never found that very satisfactory. After all, not all head & shoulders patterns reach their objective, and some abort soon after confirmation, otherwise all technical analysts would be instant millionaires.

Accordingly, having devised my own rules to deal with successes and failures at potential support and resistances, I started applying them to confirmed patterns, reasoning that if a head & shoulders (or a double top) was confirmed by a 3%, 2% 1% or 0.5% break, dependent on which market I was looking at, it was logical to consider that the confirmation had gone wrong as soon as price re-crossed the neckline etc by the same percentage.

A glance tells all, so here is a recent example of a confirmed head & shoulders that went wrong.

Chart 4-5: confirmed head & shoulders that went wrong

The chart is €/$ between 2003 and 2006. But what it is doesn't matter; it's a chart

The chart tells all

The confirmation of the pattern occurred where indicated, following a close 1% below the neckline; the abort 1% above it. When a head & shoulders aborts following a close at the appropriate level above the neckline (below it if the pattern is an inverted head & shoulders), the inference then becomes a further advance to the right shoulder.

If price closes above the right shoulder by the relevant percentage, as €/$ did several days before this chart was made, the inference is a return to the head[7].

If price subsequently exceeds the head, closing at the appropriate level above it, the inference is an eventual advance equal to the percentage differential between the aborted pattern's head and its neckline. In the present case, that differential having been 14%, provided the head is overcome by 1% at a close, the inference/objective will become 1.5400.

[7] When I wrote the foregoing in April 2006, €/$ was 1.2760. By August 2006, when I started editing this chapter, €/$ had already tested the head.

Points arising

1. A head & shoulders doesn't ignore the rules, whether they concern trend lines, trend channels or potential support and resistance levels.

2. The pattern is concerned with probability, not timing. There is no time limit for reaching an objective, but the latter can be over-ruled in the manner already described, also by (1) above or by a pattern being formed in the opposite direction.

The head & shoulders as continuation pattern

Usually, the head & shoulders is a reversal pattern, reversing the trend that precedes it. But sometimes price forms a head & shoulders top following a significant advance, at others, an inverted head & shoulders after an extended decline. If it does so, the rules already set out apply.

Chart 4-6: head & shoulders as continuation pattern

Following the S&P's Q1 2004 high, the neckline of an inverted head & shoulders appeared very near that potential resistance. But neither neckline nor high became actual resistance. If you argue that the pattern was not at the absolute peak, I don't think it matters: either way, having overcome the resistance at the high, the S&P went on to fulfil the objective.

The move to be expected following confirmation of a head & shoulders

Once a head & shoulders has been confirmed, a move equal to the percentage differential between the head & neckline is the minimum expectation, not the maximum.

To qualify as an investment, as opposed to a speculation, any commitment to the market must have an objective, therefore if you buy because of a head & shoulders' confirmation and objective, taking a profit once the latter has been reached isn't necessarily a stupid thing to do. And sometimes the minimum move does turn out to be all you get, so taking your profit then becomes a very sensible thing to do.

But in this far from easy business there is always an on-the-other-hand.

The-on-the-other-hand here is that the trend is your friend. When price reaches a head & shoulders' objective, it isn't hard to understand that there is unlikely to be anything wrong with the trend. In the case of a head & shoulders top however, price might be at potential support, at potential resistance if it's an inverted head & shoulders. But it might be at neither.

What do you do then?

Use your judgment and experience, and hope for some luck as well. You also need to be totally disciplined. It also helps to have no heart: that way, you have a chance of being flexible. Investing isn't easy; but it is indoor work and there's no heavy lifting.

Chart 4-7: FTSE250 index since 2002

If you'd bought the index because of the inverted head & shoulders that appeared at the end of the bear market in Q1 2003, you'd be feeling a tad disgruntled if you sold when the 4360 objective was reached just two weeks later.

If you had obeyed the rule concerning reversal of a trend however: no trend has reversed until the last significant low on the way up has been broken at three successive closes, you'd still be long, even though the original up trend line drawn from the head through the point of the right shoulder (not illustrated) was broken as long ago as end- 2004.

You might like to try drawing all the trend lines that have been broken since then. But I wouldn't bother: I've already done so, and there aren't any because not one has been broken by the 2% required in an index.

The chart of the FTSE250 index shows that the inverted head & shoulders took three months to form, whereas €/$'s head & shoulders top, shown earlier, took two years. It makes no difference to the pattern how long the formation takes to appear: all are equally valid; whether the period is long or short.

A head & shoulders can take as little as six days to appear:

1. rise to point of left shoulder;
2. fall to point where neckline might appear;
3. rise to new high (the head); fall to approximately the same level as 2;
4. rise to point of right shoulder;
5. fall that breaks neckline.

It can also take several years to form. But the time taken to form a pattern does not determine how long it is going to take to achieve the objective, although most are reached in far less time than that taken to form them. As I've already written: *the pattern is concerned not with timing but with probability.*

Chart 4-8: $/DM

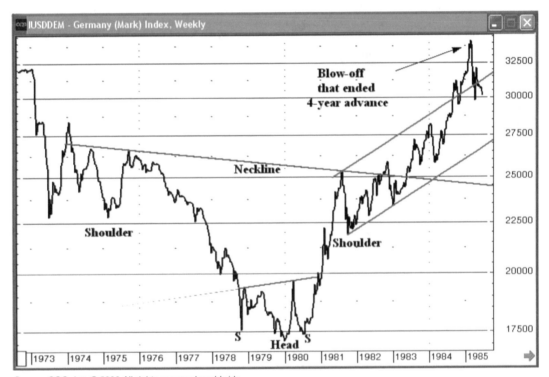

Source: CQG, Inc. © 2006 All rights reserved worldwide.
www.cqg.com

Although a two-year wide inverted head & shoulders was confirmed in December 1980, this weekly chart also shows that it took nearly eight years for $/DM to form a second one.

The objective was DM4.0000, and even though the highest point reached was only an intraday DM3.5700, the point to remember is this: the pattern was confirmed after $ was more than 100% above the 1979 low and had already been rising for 3½ years, and although the full objective was never reached, in 1983 when received wisdom had it that, from a fundamental point-of-view, $ was overvalued at DM2.5300, the pattern had it (for me, anyway) that $'s direction was up, and likely to remain up for some considerable time.

By 1985 however, the received wisdom had it that $ wasn't overvalued at all; it was still expected to advance. But the Q1 blow-off that year told me that $ was going wrong and that DM4.0000 was therefore very unlikely to be achieved.

But from a fundamental point-of-view $ had also been overvalued at its 1979 low. "Going to hell in a hand-basket" was the cry.

Guess what the reason was?

The budget deficit, exactly the same reason as that being touted now and, indeed, ever since the 2004 low. And just like today, the received wisdom had it that interest rates wouldn't be allowed to rise; couldn't rise. Ho! Ho! What couldn't happen did happen, of course.

Naturally, no one had believed my call in 1983, when, with $ at DM2.5300 I had called it up to DM4.0000. Indeed, lunching at SG Warburg on $'s high day in 1985, I was told by a senior banker that when I had made that call, he and his colleagues all thought I had gone mad.

At that lunch the senior FX dealer said I was still mad, telling me that with $ already Pf15 up that morning anyone who wasn't long $ must be crazy. My answer was that anyone who was long $ would regret it. It turned out to be the high day. The dollar went down; the dealer went the way of all dealers. The banker, even more senior today, is still a client.

Two weeks earlier I had been lecturing in Singapore, and told delegates to the seminar, and the assembled press, that $'s rise was ending. I wasn't believed there, either. The trend was being extrapolated; it was already vertical; the fundamentals were wonderful; and in any case, the press told me that I must be wrong because the dealers were bullish of $.

I asked the press if *all* the dealers were bullish, and when assured that they were, I *knew* I was right. The crowd is always wrong.

One more head & shoulders before we go on

Chart 4-9: The Diamond

SPC5 - Standard & Poor 500, Daily (Delayed by 10 mins)

Source: CQG, Inc. © 2006 All rights reserved worldwide.
www.cqg.com

The diamond, also called a head & shoulders with a bent neckline, can be a top or a bottom, i.e. a reversal, or, as in the present case, a continuation pattern.

When it began forming in August 2005, having started in October 2005 from 776.76 the bull market, already 22 months old, was certainly no calf, and if it had been April/October's up trend that had been broken, this diamond *would* have been a reversal, not the continuation pattern it became when August/November's down trend was overcome.

Measurement of the objective once confirmation has taken place

Confirmation is a close 3% above the down trend line or above the up trend line for a share, 2% for an index, 1% for a currency or a bond, 0.50% for a currency or bond index.

The objective, measured from the breakout-point, is equal to the distance between the head and the neckline, measured vertically upwards in a diamond bottom or bullish continuation pattern (point O, is vertically above H on the chart), downwards in a double top or bearish continuation pattern.

The diamond being considered, appearing as it did following a significant advance, was a bullish continuation pattern. The objective, measured from O, and equal to the distance between O and H, is 1335, nearly achieved at 1326.53 high; not bad when you consider that when the diamond was confirmed the S&P was a lowly 1258.

Will 1335 be reached?

Provided May's high doesn't reverse the current advance, there is no reason why it shouldn't be, especially since the latest close, as I write this, was 28th August's 1301.78, less than 2% below that peak.

Double Tops and Bottoms

Like the head & shoulders, the double top is one of the major reversal patterns. Alternatively, dependent on the direction of the eventual breakout, it can become a continuation pattern.

- **The first requirement** is an advance: how else could you get a top?

- **The second requirement** is a reaction: Price falls. How much? If you're looking at a share, price must fall more than 3%, in an index, more than 2%, in a currency, more than 1% etc. How much more? That's for you to decide, but the bigger the reaction, the better, because the size of the initial fall eventually determines the size of the decline to be expected, once the pattern has been confirmed.

- **The third requirement** is that the reaction ends: for whatever reason or, as sometimes happens, without any technical reason at all, price stops falling.

Chart 4-10: BP 1999-2000, double top

Source: CQG, Inc. © 2006 All rights reserved worldwide.
www.cqg.com

- **The fourth requirement**: price rises and tests the high. If you've forgotten, a test of a previous level is an advance to a close within 1.50% of it if it's a share, 1.00% if it's an index, 0.50% if it's a currency, etc.

The high is potential resistance because there were some investors who bought there who are waiting to get out even: if they do, they can convince themselves that they weren't wrong to have bought at that level in the first place. Others, having seen that price had fallen from that point, persuade themselves that it will fail at it the next time.

If a double top is going to be formed, following the test of the initial high the first clue appears if (a) price falls 3% (at a close) from its highest close within 1.50% of that high, or, (b) if it has closed above the first high, but not 3% above it, price falls to a close 3% below that first high.

At this stage there is no double top. All that has happened is that price has failed to overcome the potential resistance apparent at the first high: potential resistance has become actual resistance on that occasion or, to put it another way, the potential resistance has worked or appeared.

- The fifth requirement: the low following the decline from the first high is tested. That low is potential support: observers of the previous advance from that point think it must be a good level at which to buy, while those who sold then can reinstate their original long position without loss of face, or money. If buyers do appear in the region of that low, and price rallies 3% at any close, support has appeared, creating the possibility of a further advance.

- The sixth and final requirement for a double top: with or without the intervention of a rally when the low is tested, it is broken by 3% at a close.

Following that close, not before, a double top is confirmed.

The requirements for a double bottom are the same: simply read low for high and high for low.

Chart 4-11: British Land 2004-05, double bottom

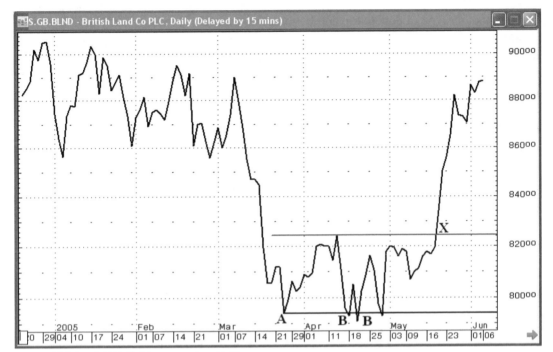

Source: CQG, Inc. © 2006 All rights reserved worldwide.
www.cqg.com

Points BB were lower than A, but less than 3% below it, so A was never broken, merely cut.

The pattern was confirmed following a close 3% above X.

How great is the expected fall (rise) following confirmation of a double top or bottom?

The distance between the top (bottom) is likely to be repeated: if the difference between the highs and the intervening low is 10%, the decline should be at least 10% beneath that low.

If you go back to the double top illustrated by the chart of BP, your eye will tell you that the Q1 2000 low was the same distance beneath the red line as the latter was below the two tops. On 24th February 2000, BP traded at 440, exactly fulfilling the double top's minimum objective, which in this case is all the bears got. If they went for more, they were disappointed....they got less, because February's was the absolute low.

Contrast this result with British Land's double bottom. Here the bulls got far more than they bargained for, and if they felt satisfied when taking their profits as soon as the 856 objective had been reached, they didn't feel that way for long: the shares hit 890 just two weeks later.

The Brahmin

There is another type of double top and bottom, the *Brahmin*. It looks exactly the same as an orthodox double top or bottom but may be less than 3%, 2% etc tall. The significance of a Brahmin is not its size but the fact that it has appeared at all. Why? Because, again with exceptions that will be explained later, the double top and bottom, whether orthodox or Brahmin, are reversal patterns: they reverse the direction of the preceding trend.

The chart of British Land, specifically the points marked B, formed a Brahmin bottom reversal as soon as the peak between them, which was less than 2% higher, was exceeded at a close. Its objective, less than 2% above that peak, was reached almost immediately. Insignificant? Not at all, the Brahmin having made an appearance was the harbinger of bigger things to come, as BB turned out to be part of the far larger double bottom.

Chart 4-12: AstraZeneca 2003, Brahmin Top

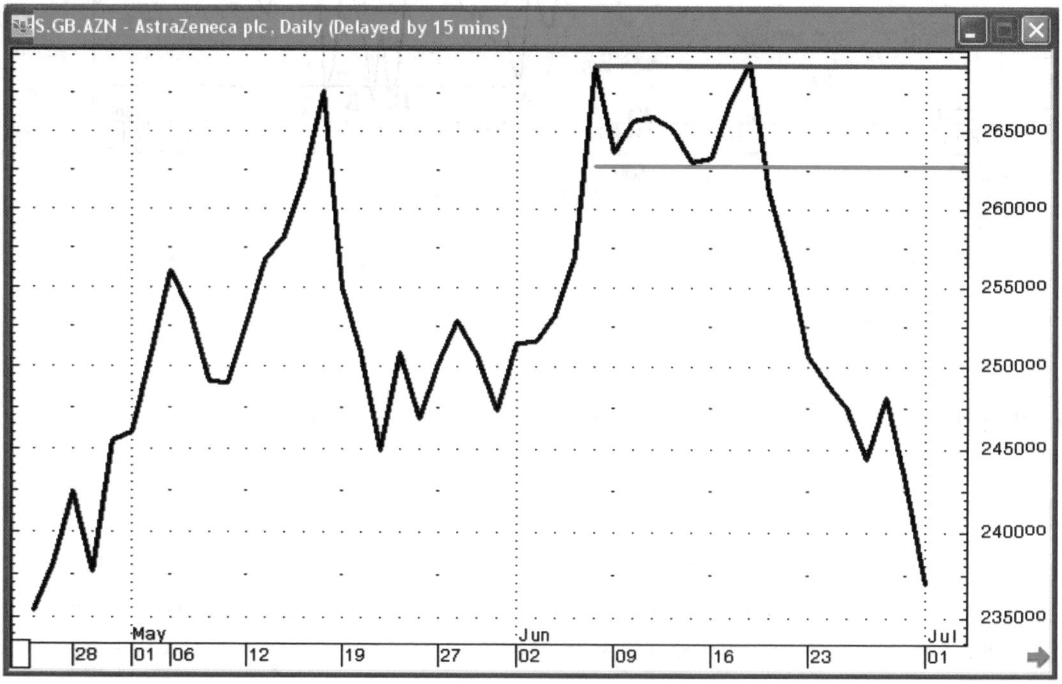

Source: CQG, Inc. © 2006 All rights reserved worldwide.
www.cqg.com

This Brahmin was less than 3% tall, but the fall it heralded turned out to be far greater.

Double tops and bottoms as continuation patterns

Price rises, then falls; it rises again, testing the first high. The test fails and price then falls and tests the low, which acts as support. There is now a trading range: two tops and two bottoms; the former are potential resistances, the latter, potential supports.

Eventually, all trading ranges are broken. The one on chart 4-13, which had looked as if it was going to be confirmed as a double bottom following the decline from October's high to January's low (1), never made the 3% upside penetration required to overcome the high at 2; 4 having been only six points above it. At 4, the red down trend line was cut, but that cut having also been less than 3%, the line remained unbroken, not only then but also two months later at May's high.

In other words, the potential resistance at that line, had worked twice, which did not make it stronger however, potential resistance and support never being any more or any less than that, i.e. potential.

2 was, of course, the peak between 1 & 3 (the latter having been less than 1.50% above the former, was, for technical purposes, at the same level – see chapter two).

5 was another attempt to break the potential support at 1; May's high an equally unsuccessful attempt to overcome 2 & 4.

Chart 4-13: Double Top as continuation patterns

Finally, the range was broken, as all ranges are. This one became, not a double bottom reversal pattern, as had at first seemed likely, but a double top continuation pattern.

Once again, like a double top or double bottom reversal, a double bottom or double top continuation pattern creates the legitimate expectation – also called the objective – of a further decline equivalent to the distance between the highs and lows of what had been, until 6 was broken in this case, a trading range that could have been resolved in either the bears' favour, as it was, or in the bulls'.

Chart 4-14: Glaxo Smithkline 2004-05, Double Top?

Source: CQG, Inc. © 2006 All rights reserved worldwide.
www.cqg.com

Is this a Double Top?

It certainly looked like one where I have stopped this chart in August 2005.

Or did it?

There is no such thing as making a top or base area, except in brokers' minds as they try to nudge clients to do something without really saying anything. A base or top area is only a base or top area once it has been confirmed by a close 3% above or below the relevant breakout-point.

In GSK, last August's low was nine points beneath June's 1327, needing to be nearly 40 points beneath it to confirm the range since May as a double top. Look what happened next.

Chart 4-15: Glaxo Smithkline 2004-05, double bottom continuation pattern

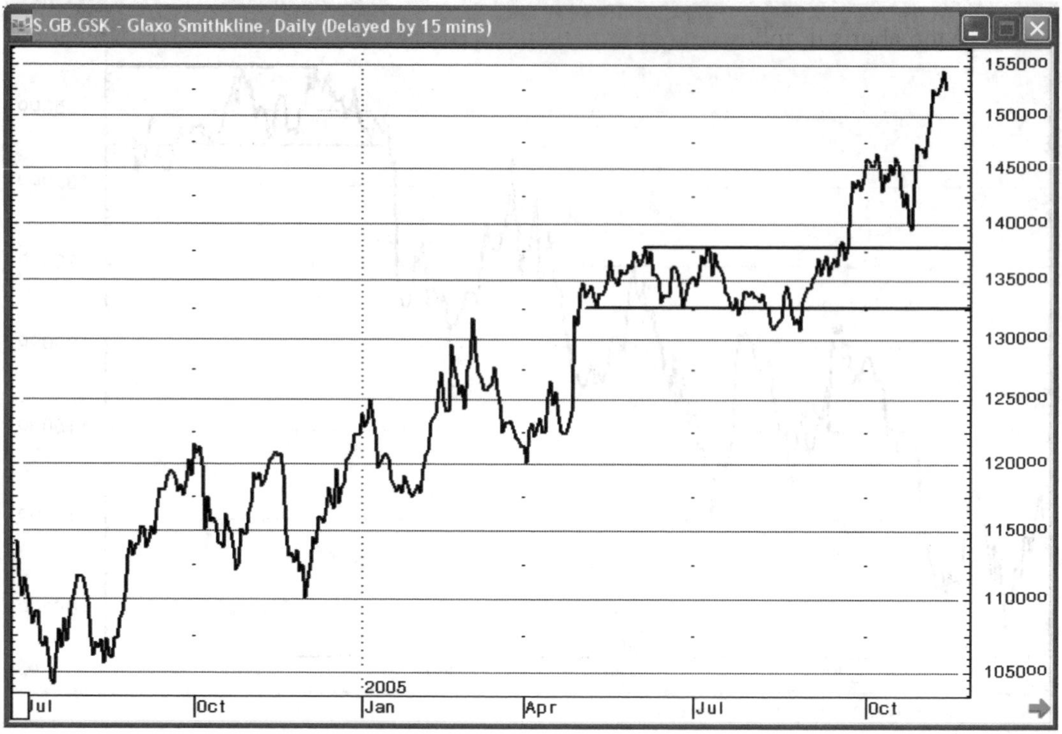

What looked as if it might become a double top became a double bottom continuation pattern, although you might just as easily call it a double bottom continuation pattern. But it doesn't matter what you call it as long as you didn't call it a double top at August's low, which (as already pointed out) did not break June's by the amount needed for confirmation of a double top.

NOTE Never anticipate the direction of a breakout.

Double top or bottom: the abort

A double top aborts if, following confirmation, price reacts and penetrates the horizontal line drawn on the two highs by 3% etc at a close. A double bottom aborts if, following confirmation, price advances to a close 3% above the low/lows of the pattern.

The foregoing is what happens according to my rules: the books say that the pattern remains valid unless the mid-point is subsequently re-crossed at any close.

I say that at best this means you lose too much money, at worst it's rubbish. The pattern aborts following a 3% re-penetration of the patterns' border; price then tends to test the mid-point, and if that is broken at any close, it remains potentially vulnerable to a further decline to the base of a double top; to the upper limit of a double bottom.

Supposing the mid-point, having been crossed, is re-crossed in the opposite direction?

Price is still in a trading range, i.e. it is undecided. If price is undecided, you should remain undecided too. Whatever position, you have, long short or square, there is no need to alter it.

To revive/reinstate a confirmed double top or bottom that has subsequently aborted, price must rise above the highest/lowest close posted before the 3% re-penetration of the upper/lower horizontal lines that made the top or bottom. The original objective/expectation then becomes valid once more.

NOTE	In view of the foregoing, it follows that there is no such thing as a triple top or bottom, thought by many as being more significant than a double top/bottom. A "triple" top or bottom is nothing more than a failed double top or bottom that got reinstated.

Triangles

It doesn't matter what type of triangle it is, and there are several, *this pattern signifies indecision*. But until confirmed by the appropriate breakout, all patterns signify indecision, even though the books don't apply the term except with regard to the three-cornered variety.

Chart 4-16: The isosceles triangle

Source: CQG, Inc. © 2006 All rights reserved worldwide.
www.cqg.com

It will come as no surprise that the down trend line converges on the up trend line. How else could you have the beginnings of a triangle without two converging sides and a base? I'll tell you how: in technical analysis. As I wrote the preceding paragraph, I realised for the first time that in technical analysis there is neither base nor third side to any triangle.

What we call a triangle should be called an arrowhead flying from left to right. And if isosceles means to you that the sides converge on each other at the same angle, then it shouldn't be called isosceles either, but a pattern with converging trend lines.

Initially, these two lines each have only two contact-points, which breaks the Rule of Four explained in Chapter Two. That rule stated that to draw an up trend line you must have a low, a high, a higher low and a higher high (a down trend line requiring a high, a low, a lower high and a lower low).

But a triangle is formed when the down trend line has only a high, a low and a lower high converging on an up trend line that only has a low, a high, and a higher low.

The points of contact with the down trend line must alternate with those points on the up trend line.

Thus you can see that the triangle *must* imply that the market is undecided: while buyers are happy to enter positions at progressively higher levels, sellers are prepared to accept successively lower ones. If this state of play continues all the way to the apex, the market has no direction; it is without a trend.

> **NOTE**   A market with no trend (a trading range) is the technician's worst enemy.

The problem with trading ranges is that you don't know you're in one until you have seen at least two points of contact with the upper line and two with the lower, and it doesn't matter if the lines are parallel, diverging or, as they are in a triangle, converging: less than two points of contact with any line means that it is speculative (the Rule of Four hasn't been applied).

Because we are certain to lose on the roundabouts, our aim must be to make money on the swings. Better to sit out the former and climb aboard the latter, although the former can provide a comfortable ride, provided you don't take it (that's the hard part) until the range has become an established fact rather than a hypothesis.

> **NOTE**   During the formation period of a trading range (the four initial moves, two up, two down), it is very easy to lose money. But once you can see that the range exists, making money out of it isn't hard, although it is contrary to human nature.

All you have to do is sell short at the top of the range, take your profits at the bottom and go long.

Anything else?

Yes; each time you deal, use a protective stop 3% outside the range, and pray that it lasts forever. It won't of course, but when you get stopped out of your final position inside the range, you are off the roundabout, so take your turn on the swing by going long/short as the new trend begins.

> **NOTE**   If you have a holding in any market that is triangulating, hold. If you have no position, don't open one. Since the market can't make any decision, why should you try doing so?

As with all trading ranges, triangles are eventually resolved, the best breakouts occurring at a point between two thirds and three quarters of the distance between the first point of contact with the up or down trend line and the triangle's apex.

"Best"?

If the breakout occurs any nearer to the apex than one quarter of the distance between the latter and the first point of contact with the relevant up or down trend line, there is a greater chance of it proving illusory or false.

It isn't hard to see why: the rallies and reactions within the triangle have become progressively shorter, illustrating that the division of opinion between buyers and sellers has become smaller.

Breakout from an isosceles triangle

If it is to be in favour of the bulls, the confirmation is a close above the second point of contact with the down trend line; in favour of the bears, a close below the second point of contact with the up trend line.

It isn't hard to see why: as soon as either has been passed at any close, the Rule of Four is satisfied and the speculative trend line forming the down or up side of the triangle ceases being speculative at all. It has become a valid up or down trend line.

Following confirmation of such a triangle, what is the objective?

If the breakout has been north-east, i.e. in the bulls' favour, draw a trend line parallel to the new up trend line from the first point of contact with the now broken down trend line: eventual contact with that line becomes the no time limit objective.

Chart 4-17: objective after triangle breakout

This chart is an extended version of the previous one. When that chart was drawn, price had not broken out of the pattern, i.e. the triangle had not been confirmed (see the section above on breakouts from triangles): there had been no close above the second point of contact with the down trend line until early October's advance.

It then became correct to draw the red line parallel to the blue up trend line: contact with that line became the triangle's objective.

Having appeared following an advance, October's upside breakout confirmed the triangle above as a continuation pattern. If the breakout had been south-east, the breakout would have confirmed the triangle as a reversal pattern.

Chart 4-18: triangle breakout as reversal pattern

The green triangle also appeared following an advance. But the May close below the second point of contact with the green up trend line confirmed this one as a reversal pattern, whose objective became the dark green line. Contrast the green triangle with the pink one. The latter was a continuation pattern: objective, the upper pink line (the return line) drawn parallel to May/September's pink up trend line.

What about potential resistance/support on the way up/down?

The confirmation of the triangle doesn't suspend the laws of potential support or resistance. Bearing in mind one of the first comments made about trend channels, the presumption that they are likely to be parallel, the first potential resistance will be the new up (down) trend line's parallel return line, although it could just as easily be the high (low) where the triangle began.

When does an isosceles triangle abort?

After confirmation has taken place, and whether or not it has been reached, if price closes beneath a horizontal line drawn through the apex.

Chart 4-19: aborting of a triangle

Source: CQG, Inc. © 2006 All rights reserved worldwide.
www.cqg.com

The triangle had been confirmed as an ascending continuation at X, a close above 2. It aborted several days later when price closed below the green line. On this occasion a move in the opposite direction then took place. But such developments are not mandatory as explained in the following paragraph.

The aborting of a triangle, unlike the aborting of a head & shoulders, doesn't create any objective in the opposite direction. What happens after a triangle aborts depends entirely on the market's technical condition at the time.

Ascending right angle triangle

Chart 4-20: ascending right angle triangle

Source: CQG, Inc. © 2006 All rights reserved worldwide.
www.cqg.com

While buyers are prepared to pay successively higher prices, sellers are happy to accommodate them, but unlike an isosceles, in a right angle triangle the sellers won't accept progressively lower levels.

Therefore more ascending right angle triangles are resolved by an advance above the horizontal side than by a close beneath the up trend line. But anticipate the direction of the breakout at your peril.

Actually, as the intending buyer/seller, you can do what you like, of course, but I earn my living as an adviser, and as an adviser I never advise anticipating the direction of the eventual breakout from any triangle; and as an investor I always listen to my own advice, mirroring that given to clients.

Ascending right angle triangle: the objective and the abort

If the breakout is north-east, a line parallel to the up trend line becomes the objective (the red line on the above chart). The abort is renewed close 3% beneath the horizontal.

Descending right angle triangle

Chart 4-21: descending right angle triangle

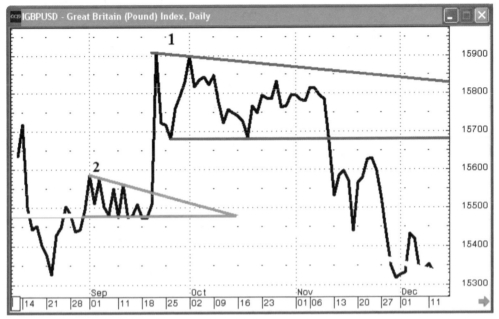

In this pattern (1 on chart), buyers keep appearing at the same level, but sellers reduce their limits. The inference is that resolution of the triangle will be made through a close 3% beneath the horizontal line (1% in this chart: it's an FX rate – £/$ in 1995).

You have the luxury of anticipating that outcome, yet once again my advice is to avoid self-indulgence, even though you'd have got away with it on this occasion. You wouldn't have done so in triangle 2 on that chart however. Nor did I get away with it in 1995 when I thought a downside break would occur. I was wrong. Technical analysts are not meant to think but to interpret what the chart is saying.

If it's a share, breakdown from a descending right angle triangle is a close 3% etc beneath the horizontal line, the upside breakout, a close above the second point of contact on the down trend line (12th September's, here). The inference of such a close is a further advance to the start of the down trend line, potential resistance because some poor fools bought there and, wanting to break even on what became a wrong decision as soon as the position was taken, are willing sellers.

If that point is overcome as it was in triangle 2 (you know the rules by now), the advance is free to continue. But if that potential resistance isn't overcome, you have the beginnings of a potential double top, although it only becomes one if the low between the two highs is broken by 3% etc at a close.

Wedge

As with all triangles, the sides converge. But unlike the isosceles and right angle triangles, in a wedge both sides are moving in the same direction: up in a rising wedge, down in a falling one.

You will recall the presumption that trend channels run between parallel lines. They aren't always parallel of course; it was only a presumption, a working hypothesis, if you prefer, not a rule.

Chart 4-22: rising wedge

A **rising wedge** illustrates that each successive up-thrust is gaining less ground than its predecessor, a market that appears to be running out of steam. It hasn't done so completely however unless/until the up trend line has been broken, at a close, by the required percentage.

As long as that line and the upper return line remain unbroken however, there is always the possibility that it will be the latter that gets broken, not the former.

A **falling wedge** illustrates that it is the down-thrusts that are becoming progressively weaker. But you shouldn't presume that all such patterns are resolved by upside penetration of the down trend line, even though the majority are.

Breakout from or confirmation of a falling wedge

If the down trend line is broken by an advance 3% above it at any close, as in the chart of BSkyB below, do nothing apart from watch and wait because what tends to follow is a rounding bottom, which looks exactly like it sounds, but which takes a long time to be formed.

Think half-circle, diameter on top. When that horizontal line has been broken by the appropriate close, a bottom reversal is in place. Then you buy.

Chart 4-23: breakout from a falling wedge

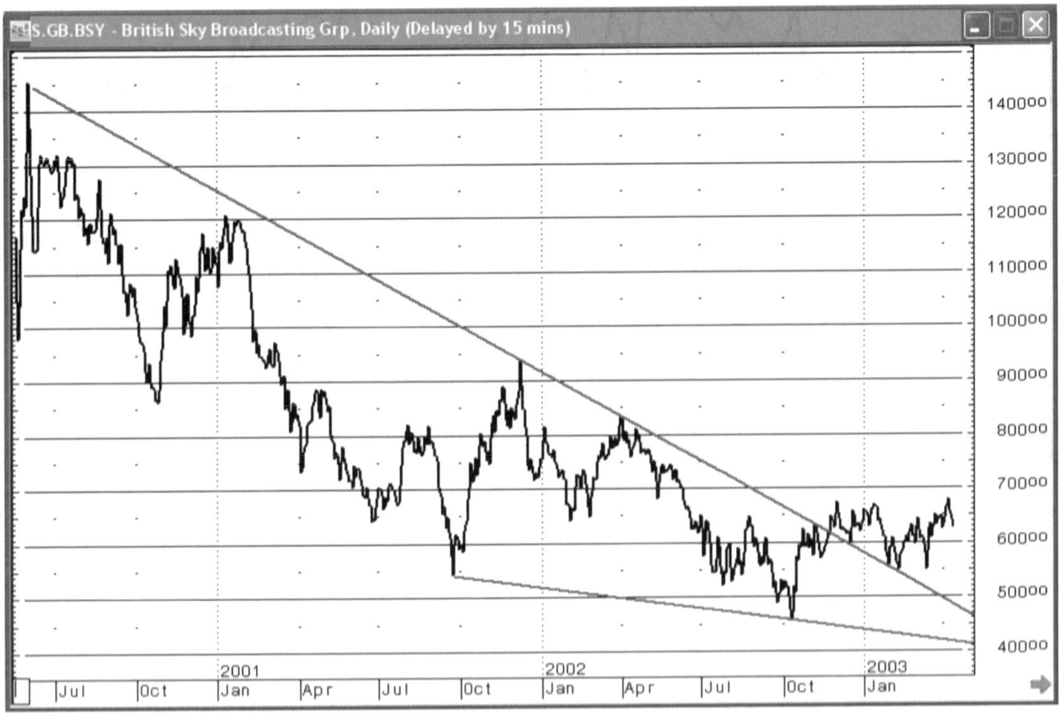

Source: CQG, Inc. © 2006 All rights reserved worldwide.
www.cqg.com

If it is the lower return line that is broken, draw a line parallel to the down trend line from the first point of contact with what had been the lower return line and look for an eventual second contact with it, i.e. a longer decline than the immediately preceding one.

The pattern is frequently seen in the shares of large, old-established companies.

Breakout from or confirmation of a rising wedge

If the up trend breaks, most if not all the ground gained during the pattern's formation is likely to be lost.

Chart 4-24: breakout from a rising wedge

If it is the upper return line that is broken by an advance above it, draw a line parallel to the up trend line from the first point of contact with what had been the converging upper return line, and in due course a second contact with the new upper return line becomes the expectation, and in the chart of the S&P below, was the realisation.

Chart 4-25: breakout from a rising wedge

Between January's high and March's, the S&P looked as though it might be going to form an ascending right angle triangle, but when the January and February highs, potential resistances, of course, chose to become actual ones, and neither of February's lows provided support, the range became a double top when the first of them gave way.

Broadening tops

The best way to describe the formation is to show you a chart.

Chart 4-26: broadening tops

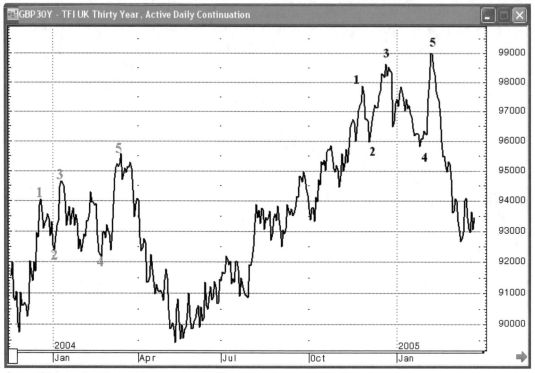

This chart, a 30 year U.K. Gilt, has two broadening tops that appeared within months of each other. Considering that the technicians' bible says such patterns are extremely rare, this chart is equally so.

The pattern, always a top, never a bottom, is said to appear only following an extended advance (Edwards & Magee on such formations: "make their appearance as a rule only at the end or in the final phases of long bull markets") at a time when the public is "excitedly committed", and the market is being swung about by wild rumours. When isn't it?

I can't recall if the public was in the market when these patterns appeared in 2004, but the Q3 low was the absolute low, and since May/February doesn't qualify as a long bull market, perhaps the nature of markets has changed, at least as far as this pattern is concerned.

What I can recall is making the call that a fall was due on both occasions, as soon as the pattern was confirmed: a close 1% (the norm for a bond) below point 4. Where I made my mistake was in remembering the comments about the pattern tending to appear only in the final phases of a long bull market, which made me believe that the fall would be long-lasting as well.

Following the confirmation of a broadening top, the decline should equal the distance between point 5 and 4, measured due south from the latter.

The reason for the name is obvious: the second peak is higher than the first; the third, higher than the second, while the second low is lower than the first.

Before we leave this pattern, I have three final thoughts,

1. If you see a broadening formation below the other highs, beware! It's the sign of an unstable market, even if there is no immediate fall.

2. Even so, if a rally crosses the mid-point of the line between 4 and 5, it aborts the broadening top.

3. Although there is supposed to be no such thing as a broadening bottom, there would be if £/$ made a broadening top because, quoted as it is in U.S. as $/£, that top would be a bottom.

All the patterns discussed so far were concerned with probability rather than timing. Indeed, the only pattern I know of that shows probability and timing is the flag.

Flags

Chart 4-27: flags

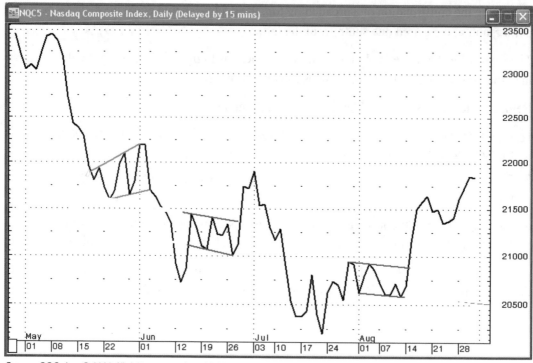

The ranges within the red and blue lines are all flags.

The rules for flags:

1. Flags need flagpoles, so the first move required to produce one is virtually straight, but does permit two successive up-days if that move has been down; two successive down-days if it has been up.

2. The initial move is down for a bearish flag, up for a bullish one. That move starts following the most recent high/low or consolidation.

3. The flag is the range between the red/blue lines. Both sides must be contacted at least twice, the first and third contacts are on one side, the second and fourth on the other.

4. The flag can point up down or sideways; the sides can be parallel, converge or diverge.

5. A flag is a flag only on a daily chart, and must be completed, i.e., confirmed, in no more than fifteen trading days, including the breakout from the pattern.

6. Breakout: if the first move (the flagpole) has been down, completion/confirmation is a close beneath the lowest in the pattern; if the first move has been up, above the highest.

7. The flag flies at half-mast, but is no cause for mourning.

8. After completion/confirmation of the flag, always in the same direction as the initial move, the second move begins, measured from the point where price last crossed the pattern's side.

9. The expectation is that the move will be approximately as large as the initial one.

10. The move must take no more than the same number of days as the initial one.

11. If the flag fails to achieve that objective in the time permitted, the pattern aborts.

12. With shares, the flag also aborts in a down-move following three successive up-days (two for an index) or a close 3% above the lowest (2% for an index); whichever occurs first; in an up-move, following three successive down-days or a close 3% below the highest, whichever occurs first; in an index, two days and 2%. In currencies, the abort occurs following two successive down or up-days (whichever applies) or a close 1% above (beneath) the lowest (highest). In a currency or bond index, reduce that to 0.50%.

13. Frequently, but not invariably, if a flag aborts according to the provisions of rule 12, the short-term trend reverses, but not if it aborts through application of rule 11.

I repeat chart 4-27 on page 156.

The **red flag**: an up-pointing pattern in a down-market. The objective resulting from this flag confirmed at 6th June's 2162.7 close was 1996, 8% below the breakout from the pattern, this being the size of the decline from May's high to the flag's low-point. But the lowest point reached was only 2062.1. The pattern aborted at 15th,'s 2144.1 close, the second successive up-day.

The **first blue flag**: down-pointing in an up-market. The upside objective was achieved.

Chart 4-28: flags

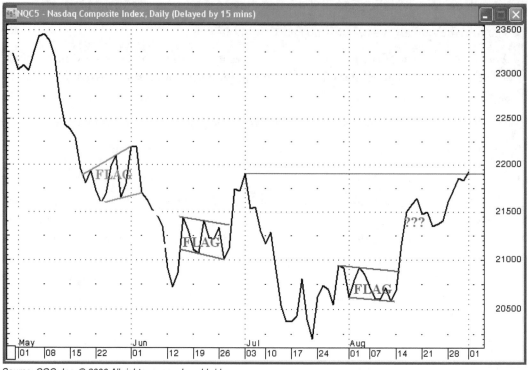

Source: CQG, Inc. © 2006 All rights reserved worldwide.
www.cqg.com

The **second blue flag**: The objective was reached, and exceeded.

The **green question marks**: a down-pointing flag in an up-market. The objective was 2249, 5% above the breakout-point, equal to 11th/18th's advance, but needed to be reached in no more than five days. Accordingly, it aborted at 1st September's close, the fifth day (I am writing this on 2nd September), yielding a profit of 2.47%.

Final notes on patterns

1. Flags don't always work; nor does any other pattern.

2. In 1998 I presented a paper to the Society of Technical Analysts demonstrating that during the previous sixteen years there had been several head & shoulders tops, and that none of them had worked.

3. Since patterns don't always work, use the stops.

5

By The Way...

You've used the expression many times, and heard it just as often, but have you ever thought, by the way, what follows? Almost invariably, something very important that belies those three little words.

By the way, I've won the lottery...I'm leaving you.

By the way, I wrote that in late May, 2006, just before the Court of Appeal's decision concerning the division of spoils in a spoiled marriage. So, by the way, I haven't won the lottery, but I'm still leaving you...

By the way, you'll be on the substitutes' bench on Saturday...

By the way, those shares we bought have come off a little, but the fundamentals are fine.

So this is a chapter about all those not so trivial things that happen in the investment business that don't lend themselves to a whole chapter but are nevertheless important.

[By the way, you will have read some of what follows elsewhere in these pages. If you don't remember, that's fine. If you do, then those comments must be worth repeating.]

By the way...

- If you are unfamiliar with the book of Sysilana, an excerpt of which appeared in the Prologue, tried to find out about it by looking up ©Chatline on the internet, and failed, try an anagram of the latter and spell the former backwards.

- In fundamental analysis it's always, "this time it's different". But technical analysts know that it's always the same. Nothing ever changes. People don't; why should markets?

- Technical analysis is huntin', shootin' and fishin'. Hunt for a trend; don't fish for a bottom nor shoot for a top.

- When people hear "buy", they think they will never get a better opportunity to do so, when they hear "sell", which they seldom want to hear anyway, they think that means the share or market will never, ever, go any higher than it is at that precise moment.

- Technical analysis without fundamental analysis does far less harm to your capital than fundamental analysis without technical analysis.

- The investment business is indoor work and no heavy lifting (John Owen).

- Investment genius is a short memory and a rising market, whereas investment intelligence is acquired only through a long memory of falling ones.

- Pride comes before a fall, they say. I say pride comes after a fall, but only if you forecast it.

- Most technical analysts were originally fundamental analysts. I've never heard of anyone who made the journey in the opposite direction.

- If everyone in the world who needed a currency that year was obliged to buy before any speculation was allowed, when do you think the doors of the casino would open? 3rd January.

- Thinking is what causes the really big losses. Why not let the market do the thinking for you! Stick to interpreting.

- In technical analysis, being clever starts with not trying to be clever.

- When the chart is saying something strongly enough, the fundamentals needed to make price behave the way the chart says it will appear.

Rain in Iowa

Purely by reference to the three month rate-of-change, an extremely important indicator explained in Chapter Six, in the 1980s I called the end of a drought in the American corn-belt.

It was simple, really. Because of this drought, wheat, corn, you name it, went through the roof. So did copper and hog bellies. You think I'm joking? The copper and hog bellies pits are next to soft commodities. Enthusiasm for corn and wheat spilled over into other pits. Crazy? Of course it is, but that's the way markets behave.

All I had to do was look at the overbought condition revealed by the rate-of-change. When it became extreme, *and* its trend had reversed (the trend of everything, indicators as well as price, is always your friend), I announced on Reuter's public screen, "Within five days, it will rain in Iowa". It took two.

How could that be?

The overbought indicator couldn't know it was going to rain, could it? It couldn't, and didn't. But in the end, price takes care of everything, and price was too high: the indicator was saying it. But the only fundamental that could trigger the selling required to unwind the overbought condition was the reverse of that responsible for the buying: rain in place of no rain!

- Bull markets end when the news is good. The only markets that end when the news is bad are bear markets.

- There are two good days in partnerships, the days you say hello and goodbye.

- I am frequently asked what my best calls have been. The ones no one remembers. They don't remember because they don't want to, having almost invariably been on the wrong foot at the time, preferring to extrapolate the existing trend than change their minds.

- The potential for loss when gambling on certainties is infinite. (Winston Churchill)

- People who use technical analysis just to confirm what they are already thinking, yet reject it when it does the opposite, are barking up the wrong tree.

- You can buy all of the shares some of the time, some of the shares all of the time, but you can't buy all the shares all the time.

- Correlations are a fundamental concept, therefore suspect: if correlations really worked, economists would have a better track record.

- When downsizing, J.P.Morgan chase, Goldman sacks, Merrill lynch.

- When all else fails, put on a costume and sing a silly song. (Sam Walton of Wal-mart)

- Although there are people who make money on the big tables at Monte Carlo, if you haven't got the stomach for it, you're better off on the beach. (David Blackwell)

- You can always tell an out-of-the money options trader by the way his hands shake when he asks "what's the market doing today?". (Joe Granville)

- If you hitch your wagon to a star, beware the nuclear fall-out.

- In the middle of the 20th century, the 100 year average was 1950. How did that help in...1999, or 1901? And if you take the long-term average into account, although the average dead man has been dead for years, his average age hasn't changed at all.

- In markets the only thing likely to fall in your lap is your soup.

- Board members should always be an odd number, and three is too many. (Gianni Agnelli)

- There is no substitute for intelligence, but you can get the same reputation merely by keeping your mouth shut.

- There is no such thing as "making a top area". A top area isn't a top area until it has been confirmed; until then, it is a trading range, which might just as easily be resolved by an upside as by a downside break. "Making a top area" is an opinion, not a fact. There is no such thing as making a base area either; by the way.

- The straw in the wind may be the one that breaks the camel's back, and the light at the end of the tunnel is sometimes just that.

- Nothing is more suicidal than a rational investment policy in an irrational environment. (J.M. Keynes)

- A study of economics reveals that the best time to buy anything is last year. (Marty Allen)

- It is often said that you're only as good as your last call. If only it were true; you're only as good as your next one.

- Price responds not to value but to people's opinion of future value. If price did respond immediately to value, there would be no market.

- Old forecasters never die, they just make fewer calls; old brokers never die, they just get fewer calls; old chartists never die, they just lose relative strength; old traders never die, they just lose their nerve; old speculators never die, they just lose their money.

- If fundamental analysis is really that effective, how did technical analysis come into being?

- It is neither necessary nor possible to understand the market; the one essential is to come to terms with it.

- There is a tide in the affairs of men which, taken at the flood, leads on to drowning. (Shakespeare/Marber)

- When they were called personnel officers, they looked after you. Now they're called human resources, all they do is waste you.

- The City is a lousy place…(in which) to make a lot of money.

- Good shares are like good parties; it's hard to say good bye to them. But shares don't know you own them; they're for buying and selling. If you want to buy and hold, antiques are your game.

- Wall Street is the only place to which people ride in a Rolls Royce to get advice from people who ride the subway. (Warren Buffett)

- For an honest man there are no conflicts of interest; or for a dishonest one.

- It's better to stand up and be counted than lie down and be counted out.

- Charting's tough and then you're wrong.

- Collegiate investing decisions may make those present feel good, but don't do much good for investors.

- Things go on in club committees that you wouldn't tolerate for five minutes in business.

- If you're committed, don't sit on committees.

- Investors are never more emotional than when trying to justify a position which, rationally, they have already started to question.

- The meek shall inherit the earth, but not the mineral rights (Jean-Paul Getty). A mine is a hole in the ground with a liar at the top (Mark Twain). Many a good mine has been ruined by sinking a shaft (stock market lore). More oil has been discovered on the floor of the stock exchange than ever came out of the North Sea (ditto).

- Food finds it easier to land on light-coloured ties than on dark.

- Life is a bear market with ever more feeble rallies; getting older is better than the alternative; death is nature's way of telling you to slow down.

- Long-term forecasting is for those who have no idea what's going to happen in the short-term, and as J.M. Keynes so brilliantly observed, in the long run we're all dead.

- Life is short and then you die. (Woody Allen)

- No man is a prophet in his own country (Arab philosophy). If you want people to pay attention, go abroad to forecast.

- Virtue is its own reward; also it's only reward.

- Winning isn't everything, but losing isn't anything.

- You may make money and will undoubtedly feel clever by dealing against the trend, but does it make sense? Not to technicians; we know that the trend is your friend. Why lose a friend?

- You can't win 'em all, but you don't have to.

- When you make money, you got lucky. When you lose it, it's your own fault.

For your bumper sticker: *Technical analysts do it, by the way, when the market closes.*

6

Indicators

Accumulation/Distribution	MACD	Price Channel
Alexander's Filter	MACD Forest	Rate of Change
Alpha/Beta	Majority Rule	Ratio
Bar Chart	Market Profile (CBOT)	RSI
Bollinger Bands	Momentum	Scatter Chart
Butterfly Spread	Money Flow Index	Spread
Candle-stick	Moving Average	Spread MA
Chaikin Oscillator	On Balance Volume	Stochastics Fast
Commodity Channel	OBV – Weighted	Stochastics Slow
Counter Clockwise	Open Interest	Ultimate Oscillator
Directional Movement	Oscillator	Volatility
Ease of Movement	Parabolic Time/Price	Volatility Index
Ichimo Kinko Hyo	Per Cent R	Volume
Kairi	Point & Figure	Volume Price Trend
Line	Point & Figure Hi/Lo	Weighted Close

When I compiled the above list from the Reuters' menu, I was going to point out that since they are given away free when you take the service, they were unlikely to be of any use because free advice is worth precisely what you pay for it. Then I realised that in this book I have already given away the secret of one of my indicators, and will shortly do the same with a second.

There are two explanations: either inventors of indices know their indicators don't really work or we are all frightfully nice chaps.

The indicators underlined above will either be rubbished or explained somewhere in this book.

My list is a third the size of the full one, but is really even shorter: I don't use the term indicator to describe bar, candle-stick, line, point & figure or price channel, considering the terms momentum and rate-of-change to be inter-changeable, and volume as having no use at all.

Coppock Indicator

Many years ago, in a paper titled "Emotions Make Prices", the eponymous Edwin Coppock devised an indicator that tells investors when to buy shares for the long-term. As he wrote at the time,

> *"Do major long-term buying of strong stocks when the curve...turns upwards from below...zero line".*

Don't worry; what Coppock meant by that will soon be explained. As for the zero line, in my experience (I have worked with this indicator for more than forty years), signals given at and just above the zero line are equally valid.

I first read about Coppock in a 1963 issue of the *Investors Chronicle*, in an article by Harold Wincott. It was one of the major factors influencing my conversion from fundamental to technical analysis, although, strictly speaking, it isn't a technical signal at all. Edwin Coppock was an econometrician.

Like everything else these days, Coppock's Indicator has been dumbed down. Who by? Traders of course who do little research from either a fundamental or technical point-of-view, just buy and sell and, if they're hedge funds, sell and buy as well.

Not being able to look beyond the bridge of their noses, traders cross bridges before they come to them, or jump off before they're even halfway across, which is why they often go under water.

"Emotions Make Prices" reminded readers that,

> *"The technique is of no value whatsoever to an in-and-out trader.*
> *It is a technique for long-term investors; their long-term buying guide".*

The Coppock Signal is not the sign of a trend reversal, but shows when the risk factor in the market is low, and usually heralds a sustained advance.

Although Coppock applied his signal only to the Dow Jones Industrial Average, its rationale makes it applicable, at least in theory, to all markets, and I have used it successfully in many. The only non-performer being the foreign exchange market, I never use it there.

> **NOTE** Since 1919, in the S&P 500 Index Coppock's technique has given only one "bad" signal, in 2002.

Chart 6-1: Coppock Indicator, S&P500

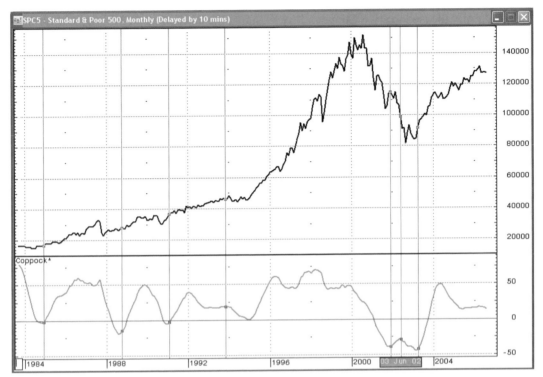

The indicator's record since 1984

Wall Street

But the indicator was not devised for traders buying the index but for long-term investors buying "strong stocks" researched on a fundamental basis, and following the 2002 signal you would have stopped buying at the red line on the chart, placed where the curve started falling from a position below zero (my innovation), and started buying again not long after the bear market low.

I don't know what shares you would have bought following either signal, but if you average the two purchase levels, your long position, in well-researched stocks, was at 1033.9. How bad is that?

London

I was naturally pleased to see a Coppock Buy Signal at the end January 1975, especially since I had called the end of the 1972-74 bear market on 8th (the low had been posted on 13th December 2004).

When a bull market starts few believe that what they are seeing is anything more than a dead cat bounce, so most institutional clients, especially my former colleagues in the investment department at N.M. Rothschild, greeted the Coppock signal with derision, just as they had greeted my 8th January call, one of them going so far as to say cattily (his name was Katz) "Brian Marber always was mad".

Contact with Edwin Coppock

The Coppock critics' argument was that markets had changed, cycles were shorter, this time it's different etc; in other words, all the usual rubbish trotted out at market turns. To silence them, I contacted Edwin Coppock, who sent me a taped reply. This is the gist of it.

He was a devout Episcopalian. Having been asked by administrators of church funds to devise a long-term low-risk signal to enable them to know when to increase their equity holdings, and when to stand aside, Coppock asked a number of ministers how long it took for the human mind to adjust to bereavement, divorce, illness, unemployment, losing money, moving house, retirement etc, i.e. the greatest stresses people have to cope with.

The answer was "11 to 14 months". In case you've heard versions of this story from other sources, then you heard them from people who heard them from other people who heard them from me, and went wrong along the way. As you can see, the indicator has nothing to do with market cycles but everything to do with human nature. Coppock set to work. Here is the result of his labour as amended by me.

Creating the indicator

1. Compare the end-month close with the closes 11 and 14 months previously.

2. Express the differentials as percentages of the current month.

3. Combine the two results and multiply by 10.

4. Repeat the exercise for each of the preceding nine months: the numbers of the one immediately preceding the current month are multiplied by nine, of two months previously by eight etc. After ten, you have a weighted average of the monthly data going back 24 months.

5. Plot the indicator below the monthly chart of the index you're monitoring.

6. Buy when the curve, having fallen near to (Marber amendment) or below zero, turns up.

7. Stop buying if the curve turns down below zero (Marber amendment).

8. Finish buying by the time the indicator has risen to zero: if it turned up near zero, finish buying in accordance with shorter-term technical signals.

9. Enjoy the ride: after zero has been exceeded the big amplitude move of the bull market starts.

Sell Signals

The indicator doesn't give sell signals because human beings don't need 11 to 14 months to turn from elation to depression.

Chart 6-2: Coppock Signals in FTSE100 since its inception

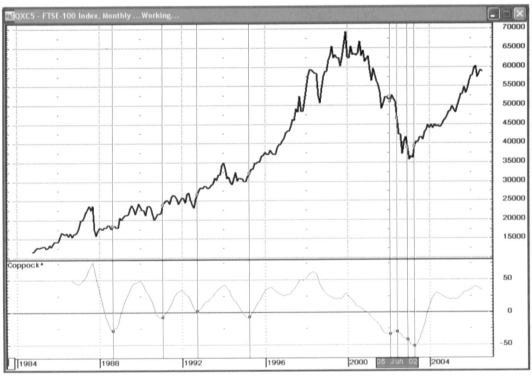

Source: CQG, Inc. © 2006 All rights reserved worldwide.
www.cqg.com

Since 1945, there have been two "bad" signals, the first in 1948. Not in FTSE: it hadn't been thought of at the time, but in the Industrial Ordinary Index, which was superseded by the All-Share. The second one was in 2002, and matches that in the S&P, already described. The arguments used to explain why the S&P signal wasn't so bad after all apply equally to FTSE.

> **NOTE**　　　When Coppock signals appear, the fundamental outlook is invariably poor. But history tells us to be guided by the signal rather than the outlook, even if not immediately. For example, four months after the 1988 signal, FTSE was off 4.8%. Six weeks after 1991's & 1992's, it was off 5.1% and 4.3%.

In 2002, in an article in the *Financial Times*, Philip Coggan poured scorn on the indicator when the market fell substantially following the 2002 signal: two errors in more than 60 years. I can only conclude that this distinguished journalist, who learned about Coppock from me, didn't distinguish between trading futures and long-term investment.

The Rate-of-Change (ROC), also known as momentum

If you're an opera-lover and learn that the price of tickets has just been doubled, you will probably cut down on visits. But supposing prices are going to be gradually increased over the next two years until they have doubled, will you still cut down on visits? Maybe not.

Markets work the same way. Buy something that falls 5% immediately and I'll bet your emotional reaction is totally different from what it would be if the fall took place over a year.

$E^2 = MC$

If you think you've seen something like this equation before, yes you have. But $E = MC^2$ is very old hat; $E^2 = MC$ is Marber's Law of Relativity: the market obeys all the laws of physics; none is up for change when E=emotion, M=movement and C=course of time, then the bigger the movement and the shorter the time period, the greater the effect on the emotions..

Roll a ball down a hill. Until you let go, your arm has all the momentum; the ball, none. But as soon as you release it, the ball starts gaining downside momentum, and the further it falls, the greater that momentum or rate-of-change becomes, reaching its peak at the bottom.

What happens when you throw a ball in the air? Although its momentum (rate-of-change) starts decreasing as soon as you release it, the ball still keeps rising until upside momentum reverses. Only then does the ball start to fall. By all means keep your eye on the ball, but pay more attention to its momentum if you want to know when the change from up to down is about to take place.

The market is the ball

Concentrate on the former. Momentum is what creates emotion, and it is emotion that moves the market: the faster the market moves, the greater the effect on the emotions.

Looking at the question in another way, if your sales were up 10% last month, that's good news. But if the increase over the three preceding months was 14%, 16% and 18% respectively, then the latest news is relatively less good than at first appeared: sales are increasing but at a diminishing rate, therefore it may be only a matter of time before they not only fail to increase but also start to fall.

Creating a momentum or rate-of-change indicator

Express the latest price as a percentage deviation from price at your chosen date in the past. My chosen date is three months (63 trading days). This isn't, nor ever has been, a whim: I've been there, done the work, bought the T-shirt, thrown it away and moved on. But my chosen time period hasn't.

I doubt you will have to draw your own indicator, as I had to for the first twenty years I used it. But to create one, you look back 64 trading days, not 63, for mathematical reasons that should be obvious; calculate the difference between price now and then, and express the latter as a percentage of the former.

Why three months?

Empirical observation; if, having fallen for some time, price reverses and then advances, let's suppose that eleven days after the low it has advanced 5%, empirical observation tells you if it hasn't liked such extremes in the past, i.e. if it has tended to react when the rate-of-change has reached 5%. If so, 5% is an overbought condition.

Reading the Rate-of-Change's chart

The chart of the rate-of-change(ROC) is read exactly like any other; at extreme levels the indicator not only shows overbought/oversold conditions (the extremes vary according to which share, rate, index etc. you're reading, and also the stage of the bull/bear market you're in) but also makes patterns and trends, potential support and resistance levels.

Finally, the principles of averages described in the previous chapter also apply.

I have already told you that I use a 63-day rate-of-change; I also use a 10-day average of that period.

> **NOTE** Momentum reversals occur when the indicator's average reverses direction, and the relevant up or down trend line has been broken by 1%.

What is the relevant up or down trend line?

I use a 63-day period in London (64 or 65 days when the market being monitored demands it).

The rate-of-change is a *leading* indicator (where it leads the market tends to follow). Accordingly, the reversals I look for are those that tend to occur after price has been moving in a trend that has lasted approximately three months. That having been said, it is vital to bear in mind that all trends can end at any time, often without warning. But the great merit of the ROC is that it tends to make a reversal just before the trend's direction changes.

Supposing price has been falling. Then the rate-of-change's down trend line is broken by 1%, and its 10-day average starts rising (the two events don't have to be in that order), then – see above – a momentum reversal has occurred.

Following a momentum reversal, the odds have moved against continuation of the previous trend, and if it hasn't already done so, price is likely to start reversing at any time, although there is no obligation for it to do so immediately, or indeed, at all.

When driving and you put out your indicator (actually, I don't think it's called that any more – isn't it now the blinking light or blinking blinkers?), you are telling others that you are about to change direction. You don't generally flick the switch three roads before you turn. But sometimes you might do so, at others you might change your mind after it has started flashing; going straight on or even turning in the opposite direction to that originally indicated.

NOTE	The indicator is just that; an indicator, not a dictator.

There are times when price posts a new rally high or reaction low, but not the indicator. If so, the peak or trough in price is accompanied by a *momentum divergence*. A momentum or rate-of-change divergence is never good news, usually pointing to trouble in the not-too-distant future.

What does "not-too-distant" mean?

That's the problem: it varies. But if you trade against the trend of the indicator, you might make money (if you trade against the trend of anything, you might make money), but you are taking a risk that I wouldn't take, and acting against my advice; therefore wasting my time in writing this book, and yours in reading it.

I have never read anything in any other book about trends and averages being applied to the rate-of-change indicator, nor patterns: what you are reading is pure Marber. The techniques described so far in this chapter, and in the following paragraphs, like my technique for dealing with potential support and resistance, are my own invention. *They have never been revealed before, not by me, anyway.*

I use those techniques because they work. Not all the time however: technical analysis is not an automatic process; and although I have said it is a religion, it is also dependent on the skill and experience of the person reading the chart: knowing what to use, and when. In technical analysis, the only thing that works all the time is the technical analyst.

Where the ROC points, price tends to follow

Exception

There is one occasion when the rate-of-change frequently goes in the opposite direction to price: during price's second advance in an up-market, its second decline in a down-market.

Up market: The first significant overbought condition having been unwound ("significant" meaning an overbought greater than any in the preceding down-market), the second advance takes place with price going up at a slower rate than it had done when that first overbought excess was being created, causing a divergence between price and momentum (the ROC).

Down-market: The first significant condition having been unwound (see above for the definition of significant), the second decline takes place with price falling at a slower rate than it was when the first oversold excess was being created, causing a divergence between price and momentum (the ROC).

Momentum divergence: price rises but the ROC falls *or* price falls but the ROC rises.

Chart 6-3: ROC

The daily chart on the previous page is the dollar index from the end of the 1998 decline to July 2006's peak and shows that the advance between April and late June took place despite a decline by the ROC.

Would the green line, the index month average, have kept you in the market as it frequently does during an extended rise in price? Not for the whole period: in May the average started falling, switching roles from the potential support it had been when rising to the potential resistance it then became as it fell.

Would anything of a technical nature have kept you long?

Let's see: the last low on the way up to end-April's high, potential support, was also broken, the three month average wasn't tested (I like to see a renewed close above an average following one or more beneath it before allowing that a true test has been made); at $'s May low the ROC certainly wasn't showing any oversold, nor were stochastics, the RSI and MACD. None of these indicators are shown here because I haven't yet explained them.

Does the foregoing mean that on this occasion technical analysis failed?

If you like to say so, yes. But as I've said before, and will say again, it's an art not a science, and won't show everything all the time.

Price/ROC divergences

Do price momentum divergences only tend to appear in the early stage of a major market reversal? No.

What about trying a different period?

Would a much shorter or much longer period than 63 days be better? No. I've done the work and got the answer: 63 days works best.

Of course, regression analysis could find an indicator that would have kept you in $ during May's decline, after the event, of course. You can always find an indicator that, post hoc, would have got you out or kept you in any position, but that doesn't mean it would work the next time.

- The first major **overbought condition of a new bull market** is almost invariably greater than any seen in the previous bear market, and usually the largest overbought of the whole bull market. If an overbought condition greater than the first appears later on, that new overbought peak tends to coincide with the bull market's end.

- The first major **oversold condition of a new bear market** is almost invariably greater than any seen in the previous bull market, and usually the largest oversold of the whole bear market. If an oversold condition greater than the first appears later on, that new oversold excess almost invariably coincides with the bear market low.

Once the first overbought condition of a new bull market (the first oversold of a new bear market) has made a top/bottom, i.e. once the ROC has made a top/ bottom reversal (explained at the beginning of the section on reading the rate-of-change's chart), a fall (advance) almost invariably follows.

Chart 6-4: first major overbought condition of a new bull market

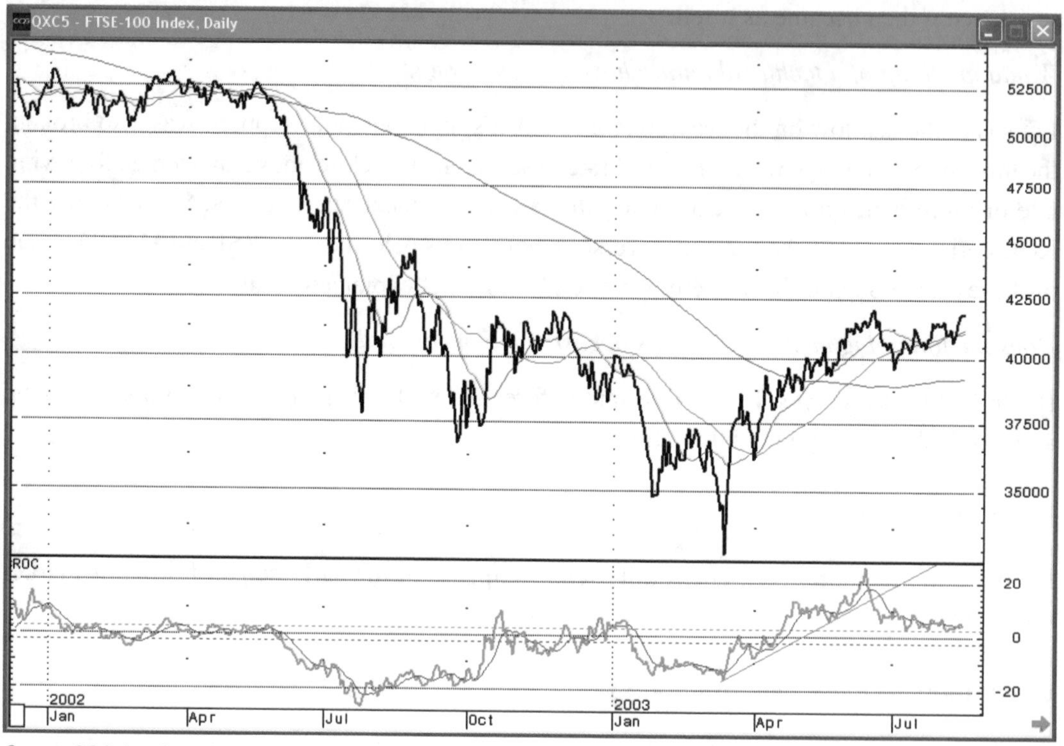

Source: CQG, Inc. © 2006 All rights reserved worldwide.
www.cqg.com

The chart is FTSE, but that's not what's important. What matters is that it's the chart of the concluding stages of a bear market, followed by the first *major* overbought condition (revealed by the ROC) of the succeeding bull market. In this case, the overbought excess recorded by the ROC in June 2003.

Why wasn't the end-April 2003 overbought condition the first of the bull market?

Because it was lower than December 2001's.

How do you know the reaction following the first major overbought condition has ended?

Judgment and experience, but not very hard in this instance: the successful test of the three month average (red line on the chart of FTSE itself), which was confirmed when the index, having closed several times beneath it, subsequently closed above that average again.

But frequently price does better than that, finding support at the one month average in the same manner as described above. At others, neither average provides support. If that is the case, you have to wait for some other signal.

Note: Do *not* compare the first overbought condition of what might be a new bull market or the first oversold condition of what might be a new bear market with the first overbought condition of the previous bull market or the first oversold condition of the previous bear market: *every bull and every bear market sets its own parameters.*

When anyone other than a technician says "the market's too high", he is actually saying "I didn't think it would go up so much"; i.e. he's wrong, but not admitting it; preferring to blame the market for being wrong instead of blaming himself and his wrong-headed thinking. But as I have already written earlier in this book, the market is never wrong; never right. The market merely is.

"The market's too high" a synonym for "it's come up too much, too soon", is another way of saying that it's worked up too much steam, or that it's current momentum is too high to be sustained.

ROC/momentum studies work because the indicator measures emotion in the market place. It is a mathematical calculation of what constitutes too much, too soon; an unemotional way of measuring the market's emotions.

> **NOTE** Don't ever forget that it is emotion and psychology (and an imbalance between supply and demand, of course) that rule price, not logic.

Other indicators can sometimes tell you the direction of the next move in price, but neither its extent nor the likely commencement date of that move before price has given any indications. It is also the only indicator that can tell the expert how long that move might last, even before it gets underway.

The long-term doesn't get to have its say until the intermediate trend has had its day. The latter is the province of the ROC indicator. If an intermediate-term move violates the relevant support or resistance, the long-term trend can be reversed.

As with everything in technical analysis, the trend is your friend. It doesn't matter how high momentum has become; until the indicator (any indicator) makes a reversal, it is always possible for that trend to continue. But momentum can and does move in trends, and once the up or down trend changes its direction, believers in price and price alone are likely to receive unpleasant surprises.

Unfortunately for me in my advisor's hat, but fortunately not for you as an investor, the calls I can and do make based on the ROC are seldom believed because few clients bother to read anything apart from the conclusions without trying to understand the indicator's rationale. Seeing nothing suspicious in price, they confine their suspicions to the indicator.

The most important considerations are–

Is the market overbought/oversold?

In which direction is the ROC's trend?

Once the indicator has reversed, the odds favour a market reversal, but do not make it a certainty. In this business there aren't any certainties, merely probabilities and possibilities.

System assessed

In the early 1980s, the techniques explained in this section, as applied in my analysis of £/$, were assessed by a client company running a "what if" programme.

Over the test period (two years), in a test not confined to ROC/momentum studies but including anything and everything in technical analysis that those involved could think of, only one system of any kind out-performed the techniques I use (the indicator breaking a trend line and its 10-day average reversing direction).

What was this wonder-system?

Replace my 10-day average with a 9-day one.

In 1980 I was in Princeton visiting Commodities Corporation, a stable of traders playing any market that moved. At that time, the foreign exchange market was one of the big movers and shakers, shaking everyone except a few technical analysts.

I told the traders how I used the ROC, emphasising that the market becomes high risk if you continue trading any rate in a trend's existing direction when the currency is already extremely overbought or extremely oversold. One voice kept interrupting, "that's when you make the big money".

I kept on talking about the high risk; the voice kept on repeating the mantra, "that's when you make the big money". It taught me a lasting lesson: don't anticipate the end of the trend, in price, in indicators, in anything. Taking some money off the table is a good idea, of course, but don't reverse positions until the ROC tells you to do so.

NOTE	Technical analysis is about interpreting what the chart is saying; not about thinking.

The latter is how you lose the big money.

The voice was Mike Marcus's, destined to make enormous sums of money in FX trading, and immortalised in Jack Schwager's *Market Wizards*, a book I couldn't recommend more highly if you want to learn about how the really successful traders trade and think. Whether, having met me, Mike Marcus then eschewed high risk, I am not able to say, but I doubt it.

One thing I can say: It's no good trying to take the risks other people are able to take unless you are capable of doing so. As George Goodman, aka. Adam Smith, remarked in his book *The Money Game* (a must-read for anyone interested in this business, even though the author is not in love with technical analysis), "if you don't know yourself, this is an expensive place to find out".

Now for some other indicators, but none I rate as highly as the ROC.

Stochastics

The indicator, according to what I was told a long time ago, was born in the commodity market. I never checked this out. I never read about it either, because (1) I couldn't understand the mathematics; (2) I didn't care; (3) I gave it a try and it appeared to be of some assistance, sometimes; (4) technical analysis, in my submission, anyway, is all about "if you can't beat 'em, join 'em".

Briefly the theory behind the indicator is that in a rising market price tends to close near the top of the daily range; in a falling one, near the bottom. Enough said.

The indicator is an oscillator, scaled from 1 to 100. When levels in excess of 80 are posted, the oscillator is showing an overbought condition, whereas at levels below 20, it is showing that the market is oversold.

The "signal" to deal

Some would say that you sell above 80, including selling short; buying to cover shorts and go long below 20.

I say "rubbish" to both.

As you can see, the indicator has an average, and if you want a "sell" signal, and a "buy" signal for that matter, wait for levels above 80 or below 20 to be posted, dealing only after the average has changed direction as well: sell when the indicator has risen over 80 and the average starts falling; buy when the indicator has fallen below 20 and after the average has started rising.

Why the inverted commas?

Because I don't believe that dealing purely according to the movement of stochastics will do anyone much good, if any, in the long run.

5-day stochastics:

Coming from the commodity market where five days is the long-term and positions are frequently sold out by the weekend, the indicator is unlikely to start rising until after the market has already done so.

Chart 6-5: 5-day stochastics

The indicator's average starts rising later still. Then, if the movement only lasts around five days, and you use a downturn by the average as your reason to cover the position, by the time you do so you've probably made a round trip – a euphemism for losing money.

> **NOTE** You cannot found an investment policy or a trading one (in my submission) on a 5-day period.

Where 5-day stochastics can help is when you have made up your mind to buy (or sell) and want to introduce an element of short-term timing in order to find an entry or exit-point.

34-day stochastics

I know no one who uses this time period unless he learned it from me. I use it because it works. It does so as follows: once levels above 80 (75 if you prefer) have been posted, the indicator, though overbought, frequently stays above 80/75 for long periods; it isn't primed to unwind that condition until both indicator and average have fallen below your chosen horizontal. When indicator and average fall below 25/ 20, registering an oversold condition, the latter frequently lasts for long periods.

Chart 6-6: 34-day stochastics

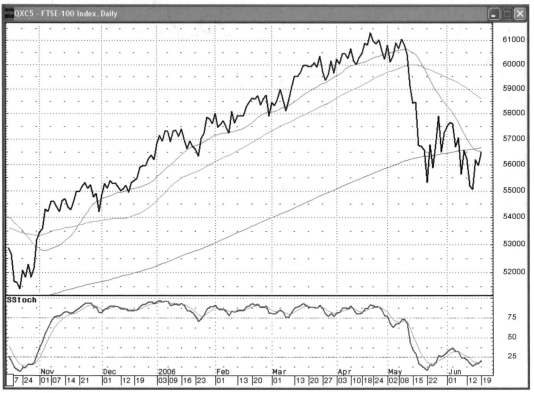

Even though the criteria for the overbought condition to start unwinding were met in January and February 2006, FTSE's one month average never stopped rising, never ceased to act as support for price. Using a second filter to dissuade you from acting without sufficient reason has to be a good thing.

A problem arises when indicators give conflicting signals. That's when you need judgment and experience; when those who think they're "a bit of a chartist" fall by the wayside, deciding that technical analysis is no good. That's good; the less technical analysts there are, the more effective does technical analysis become.

> **NOTE** With 34-day stochastics you are kept in the market, or out, when other indicators covering shorter periods have done you no good at all, enriching no one apart from stockbrokers.

Why did I choose 34 days?

It's a number in the Fibonacci series. Illogical? With a number of indicators the standard default is 14. Why? A 14 day period equals half a lunar month. But a lunar month includes weekends, whereas the standard 14-day default doesn't. Now that's what I call illogical.

34 day stochastics fills a niche. I try to cover a number of different time periods:

- **5 days** (short stochastics),
- **9 days** (the relative strength indicator),
- **21 days** (one month average),
- **63 days** (ROC and three month average), and
- **252 days** (one year average in the UK stock market – 261 days in the FX market).

Relative Strength Indicator (RSI)

Devised by Welles Wilder, the oscillator is one of many created by this American, and if this raises the question that if this one's any good, why did he feel the need to devise any others, that's a very good question (a synonym for: "I'm not sure of the answer").

In FX markets in the 1980s, it was all the rage. I investigated it, and found it didn't work very well for me. But the oscillator does apparently work for some technicians, so here is a description of how it works…for them.

Oscillators are scaled from 0 to 100. Like stochastics, the RSI (relative strength indicator) shows an overbought condition when it rises above 75 or 80 (the choice is yours) or falls below 25 or 20 (same thing applies).

Relative strength: what strength and what is it relative to?

The oscillator calculates the ground gained on days when price is rising compared with the ground lost on days when it is falling.

Chart 6-7: RSI

Source: CQG, Inc. © 2006 All rights reserved worldwide.
www.cqg.com

I have used the standard default, 9 days (trading sessions) for the oscillator/indicator, 21 days, the standard default, for its average.

If it was your strategy to buy only when the oscillator was oversold, and only to sell when it was overbought, you bought in October 2005 and sold in November, buying again in May 2006, making one profit and running one paper loss.

Using changes in the direction of the average (see the red and blue vertical lines on the chart), you traded far more often. And if you had substituted a shorter period than 21 days for the average, you would have been even more active.

Proponents of the RSI also draw trend lines as described in chapter two (I have drawn three on the chart), combining them with upturns and downturns of the average, and including, where relevant, overbought and oversold conditions to indicate when to buy and sell. But that's not all: they also pay attention to the relevance, if any, of crossing the mid-line at 50.

The possibilities are almost limitless, but I'm not finished yet. Divergences between indicator and price are also taken into account. As an example, between November 2005 and May 2006, the S&P was trending up while the RSI was trending down, a bearish divergence.

It can't be denied that the index fell out of bed in May, but was the divergence the reason? If so, why didn't the former fall out of bed in any of the first five months of that divergence, it having been equally apparent during all of them?

Chart 6-8: RSI

Source: CQG, Inc. © 2006 All rights reserved worldwide.
www.cqg.com

In gold the indicator has worked much better, certainly since May 2005.

What does this tell us?

Once again, that there are no certainties, just probabilities and possibilities. If you are thinking about using the RSI, look at its record in whatever chart you're analysing and see if it has been good or bad.

In the early 1980s the senior dealer of BP, then a client, became hooked on the RSI, but in a much more simplified way than the examples given above. He swore by covering long positions in cable (£/$) whenever the oscillator advanced above 80, going short (selling £) whenever it fell below 80.

I investigated: at the time, I didn't come up with any favourable conclusions despite changing the time period of both oscillator and average.

But, as frequently pointed out, if something works for you, use it, and I have recently decided it does work for me, and since I didn't have any other indicator for two-week periods, I look at it, having incorporated it into my work-sheet.

Moving Average Convergence & Divergence (MACD)

I would be cheating if I didn't quote my sources, a variation of one I first used many years ago, and heard about from David Upshaw, a friend in America.

MARS is what David called his study: an acronym of Moving Average Ratio Series. It plots the percentage differential between a shorter and longer moving average.

As prices rise, the differential between shorter and longer widens until, like a piece of elastic stretched too far, the two ends (the level of the averages) snap back, if not together, at least towards each other. When prices fall, once again this differential appears until it gets too great (what is too great you must discover through observation), when, once again they snap back towards each other.

The only way this can happen is if price falls or rises.

The mathematics of technical analysis

So far in this chapter, when introducing indicators apart from the ROC, I have been apologising for not explaining the mathematics. I've just realised that there is no reason to apologise because it isn't necessary to understand the maths; the only thing that matters is, does an indicator work?

If you are already using technical analysis, or decide to after reading the book, you are very unlikely to have to do what I had to do for most of my working life, calculate the indicators yourself, because it is all done for you by whatever service to which you subscribe. Whatever that service may be, it will also explain each indicator better than I could, and by mathematicians.

It may not be an intellectual approach, but since technical analysis is about empirical observation, not theory, this particular non-intellectual technical analyst believes that if it works, use it. The investment business is not an intellectual pastime: it's about trying to make profits and limit losses.

Supposing you embrace technical analysis but decide not to subscribe to a service; you won't have the time to calculate all the indicators even if you understand the mathematics, and this book is about technical analysis, not maths. How many accountants are good investment managers? cont...

> ...cont
>
> Since services became available, I have tried a number of them. By far the best, and one of the more reasonably priced, certainly far less expensive than Reuter's or Bloomberg, is the one I have used for the charts in this book, CQG Inc.
>
> The system is user friendly; so is everyone on the help-desk. You always find someone available and unfailingly helpful. And if a problem occurs out-of-hours, that doesn't exist as far as CQG is concerned: your call gets patched through to America.

The technical world has moved on since the word from MARS. For a start, calculators and computers have enabled exponential averages to be calculated, and although I don't use them when looking at the charts of price for reasons explained elsewhere, they are used in the MACD, the moving average convergence and divergence indicator.

Here is the indicator plotted beneath the chart of the FTSE100 index between November 2005 and June 2006. The averages are exponential, the red one covering a shorter time period than the longer. It is *not* an average of the black average.

Chart 6-9: MACD

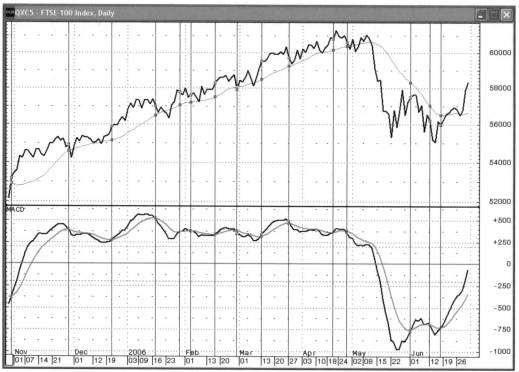

Source: CQG, Inc. © 2006 All rights reserved worldwide.
www.cqg.com

The green line on the chart of the FTSE100 index is its one month *arithmetic* average.

The indicator gives signals when–

1. the averages cross each other;

2. the averages cross the zero line.

Signals–

*   **Buy**: black crosses above red average

*   **Sell**: red crosses above black average

The vertical lines show where FTSE was when the fifteen signals described above were given.

When the averages are below zero, since the crossing of the red by the black generated a buy signal, you are already in the market by the time they both cross above zero.

The reverse applies when the red average crosses above the black: you have received a sell signal and are already out of the market when the averages cross below zero.

That being so, what is the point of the zero line?

It can only be of interest when the averages have not generated a recent signal and are trading near to that line.

In the example shown on the chart, you were given less hassle and far fewer signals purely by watching the index' one month average (green), whose rule, like all averages is that you stay in the market as long as the average is rising, a rising average of whatever length or time period being potential support.

You bought in November, sold in May and bought again in late June.

Which indicator do you use?

The choice is yours: what you choose depends on many factors–

1. your time-frame;
2. how many times do you want to be put in and out of the market;
3. your appetite for risk[8];
4. your antipathy to paying the expenses of dealing;
5. your machismo;
6. your appetite for taking decisions.

You might decide to use only one or two indicators, the second being a filter for the first; or all of them relying on judgment and experience to tell which one to use in any given situation.

Whichever indicator(s) you use, if you try using the same time periods but other indicators, all will give broadly similar signals. For example, a 9-day RSI won't tell you anything different from 9-day stochastics.

In Chapter One I wrote that price was the most important indicator of all. It still is. But my worksheet, Chart 6-10, comprises the following:

---

[8] It's no good trying to take other people's risks; no good saying to yourself, if he can do it, I can or ought to be able to do it; if you try doing that, you're bound to lose money; only take the risks you're capable of taking. Though money is made at the big tables in Monte Carlo, if you haven't got the stomach for it, you're better off on the beach.

Chart 6-10: my worksheet

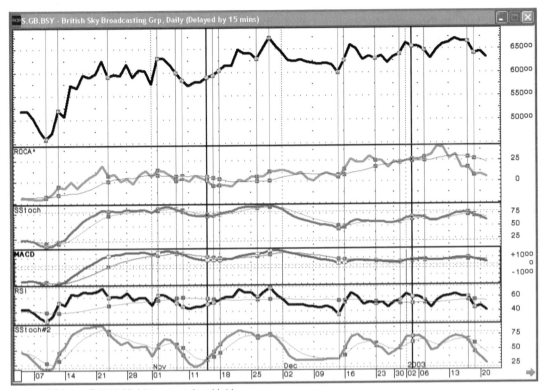

The chart (BSkyB 2002-03) shows price at the top, then the 63-day ROC followed by 34-day stochastics, 26 & 13 day MACD, 9-day RSI, and 5-day stochastics.

The indicators below price have been placed according to the time periods they cover, starting with the longest and ending with the shortest.

The vertical lines show where some of the signals to buy and sell were given: when signals were given simultaneously or almost so, by more than one indicator, for the sake of clarity I have only shown the signal given by the ROC.

Colour code

- ROC: red
- 34-day stochastics: light blue
- MACD: dark blue
- RSI: black
- 5-day stochastics: green

5-day stochastics:

When explaining this indicator earlier, I wrote that for the reasons given then you can't found an investment policy, or a trading one, on this indicator alone. As ever, the chart shows why.

When the move signalled by the indicator is an extended one, October's advance, for example, the first "buy" signal on the chart proved profitable.

But what about the first sell signal, also in October? It too appeared when the move was extended, but didn't make you any money if you were a short trader, while if you weren't, it put you into BSkyB again at a higher level than that at which you sold.

The signals are shown by the green verticals – six were profitable; five weren't. That is provided you assume that you paid no commission (which is a stupid assumption).

9-day RSI

Four signals, but only two are shown. The other two coincided with the ROC's first and last signals.

You made money on the first long trade, but were taken out of the market and/or put short on 14th November, far too soon in view of the subsequent advance which lasted until January. The re-entry then proved unprofitable: you were "obliged" to sell on the day the final red line appeared (the ROC and RSI giving simultaneous signals).

9-day MACD

The first and second signals coincided with 5-day stochastics' first and third. Both were profitable, the second being closed at the black vertical, when you were put long again, i.e. you bought.

You sold at the next red line (MACD and ROC gave simultaneous signals), and covered the position, i.e. you bought it back, at the next red line, when once again, the ROC's signal coincided with the RSI's. Your profit was taken at the final green line (MACD and 5-day stochastics giving simultaneous signals).

34-day stochastics

Your first trade was triggered simultaneously with the ROC's first; taking the profit in early-November when the two indicators' signals coincided. You bought again on 18th November (light blue vertical), taking profits when the indicator's signal occurred on the same day as the next one from the ROC.

On 13th December 34-day stochastics said buy (not marked on the chart), taking profits in mid-January.

ROC

The first trade was profitable, but you were taken out too early, on 8th November, when, if you were a short trader anticipating a fall, you also sold short, making a loss when put long again at the end of December. That position was closed at a small loss in mid-January 2003.

Conclusion

The period reviewed is obviously too short to arrive at any firm conclusions as to which indicator is likely to produce the best results. But a longer period would have been too confusing: the charts could illustrate one, of course, but explaining a multiplicity of lines far greater than those shown above would have been confusing, not only for you but also for me.

In any case, my objective wasn't to try and show you which indicator is best but how and when their signals are given, special attention being paid to those signals' relative timing.

Nevertheless, although I had already come to the conclusion, long ago, that 5-day stochastics was only useful to time buying or selling following purchase or sale decisions taken for other reasons, I find that I like the RSI rather more than I did when I started writing about it earlier on in this chapter.

As for the MACD, does it tell us anything that we don't know from observation of one or more of the other indicators?

We are left therefore with 34-day stochastics and the ROC. I like both. And don't forget that in order to make the review easier to understand, I chose not to show how averages and trend lines might have affected any decision to act.

> **NOTE**   In the end, price takes care of everything.

But discipline, judgment, experience and luck are of almost equal importance. Never forget that when you make money, you get lucky; when you lose it, it's not the market's fault or the chart's but your own.

7

Candlesticks

Candlestick chart analysis pre-dates Western technical analysis by two hundred years, but it wasn't until 1984 that it started to become known, and used, anywhere outside Japan.

At first sight, many people find candlesticks too difficult to understand. I never did, and learning about them proved most enjoyable while the results were highly rewarding.

The techniques of candlestick analysis deserve a complete book, but when I was commissioned to write this one, my brief was not to write yet another comprehensive tome – there are already too many – it was to tell readers what I use, how I use what I use, and how I came to do so.

Accordingly, I am not going to tell you about every candlestick, whether it be a single one or part of a group: you can find them all in *Japanese Candlestick Charting Techniques* by Steve Nison, published by The New York Institute of Finance.

What appears below is *not* a candlestick chart; it's the bar chart of BP between end-June and early November 2005. The vertical line shows the daily trading range, the horizontal lines, one on either side of the vertical, the opening and closing levels, the former pointing to the left, the latter to the right.

Chart 7-1: BP, bar chart

Source: CQG, Inc. © 2006 All rights reserved worldwide.
www.cqg.com

I don't know about you, but I have always found bar charts virtually impossible to understand, or read, so I don't use them.

Although bar charts appear throughout Edwards & Magee's *Technical Analysis of Stock Trends*, the authors state that it is the closing price that counts.

I have always regarded Edwards & Magee's great work as the technician's bible, and what they say goes, or did so until I started learning about candlesticks in the early 1990s, after I had already been a technician for about 29 years.

The next chart, like the bar chart, shows BP between 9th May and 30th June 2006.

Chart 7-2: BP, candlestick chart

Source: CQG, Inc. © 2006 All rights reserved worldwide.
www.cqg.com

Notes–

- Each vertical line is a candle, including both the thick and the thin parts.
  The thick white (or black) section is called the *real body*.
  The thin line is called the *whisker* or *shadow*.

- Candles are white when the opening is lower than the closing price.
  Black when the opening is higher than the closing price.

- When the open and close are the same, or nearly so, the real body is a horizontal and called a *doji*

I don't know about you, but I find candlesticks are easy to understand, and believe you will do so, once you know what they represent.

Why the thin line isn't called the wick, I haven't the faintest idea. Maybe it's to illustrate that you shouldn't burn the candle at both ends, or because few wax ones have two wicks.

Some candles only have shadows at one end, many have them at the top and the bottom of the real body.

When there are no shadows and the candle is black, the opening price is the day's highest trade, the closing one is its lowest trade, e.g. 23rd August's: black with no shadows.

When there are no shadows and the candle is white, the opening price is the day's lowest trade; the closing one, its highest, e.g. 9th September's: white with no shadows.

1. The length of the shadow/s relative to the size of its real body tells you the candle's character: a candle tells you far more than a bar or closing price can.

2. A single candle, dependent on its shape and size, can be a reversal pattern.

3. The relative size and relationship of one candle to its successor/s is highly relevant.

4. While reversals do occur following a single candle, showing that the low is in place at the close of business on the high or low day (what other type of chart does that so clearly?), some candles, while not being reversal patterns on their own, can be bullish when price has been falling, bearish when it has been rising, provided the next day's candle gives the required confirmation.

5. Not all reversal patterns are created by a single candle: two, three, four & even five candle reversal patterns are not unknown.

6. An expression ascribed to the Chinese is–

   One picture is worth a thousand words.

But when I said this at a seminar in Hong Kong, I was gently corrected. Apparently, the correct expression is,

   A glance tells all

I do hope so. Having written 377 words about the nature of candlesticks, showing only one chart to illustrate them and, even then, only to make favourable comparisons with a bar chart, here is that chart again, annotated to help you learn that in a candlestick chart a glance really does tell all.

Chart 7-3: annotated candlestick chart

Source: CQG, Inc. © 2006 All rights reserved worldwide.
www.cqg.com

When reading the following pages, you will find it much easier to do so, if you make a copy of Chart 7-3 above: you will be able to refer to it constantly, rather than keep turning back.

Description of candles

Unlike the reversal patterns described in Chapter Four, the size of the advance/decline that follows a candlestick reversal cannot be foretold. When a pattern works (they don't do so all the time, otherwise technicians would all be instant billionaires) it only reverses the immediately preceding trend, and holds good only until the next reversal pattern, i.e. one that reverses the new trend.

But that's not all: a reversal is just a reversal, not *the* reversal. While it is true that any day that any price closes below/above the high/low day might be the start of the mother of all bear/bull markets, you never know that at the time.

Advances don't oblige by ending only when a reversal pattern appears; the same applies to declines; the same as the reversal pattern-induced advances and declines already described in Chapter Four. Technical analysis is a guide, not an infallible gift from heaven.

Please remember, as I have pointed out before, that what you read in this book is not necessarily what you might read in other books. This is not an apology or a boast, but an explanation: I lost a lot of money doing exactly what I was told to do in various books; what you read here is what I read but amended through experience.

1. White Engulfing Pattern

A two candlestick *reversal*. The reason is obvious: The first is black and small relative to its successor; the second, white, preferably relatively long, opens lower than the black one's opening and closes above its close; i.e. the second candle engulfs the first.

The pattern, *only seen after a fall*, reverses the immediately preceding down trend.

(In case you're wondering if the pattern only appears after a fall, look at 6.)

2. Shooting Star

Following an advance, price opens above the previous close: the real body can be black or white. Either way, however, if a shadow appears beneath the real body, it must be very small, and frequently there is no lower shadow at all. As for the shadow above the real body (mandatory), it must be a long one; much longer than that real body.

The candle implies a fall, but not necessarily the next day. I like that next day's candle to be a black one, preferably opening lower than the shooting star's close. Otherwise, how do you know that a fall will follow? You don't. You'll only know that if one or more of the next few candles (unlike the shooting star), turns out to be a top reversal pattern.

As far as I am concerned, a shooting star without immediate confirmation is nothing at all.

Shooting Star as a bottom?

There is no such animal. But see 7 for a candle that looks like a shooting star turned upside-down.

3. Harami

The pattern consists of two candles. They can both be black; they can both be white. Or black (1), white (2); or vice versa.

The real body of the second candle must be contained within the first's real body. Harami is Japanese for pregnant and the first candle is known as the mother candle, the second as the baby.

The pattern resembles an engulfing pattern, read from right to left. But unlike an engulfing pattern, the harami is not a definitive reversal pattern. What it tells you is that the trend in being has ended.

After an advance, the harami shows that supply has increased to the point where it matches demand. After a fall (the pattern can appear following either), the reverse: demand has increased to the point where it matches supply.

What do you do when you see a harami?

Failing any supporting technical data, you do nothing except watch and wait. But if you have been long during the preceding advance, (or short during the preceding fall), and a harami appears, there is every reason to take profits on half your open position, dependent, of course, on your time frame.

4. Harami Cross

This one's first candle appeared following the second day of a one-day fall triggered by the harami that preceded it. After the second candle – a doji (explained in 5) – had completed the pattern, the following day's white candle wasn't needed to confirm it as a bottom reversal because the harami cross was a complete reversal by itself. Although there was no upside follow-through immediately thereafter, 14th's candle (see 5 below) was a low, which, on a closing basis, wasn't broken until six weeks later.

5. Doji

The opening and closing prices are at the same level, or as near as makes no difference. The books say that the doji is one of the most important of all candlesticks, but what that means I have never been able to understand. It certainly isn't always a single candle reversal pattern, not in my experience anyway, even though it sometimes acts as one.

The doji at 4 on the chart of BP, coming, as it did, after a fall, and followed as it was by a white candle was a reversal pattern however, and this one worked.

Although the shadows above and below this one's real body are long, making it a **long-legged doji** (if they had been both long and of equal length, it would have been a **rickshaw-man**), the real body's position relative to its shadows is, for the most part, irrelevant, except when that shadow is very short, indicating a narrow trading range on the day, week, month under consideration.

Provided the day's range is narrow, and the doji appears above the previous candle's real body in a rising market, beneath it in a falling one, the candle is a **Doji Star**.

Provided the doji star is succeeded by a confirming candle on the following day, week etc, (see below), it becomes a *reversal pattern*.

Confirming candle?

As far as I am concerned, following a decline, a doji star is confirmed as a bottom reversal only if the succeeding white candle closes relatively near the day's high; following an advance, a doji star is confirmed as a top reversal only by a black candle that closes relatively near the day's low. [For the rationale, please refer to the theory behind stochastics – Chapter Six, Indicators.]

6. Black Engulfing Pattern

After a rise, a small white candle is engulfed by a black one (see 3, and 1). The latter describes it in detail. The black engulfing pattern is a reversal, a top one.

7. Inverted Hammer

Nomenclature, no-brainer; it looks like one. The real body can be black or white, but must be small; the upper shadow, long. The latter must be two/three times longer than the real body. If there is a lower shadow, it must be very small. Frequently, there is no lower shadow at all.

An inverted hammer only appears after a fall.

If followed by a white candle that closes near the upper shadow's high, it is a *bottom reversal*. All those criteria were present at 7: a bottom was confirmed and a further advance duly followed.

8. Harami

This one had two white candles, but that's allowed. When the candle that followed was black, and the close not only lower than the pattern's second candle but also at the day's low, it confirmed that the harami was a top reversal, even though it didn't work. It isn't hard to see why, in view of what that candle was (see 7).

9. Inverted Hammer

Following the harami at 8, and the black candle that followed, on the face of it that harami became a top reversal. But look at the shape of the black candle: an inverted hammer, which, as pointed out in 7, is an attempt to make a bottom reversal, provided it is confirmed as such by the succeeding candle being white, which it was.

The advance that followed this confirmation only lasted one more day however. But as I've already told you in the introduction to this case history, a reversal is just that; a reversal, not *the* reversal, and can be subjected to another reversal the next day.

Live by the candle?

Does this mean that if you live by the candle, you must die by it? You can if you like, or your decision on how to act might be made subject (in no particular order) to your time-frame, the direction of the long-term trend, your appetite for risk or security, the cost of dealing; i.e. your judgment and experience.

And even though that means you have to do some thinking, that thinking is technical, not fundamental, therefore not necessarily incompatible with the maxim that thinking is what causes the big losses in this business.

Since an inverted hammer is a bottom reversal provided it is confirmed as such, as already described, what about a reversal called a *Hammer*? Is there such a pattern? Indeed there is.

The nearest approximation on this chart is the candle that follows the shooting star at 2, although it could be argued that its upper shadow is longer than a purist would care for. I am not that pure. In any case, look at the length of the lower shadow: much longer than the two/three times the size of the real body required for this candle.

There can be no doubt however that the hammer was a bottom reversal, even though the advance that followed lasted only one day.

Hanging Man and Inverted Hammer

Since both patterns require the real body to be small and the close near at/the day's high in the former, near/at the day's low in the latter, why, subject to the nature of the candle that follows, does the pattern become a top/bottom reversal?

I pose the question because in the hanging man, the market opens high, has a large intraday fall and then rallies strongly by the close. On the face of it, that's potentially bullish because the sellers are accommodated, and then overcome. As for the inverted hammer, it is the buyers who are overcome, so the pattern ought to be potentially bearish.

The answer is simple: empirical observation.

10 & 11. Harami

Confirmed, as always, at the close on the second day, when the advance ended, supply having increased to the point where it equalled demand.

When did the pattern become a top reversal? According to the principles already explained, not on the day after the appearance of the harami, but on the following one.

The reason?

Although the first candle after the two-day harami was black, its close was above the pattern's second candle: not, in my submission, a top reversal. Accordingly, it was the black candle at 11, closing below all three of its predecessors, that provided the confirmation.

12. Window

Opened when no part of the shadow or of the real body (if there is no shadow) is at the same level as any part of its predecessor. A window is the same as a gap in Western technical analysis. See also 12a, 12b & 12c.

The theory is that the window will be closed: in a down-market price should return to the level of the preceding shadow or, if there is no shadow, to the level of the real body. If/when price obliges, the window is closed, and the market's previous trend is resumed. In other words, the window is not a reversal but a continuation pattern.

Note the words "theory" and "if/when". A theory is a theory because it hasn't been or cannot be proved, and windows aren't always closed. Although the window was closed by the candle between 12 (the day after window opened) and 13, a perfect example of the theory working out, as you will see when we get to October on this chart, there are many occasions when it doesn't.

Long before I became involved with candlesticks, I had always had problems with gaps,. For my daily work, using, as I did then, only closing prices, I never saw any gaps. No problem: it did me no harm at all; exactly the same as my non-use of volume.

The problem of gaps

From time to time, in order to understand the intermediate or long-term picture I did examine weekly or monthly bar charts. Seeing the gaps, I had to learn something about them. Technical lore had it thus:

1.   gaps are closed within three days;

2.   if not closed then, they'll be closed in three weeks;

3.   if not closed then, they'll be closed in three years.

Naturally, that taught me nothing; at least, nothing of any practical use, so I asked my friend and former colleague, David, a highly experienced American technical analyst, for his view on gaps.

Given the similarity between his origins and family name, Yohannon, and Yossarian, the hero of *Catch-22*, David's reply was hardly surprising (it's a catch 22 situation), "Everything depends on what type of gap you're looking at: is it a breakaway, running or exhaustion one?"

Whether you are a day-trader; someone taking a longer view and looking at a weekly chart, or a long-term investor examining a monthly one; when the relevant candle/s appear, confirming what type of gap it is, the opportunity to trade has gone; an example of received wisdom: by the time it's received, it's too late.

My problems with gaps and windows continue.

13. Window

This one was opened at 23rd's 627, 22nd's close having been 628, and was closed two days later when the high trade of 25th August was also 628.

14. Engulfing Pattern?

No: although the black real body did engulf the preceding small white one, to make a reversal, which is what an engulfing pattern is (it is never a continuation pattern), appearing after a fall as it did, 14's candle would have to have been white.

Was the tall black candle that followed 14 a bottom reversal?

No.

That being so, why did the market start to rally the next day?

Because not every top or bottom is signalled by a candle.

15. Tweezers

A two-candle reversal pattern: a top following an advance, a bottom following a fall. But tweezers are less significant than those already described. Sometimes however the second candle combines with the first to form a second or dual reversal, making the whole pattern more significant.

Tweezers are formed whenever a high or low (close or intraday) matches that posted the day (week, month, dependent on the chart's time period) before, as the high trade on 2nd September matched 1st's 642. The pattern is equally valid if the previous high or low was posted several days, weeks etc before the second one. "Several"? That's a matter of judgment.

16. White Engulfing Pattern

It is white because that is the colour of the second candle. Two days later, 13th's low trade having been at the same level as the engulfing pattern's first candle, tweezers: an example of a dual reversal such as that described in 15.

17. Shooting Star

A top reversal; see 2. But the next candle's low trade was only 0.08% lower than the opening of the long white candle of two days earlier – as near as makes no difference, a match. Tweezers again, and the fall triggered by the shooting star was reversed.

After three bottom reversals in seven days, and even though there had been a top reversal between two and three, it is little wonder that BP then took off.

18. Window

It was closed, but not until fourteen days had passed, while in the interval BP had first risen 6.11% and then fallen 7.51%. Anyone waiting for the window to close was intellectually rewarded, but financially? I think not.

18a. Window

Same argument as above; closed five days later.

Not numbered

Wasn't 22nd's white candle a hammer? After all, while having hardly any upper shadow, its lower one was very long indeed, and it certainly looks like a hammer? No; it may look like one, but hammers *only appear after a fall*, and this one had, at the time, the highest close of the rally.

Accordingly, despite not appearing at the absolute high (20th & 21st's intraday highs were above it), 22nd's was a Hanging Man, a potentially negative pattern, although on the following day a black candle was needed (with a close near the bottom of the daily range) to turn that potentially negative candle into a top reversal.

Although a black candle did appear the next day (23rd), it did not confirm that hanging man as a top reversal because the close was near the day's high, forming a potentially bullish hammer, which was confirmed as a bottom reversal by 26th's long white candle.

19. Long-legged Doji & Black Engulfing Pattern

The long-legged doji (see 5) was succeeded by a long black candle that opened above the real body of the former. By the close, that black candle had not only confirmed the doji as a top reversal but also completed a second reversal, an engulfing pattern: two reversal patterns for the price of one. Two are more bearish than one, and this pair was even more so because it was an Evening Doji Star (to be explained later in the chapter).

20. Doji

3rd October's candle was one.

A potential bottom?

Potential is as potential does, and this one was never confirmed. On the contrary, that doji was followed by an open window which wasn't closed until 21st January of the following year.

Provided you were an investor, and as long as you knew for certain that it would be closed…eventually, you could relax while price fell from 655.50 to 599.00 during the 13 following days.

But that begs the question: would you be relaxed? Nothing is certain in this or in any other business, and as already explained in Chapter Six (Indicators), the larger the fall and the shorter the time taken to make it, the greater the effect on the emotions.

21. Window

Not closed until the following January.

22. Belt-Hold Line

A candle that looks as this one does (white, opening at or very near the day's low, closing higher, after having been higher still) and that appears after a fall is bullish.

Would it have been an inverted hammer if the shadow had been two/three times the length of the real body instead of less than two? Give me two ifs and I'll beat Tiger Woods!

The real body here is a bit big for a hammer, but even so, it would have qualified as one. But who cares? An inverted hammer is only a potential bottom reversal, whereas a belt-hold line in low ground is bullish, all by itself, even if it doesn't trigger an immediate advance as this one did.

23. Dark Cloud Cover

After just two more white candles and a strong opening on the third day that gapped up not only above the preceding candle's real body but also above its upper shadow, the sun set on the advance. Price fell back, and the close was not only below the opening but also more than half-way below the white candle's mid-point. That's a one-day top reversal called dark cloud cover: the reasons are obvious–

- There is also a black belt-hold line, bearish, naturally. But I won't describe it until I find one: a glance tells all, if you like.

- There is also a bottom reversal that looks like the candle that makes dark cloud cove; but upside down, and white. Once again, I'll describe it when I find one.

24. Black Engulfing Pattern

See 6.

25. Doji

Coming, as it did, after a fall, this one (a gravestone for visually obvious reasons) should have been a bottom reversal. But if it had been, the market would have rallied the next day: it didn't. Even so, after a fall, a doji, gravestone, long-legged or rickshaw-man, is frequently the sign that a low may not be long-delayed, as in this case, a low being posted only two days later.

But was that low, unaccompanied by any bottom reversal either on the decline's penultimate day, on the low day or on the first day of the subsequent advance, the direct result of the doji at 25? Maybe it was, but I would be unhappy to buy on such a candle without other supporting technical data.

Gravestone doji after an advance: a long white candle followed by a doji often signals a top.

26. No bottom reversal

A low without one: just one of those things. Technical analysis is an art, not a science.

27. Temptation

Is not the name of a candle, but the two white candles do look like a harami, and would have been one if only the pattern's first candle had appeared on the low day. But the "pattern" did appear only one day after that low.

Nevertheless, despite the evidence provided by 25, 26 & 27, I don't think that I would have been a buyer. I would have been wrong.

Not only for short–term traders

By now, you might be thinking that candle reversals, when they work, are all very well, but since they only indicate the direction of the market until the appearance of a candle reversal pointing in the opposite direction, they are only of interest to a short-term trader. You would be wrong.

Candles apply equally well, or better, in weekly and monthly charts, working just as well as they do in daily ones, and an investor does himself no harm at all by getting out of a position one month or, better still, one week after a high, even if he doesn't know at the time that it is the high.

But before I show you any weekly or monthly charts, you need to see a few more candle reversals on daily ones.

Chart 7-4: BP once again, but this time in late 2005 and early 2006

Source: CQG, Inc. © 2006 All rights reserved worldwide.
www.cqg.com

12 numbered candle formations appear on this chart. Some you've seen; others, you haven't.

1. Look at the chart and note the candle formations you recognise, as well as those you don't. (Please refer to the first BP chart and explanations if necessary.)

2. Name the ones you recognise.

3. Are they bullish or bearish?

4. Are they one or two candlestick patterns?

5. Which are the ones you haven't seen before?

6. Are they bullish or bearish?

The new candles are 3 & 8. But first, here are the answers to the remaining questions.

1. Black engulfing pattern: top reversal.

2. Tweezers (the lower shadows: a bottom reversal that failed to work as one).

3. [Wait for explanation.]

4. Shooting Star: potential top reversal, but one that was not confirmed by the succeeding candle.

5. Black Engulfing pattern: top reversal.

6. Hammer: potential low, but not confirmed by succeeding candle.

7. Black Engulfing Pattern.

8. Curb your curiosity.

9. Harami: buying pressure matched by selling pressure. The candle that followed was black. Accordingly, the two candlestick formation became a continuation, not a reversal pattern.

10. Harami: stasis. The candle at 11 was black, not confirming 10's harami as a bottom reversal.

11. Harami: 12 confirmed it as a top reversal and confirmed a black engulfing pattern.

Other points to note

The window opened on 3rd January had still not been closed by mid-March.

16th & 17th January's harami was confirmed as a top on 18th, but failed to work.

3 & 8. Both are Belt-hold lines

When price has been falling, without necessarily having posted a new reaction low (although it did at 3), the session (day, month, year) opens at the low, the real body is white with a close below the intraday high, but that doesn't qualify as an inverted hammer, it is a positive or bullish belt-hold line.

When price has been rising, but is not necessarily at a high, merely in comparatively high ground (see 8), a real body opens at the day's high, is black but too long for a hanging man, with a lower shadow that is also too short for that pattern, it is a bearish belt-hold line.

Now we do our ABC

Stars, plain and doji

A, B & C were all long-legged doji, but can you spot the odd man out?

The answer is B. Although in all three cases the dojis' real bodies gapped from the candle that preceded them (the first requirement for a doji star), to confirm the pattern as a reversal, the succeeding candle has to penetrate well into the real body of the candle preceding the doji.

The only doji to satisfy all criteria was B. That was when 12th's white candle was posted, confirming that it was a **Morning Doji Star**, a bottom reversal.

If the candle succeeding A had been black, penetrating deeply into 2nd January's white candle, and/or that succeeding C's had done the same with 16th February's, either/both would have been confirmed as an **Evening Doji Star**, a top reversal.

Here is an Evening Doji Star

You've seen it before, at 19, on the first numbered BP chart in this chapter.

The confirming candle following the doji star also confirmed a black engulfing pattern.

Chart 7-5: candlesticks, stars

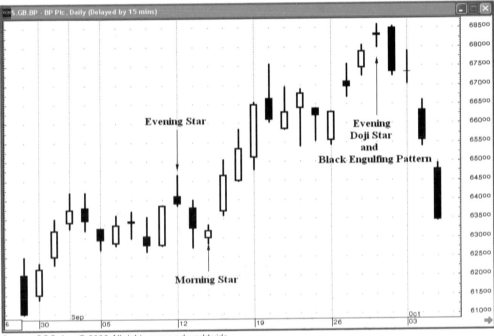

Stars with no doji: In a rising market a long white candle is succeeded by a small candle of either colour whose real body gaps up from the white one's real body. The third candle of the pattern must be black, and penetrate deep into the first's real body. The result: an Evening Star, a top reversal.

In a falling market, following a long black candle is succeeded by a small candle of either colour whose real body gaps down from the black one's real body. The third candle must be white, penetrating deep into the first's real body to form a Morning Star, a bottom reversal.

> **NOTE** While neither of the stars in the chart above had very much to reverse (the greater the preceding move, the more significant the reversal), what cannot be denied is that they did the job they were intended to do, reversing the preceding trend's direction.

The candlesticks explained so far do not constitute a comprehensive list. To compile one would take a book, but those shown do include most of those you are likely to see. I hope they whet your appetite. If they do, you'll need to read a book devoted to the subject. But we're not finished yet. What follows is a report written on 6th July 2006, just before I wrote this page.

The Tokyo Market News

6th July, 2006

TRI-STAR ISN'T JUST A PLANE

It's also the rarest reversal pattern of all.

The pattern is so rare that in the standard work in English on candlestick charts, there are no actual examples: the author couldn't find one, so he drew it.

But 3rd, 4th and 5th July 2006 the Nikkei formed a tri-star: three doji stars with the second higher than the first and third.

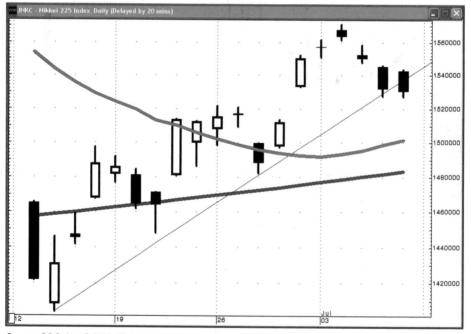

Source: CQG, Inc. © 2006 All rights reserved worldwide.
www.cqg.com

cont...

...cont

Although I admit that the middle star's real body might look a bit too big to qualify as a doji, this is partly due to the scale on which it has been drawn, while if you take into consideration that the difference between the opening and close of that real body is 0.246%, and that there is no precise definition of a doji except that the difference must be small, how small is small?

If that star is a doji, the tri-star is a tri-star plus. Plus what? Plus an **Abandoned Baby**, an or even rarer top (bottom) than a tri-star. It is formed when the gap up or down between the middle candle and the first and third ones is not only real body to real body but also shadow to shadow. Once again, the author already referred to, justly noted for the extent of his research, couldn't find one

But his book was published long before 6th July 2006, whereas this report wasn't.

In Topix, there was no abandoned baby because the middle candle's lower shadow overlapped the first candle's upper one. Nevertheless, you are looking at extreme rarity in both charts.

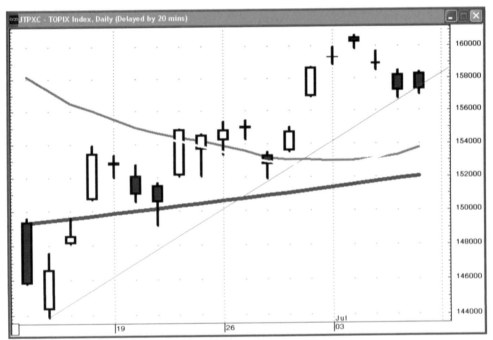

Steve Nison, who was the author of the book referred to before, the standard work written in English on candlesticks, uses the word "important" to describe some reversal patterns, including the tri-star.

cont...

...cont

Unfortunately, I have not been able to work out what he means by that.

What I do know from my own experience is that you can use some of the reversals all of the time; all of the reversals some of the time, but you can't expect all of the reversals to work all of the time.

The tri-star being a reversal, the market should fall: it has already done so today, reaching the first potential support in the form of June/July's up trend line. My address isn't Gettysburg, but holds good here as well: you can't expect all of the supports to work all of the time, otherwise prices could never break one, and there would never be any bear markets.

Support and resistance do break sometimes, which is why the words don't appear in my analyses unless preceded by "potential". I never expect support to break or to hold: I wait and see what happens.

Unless a bottom reversal pattern appears beforehand, if the trend line breaks, the one month and one year averages (green and blue lines on candle charts) will be tested: important doesn't appear to mean "certain" nor does it necessarily imply a large post-confirmation movement, either up or down.

When the latter average provided support last month, I wrote that the rally should continue and that the possibility of the highs being tested should not be discounted unless three successive closes beneath June's low were to intervene. I haven't changed my mind.

* "Japanese Candlestick Charting Techniques"

Tokyo Market News

11th July 2006

Tri-star important?

No more than any other reversal.

cont...

...cont

After the tri-star, Monday's tall white candle was a white engulfing pattern, a bottom reversal. Today's black doji converted the white one into a harami cross, another bottom reversal.

The window opened by the Abandoned Baby (Nikkei), Evening Star (Topix) is still open. If it is closed soon (candlestick lore has it that windows are closed), AND new highs are posted thereafter, my belief that the word "important" is just a word, and has no influence on the size of the subsequent move triggered by any reversal, will be given quite a boost.

The white engulfing pattern failed, but five days later tweezers (only a minor reversal compared with the important(?) and rare abandoned baby and tri-star) appeared, and worked. By early August the gap had been closed. Every reversal is as important (unimportant?) as every other.

If you are an investor as opposed to a short-term trader, you may be feeling that candles aren't anything that you need to add to your technical armoury. But what about weekly (even monthly charts)?

Weekly candlestick charts

Chart 7-6: Nikkei Index, weekly candlestick chart

Source: CQG, Inc. © 2006 All rights reserved worldwide.
www.cqg.com

1. White Engulfing Pattern

A nine week advance followed its appearance on the preceding weekly chart.

2. Shooting Star

Confirmed the following week. The market fell for another four. The tall white candle following that fall, although not marked, was a bullish belt-hold line; it triggered another advance lasting five weeks.

3. Belt-hold Line

The long black candle to the left of 3 was bearish, but the pattern doesn't demand an immediate fall; and none was forthcoming. On the contrary, the week that followed produced a long white candle. But look what came next; a long-legged doji, a sign that a top might be near, which it was. The white candle that gapped up from that doji was a star, which the next week's long black candle then confirmed as a top reversal.

Although the index then went up for two weeks, and the first of those was a bullish belt-hold line, it wasn't the only bullish event that week. The low week's candle closed below the rising three month average (13 weeks, to be precise), while the belt-hold that followed closed above the average again – rising averages are potential supports – and the support became actual, indicating a return to recent highs, *unless reversed beforehand by a top reversal candle*.

The doji in the following week proved to be a top reversal, although that only became a certainty at Friday's close, when the weekly candle was below the average, which had started falling by then, becoming potential resistance: it stopped the mid-November rally three times in the next five weeks.

Explanation of Nos. 1-5 (Chart 7-6a on page 223)

1. White Hammer

Attempt to ground, also the second candle of a **harami**, a bottom reversal pattern. Both were confirmed in the following week by a white candle which had a higher close than was seen in the week of the hammer. The advance that followed lasted ten weeks.

2. Black Engulfing Pattern

I hope you know all about these by now.

3. Gravestone Doji

Described previously.

4. Inverted Hammer & White Engulfing Pattern

The second candle confirmed the hammer as a bottom reversal and was also a bottom reversal in its own right.

5. Rickshaw-Man

Confirmed as bottom reversal by the white candle that followed.

Indicators and candlesticks

You will certainly have noticed the averages, trend lines and rate-of-change indicator, even though this is the first time in this book that I have placed any on a candlestick chart.

In answer to the question which, I hope, you've been dying to ask, yes; averages and trend lines (and potential supports and resistances) are just as valid on candlestick charts as they are on line charts. So are Bollinger Bands, which will now be explained, the combination of all indicators in a later one.

I don't know if these indicators are used in Japan, and I don't care; I use them, and this book is about what I use. The reason I use what I use is because I have found that everything I use helps me. That's why I use Bollinger Bands.

Chart 7-6a: Nikkei Index, weekly candlestick chart

Bollinger Bands

Chart 7-7: Bollinger Bands

Source: CQG, Inc. © 2006 All rights reserved worldwide.
www.cqg.com

You saw this chart (without the green and black lines) accompanying the explanation of candle formations earlier in this chapter. The green line is a 20-day average because that is the standard default in the CQG data system, and presumably what John Bollinger, who devised the eponymous bands, used, and also advised others to employ.

I have never read very much about the indicator; I just heard about it from another technician, who added something about two standard deviations from the average being employed to create the bands, one on either side of the average.

Presumably, the reason the lines don't mimic the behaviour of the average is because they illustrate price's direction and volatility relative to the average between them. That is also the reason, as I understand it, why they don't mimic each other.

I make no apology for my ignorance; this is not a handbook, it's my book, and I'm not a mathematician, but a technician: if something works, I use it.

How Bollinger Bands work

The bands are flexible trend lines. The upper band is potential resistance, the lower, potential support. Because the bands are flexible, their angle of advance or decline varies according to price's direction and volatility.

The application of Bollinger Bands to candlestick analysis

I once saw an article in the journal of the Society of Technical Analysts, written by John Bollinger. I didn't have time to read it fully, but did have time to notice that it was illustrated by a candlestick chart that had Bollinger Bands on it. That's all I needed to know: if it was good enough for Bollinger, it would do nicely for Marber.

I do remember that the theme of the article was that when price got near the upper or lower band, the tendency was for it to reverse, and in due course to test the opposite one. That wasn't good enough for me. I'm a pedant, and I want certainty, or, failing that, as near to certainty as I can get. Accordingly, I created my own rule for the meaning of "near".

Marber's Rule for Bollinger Band Reversals

Once price has contacted the lower band, and (1, referring to the previous chart) a white candle appears above the band and closes above its predecessor; (2) no part of the real body or shadow makes any contact with the band, a Bollinger Band separation has taken place. This doesn't mean that the trend has definitely reversed from down to up; it merely alerts you to the possibility that it might have done or be on the point of doing so; in other words, a time to take some of your profits if you are short.

Look at 2 & 3 on the chart: the candle to the left of 2 was black and touched the lower band. The one at 2 didn't touch the band, but it was black. The one at 3, however, didn't touch the band: it was a Bollinger Band separation, signalling a possible trend reversal, and confirmed as an actual one, chez Marber, by coincidentally being a belt-hold line (belt-hold lines are bullish but not trend reversals by themselves).

Marber's rule also applies once price has contacted the upper band, and a black candle then appears below the band, closing lower than its predecessor, no part of the real body or shadow having touched the band: a Bollinger Band separation. The candle at 6 provides an example.

In case you're saying that 6 was a Hanging Man, therefore a possible reversal by itself, I know. But do bear in mind that the numbers on the chart were placed for reasons that had nothing at all to do with Bollinger Bands: they are there because they illustrate candle formation. chez Marber, you didn't need to wait for a confirming candle, even though there was one the next day: the Bollinger Band separation + Hanging Man was a confirmed top reversal.

Candle outside the Bollinger Band

A candle totally beneath the lower Bollinger Band or totally above the upper one (no part of the real body or shadow making any contact with it), signals a short-term oversold/overbought condition.

Chart 7-8: candle outside the Bollinger Band

S.GB.BP - BP Plc, Daily (Delayed by 15 mins)

To unwind that condition however, all that is needed is a candle to make contact with the band: this usually takes place within two days on a daily chart.

18th June's low and 3rd July's high are examples of candles outside the bands, the next day's candles marking the unwinding of the oversold and overbought conditions respectively.

In the former case, the trend reversed as well, but this reversal was not the consequence of the oversold condition but of the candle itself, a morning doji star.

In addition to the Bollinger trend lines, the two straight trend lines on the chart above show you that the use of the former doesn't preclude calling on the latter to help you. Anything you feel is likely to help you is fine by me, even fundamental analysis if you must, though I eschew it totally.

Narrowing of Bollinger Band channel

Chart 7-9: narrowing of Bollinger Band channel

When the channel between the bands narrows considerably, and moves due-East, signalling a sideways trend, frequently, but not invariably, a crossing of the upper/lower band by a real body signals the direction of the following one.

(1) is an example of this, but the advance signalled by the white candle never took place because the small black candle that followed was not only a bearish belt-hold line but also, with a tall white candle preceeding it, formed a harami, confirmed as a top reversal pattern by the gravestone doji the next day.

The white candle at (2) provides another example of direction-finding by the first real body to penetrate a narrow channel. Although the black candle separation from the upper band four days later was potentially bearish, the rising average (20 days chez Bollinger, but 21 days chez Marber) provided support, allowing the up trend signalled by the candle at (2) to continue.

Conclusion

This has been one of the longer chapters so far but, as I told you earlier, whole books have been written on candles. My aim has been not to condense but to show you most but not by any means all of the things you are likely to see if you use candlestick analysis; also to lift the veil on an aspect of technical analysis that I find useful.

One thing has emerged however, at least in my mind. I started out at the beginning of this chapter thinking, as Japanese technicians must do, that candlestick analysis is stand-alone. As I end the chapter however, I realise that it is enhanced by the use of the techniques of Western technical analysis, just as the former also enhances the latter.

8

Relative Strength or Ratio

W hen I was a broker (I believe it's now called "on the sell side"), specifically, in the 1970s (I went into the beastly business in 1955, but didn't put pen to paper professionally until 1973), and writing technical reports for institutional clients in the hope that they might be read rather than put straight into the wastepaper basket, which is what I used to do with research when I had been on what is now called the buy side, I decided to concentrate on what I would have found useful during my time as an investment manager at Rothschild between 1969 and 1973, if only someone had been producing it.

Apart from the usual stuff, indices, gilts (that's what bonds were called then), interest rates and gold (oil hadn't been "invented" then, at least in investment terms), I also included analysis of exchange rates as well as market sectors, the latter in both absolute and relative terms, the bank sector relative to the All-Share index for example, the FTSE100 index not having been devised then.

I don't think my work had much influence on the target audience because, although London investment institutions voted me best technician in the City for six successive years, the market share of the firm where I was a consultant didn't get any bigger. Pearls before swine?

Relative strength works

Despite investment managers' indifference to sectors' strength relative to an index or one currency's strength relative to another, relative strength charts help, enormously, otherwise I wouldn't be using them, or writing about the concept.

Relative strength has certainly worked for me. In the stock market, it helps find sectors likely to out-perform the relevant index; and which index is likely to be the best performer. It still helps me today.

Chart 8-1: relative strength

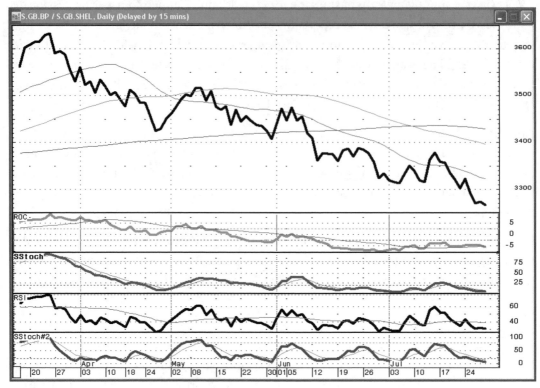

Supposing you have decided that oil shares are likely to rise, and are looking for the one most likely to rise. The preceding chart could help. It is the BP/Shell ratio. But take care: BP under-performed Shell between late March and July, that's easy to see. But this chart doesn't tell you that BP fell during that period. It did, but you need to look at the chart of BP's price to discover that.

Chart 8-2: FTSE100 relative to 250

Source: CQG, Inc. © 2006 All rights reserved worldwide.
www.cqg.com

From the chart above it is easy to see that between November and May it was all downhill for the FTSE100 index relative to the FTSE250 index. But was it downhill for the FTSE100 in absolute terms? Not at all: the 100 index went up, but not as much as the 250.

Chart 8-3: FTSE100

Between early May and June the 100 out-performed the 250. But did the 100 go up? No, it went down.

Chart 8-4: FTSE250

FTSE 250

So did the 250, but as the chart at the top shows, the 100 fell less than the 250.

Chart 8-5: TOPIX/FTSE100

The chart of Topix divided by the FTSE100 index since 1988 illustrates that from 1988, its all-time relative high, to 1998's relative low, Topix (the one on top) under-performed FTSE. Since 1998 however, the game has changed completely, with Topix out-performing FTSE.

The average is the one year (twelve months, to be precise, this being a monthly chart), and since it is rising, and the long-term down trend line has been broken, the 2000 high exceeded, and a sequence of higher highs and lows has come into being since 1998's low, if you're looking for a long-term view, it is that *Topix should continue to out-perform FTSE*. However, the chart doesn't show how that out-performance will actually take place.

The following chart of the FTSE/S&P 500 ratio shows that the former under-performed the latter from 1994 to the beginning of 2004, since when it has out-performed, a trend that will continue until it ends.

Chart 8-6: FTSE/S&P 500

FTSE up, S&P down?

Not necessarily; they might both go down, the latter more than the former.

Relative and absolute performance

At Rothschild, fed up with writing reports for the unit trusts I was managing, when trying to justify indifferent actual performance in a bear market, one Christmas I wrote:

> *God rest ye merry, gentlemen,*
> *Let nothing you despair.*
> *Although last year was difficult,*
> *The future outlook's fair.*
> *Your fund is down 19%,*
> *One less than the All-Share;*
> *Oh glad tidings of comfort and joy.*

I didn't like losing money, even if I was losing it at a slower rate than that at which the indices were falling. There weren't any tracker funds then, but if there had been, I wouldn't have liked them either. I still don't.

Tracker funds are all very well, but since bear markets are no more abnormal than bull markets, and investment managers eschew large holdings of cash, what do you do when the former hits? Unless you are fortunate enough to be holding Anthony Bolton's fund, and that didn't exist in 1970, you have to grin and bear it: "bear" meaning put up with, not sell short; hedge funds did exist in 1970, but they weren't allowed in the UK at the time.

Never forget that investment genius is a short memory and a rising market, whereas investment intelligence is acquired only through long experience of falling ones; particularly at present (July 2006) when the current bull market, at three years four months, is the third longest of the past 24 years. Since the end of the last bear market young investment geniuses have become ten a penny. How many of them will still be investment geniuses at the end of the next one, I wonder.

Relative strength and the foreign exchange market

In the FX market, a currency is not an absolute; it's a relative. One rate is always relative to another. When the man in the travel agent's asks what £ is doing, he usually means £/$.

The way the rate was expressed confused me greatly when I first became involved in FX markets. £/$ ought to tell you how many pounds you get for a dollar. It doesn't; it tells how many dollars you get for a pound. As for €/$, it should tell you how many euro you get for a dollar, but actually tells how many dollars you get for a euro. $/JPY tells you how many yen a dollar will buy.

Since £/$ expresses how many dollars you can buy with a pound, it ought to be expressed $/£: it isn't. The way rates are expressed (but not calculated) is the opposite of other relative strength charts, where the first-named of the pair you've chosen is divided by the second: the more the chart rises, the greater the out-performance of the former relative to the latter.

My involvement with FX

In the 1970s, although still working as a stockbroker, I wrote a great deal about whether £ was likely to out-perform $, Yen, DM and CHF, believing that FX was another area which ought to be of vital interest to investment managers,

I was wrong, of course, about investment managers being vitally interested in FX movements. For the most part they were completely indifferent to (unaware of?) the risks of their exposure to foreign exchange markets whenever they bought shares overseas.

Most managers tended to let their clients, institutional and private, and the holders of their unit trusts, take the strain, and the pain, of the foreign exchange market without letting them know they were doing so. Many managers haven't altered their attitude, maintaining that when unit trust holders etc make the decision to invest abroad, they know the risks they are incurring, and that therefore it isn't the managers' job to try and protect them.

G.B. Shaw, had summed up their attitude many years earlier:

> *"Foreign Exchange movements are like Saturday afternoons,*
> *which although occurring at regular intervals always catch*
> *Baker Street station by surprise."*

In the 1970s investment managers' ignorance of the foreign exchange market was matched by treasurers of major corporations and the major banks who advised them: there was hardly a bank that had heard of a chart, let alone used one.

Although at the time I had no idea that I was going to become a full-time FX consultant at the end of the decade, the work I did on exchange rates during the 1970s was what got me into the business.

In March 1979 I started writing a monthly FX commentary for Euromoney, being paid the not exactly princely sum of £100 per article (the standard rate), which, net of the swingeing tax rates in those pre-Thatcher days, netted me just £12.50 a month.

Chart 8-7: $/DM

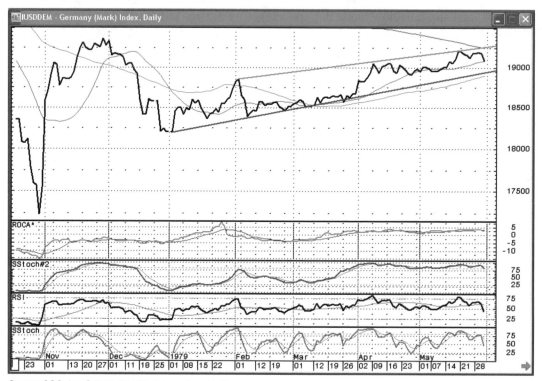

My third article, dated 1st June 1979 stated that $, which had risen from DM1.8200 to DM1.9200 in the previous five months, was extremely vulnerable (broker-talk for "going to fall substantially"). The chart accompanying that article is reproduced above.

$ did fall, almost from the moment the article appeared: if only markets were always so obliging.

Chart 8-8: $/DM

The fall that took place in June and July that year elicited a phone call from Ed Miller, treasurer of Amax, then the largest natural resources company in the U.S.A.

"If we had done what you said in that article, we could have saved the company hundreds of millions of dollars", was what he said to me. Ed came to see me in my Dickensian office; he'd never heard of charts until then. My secretary xeroxed everything I'd ever written on exchange rates, and a week later I was in the FX business, for rather more than £100 per month.

My article on $/DM, and the meeting with Ed Miller that followed, completely changed my life. Thinking the magazine was lucky for me, I wrote for Euromoney for another fourteen years. During that time, no other reader ever phoned again to tell me how impressed he was.

Ignorance and the FX market

In the 1970s, treasurers of major companies, usually accountants with no FX market experience whatsoever, were let loose in what is the largest casino in the world. They hadn't the faintest idea how to play. The FX market is the only game where, even before the first half is over, they move the goal-posts, a differently shaped ball is introduced, and the rules are altered without anyone being told.

Concern about FX movements involves making decisions not about goods but about money. Doing nothing was considered good management, deciding to cover exposures, speculative. The result: closing your eyes to FX volatility was respectable; covering exposure, suspect.

What happened?

The inevitable: rates would move to the treasurers' and their employers' disadvantage. Inactivity then became hyper-activity. The *gadarene* rush to bolt the door on the empty stable didn't end there but on the rocks below the nearest cliffs as uncountable numbers of lemmings happily leapt over.

No one apart from technical analysts knew anything about FX. And ignorance was more than matched by arrogance. The general attitude had been neatly summed up by Winston Churchill as early as 1949 in a speech in the House of Commons:

> *There is no sphere of human thought in which it is easier to show superficial cleverness and the appearance of superior wisdom than discussing question of currency and exchange.*

In the 1970s and 1980s, everyone had an opinion on the foreign exchange market, especially if he was a chairman of a major company. If the treasurers acted on their bosses' views, the money the chairmen lost for their companies would defy belief.

The rise of technical analysis in FX markets

Fortunately for treasurers, technical analysts in general and this one in particular, in December 1978 Euromoney published the results of a survey undertaken by Stephen Goodman, the Singer Company's director of treasury planning. Its conclusion was, "all the technically-oriented forecasters did remarkably well, the average performance of the poorest (being) far better than the average performance of the best econometric-oriented forecaster". Technicians came in from the cold, and not before time.

> *Econometricians get panned*
> *For the one thing they can't understand:*
> *If a rate trends or ranges*
> *On foreign exchanges,*
>
> *The law is Supply and Demand.*

Why were the technicians so good, the econometricians and other fundamental analysts so bad? Because the former operate, albeit sub-consciously, with the knowledge that markets, especially the FX market, where the decisions taken are short-term compared with those made by stock market investors, are governed not by logical but by psychological and emotional forces, whereas the latter don't.

> **NOTE** There is only one fundamental in FX markets: speculative transactions outweigh those where currency is actually needed by far more than fifty to one.

The decline of fundamental analysts' relative strength in the FX market

The buzz phrases in foreign exchange analysis in the 1970s and 1980s were *interest rate differentials* and *purchasing power parity*. Occasionally, technical analysts would be invited to debate the merits of our work with the intellectual approach of these fundamental analysts. It was no contest.

In May 1985, using the results of surveys of one year forecasts carried out by Euromoney at six month intervals since December 1980, I was able to demonstrate that fundamental analysts working with purchasing power parities and interest rate differentials had demonstrated no ability whatsoever.

At the start of the period in December 1980, 12 forecasters took part. By May1984, there were 33. By May 1985 there had been seven forecasting periods. In four of them none of the forecasters was correct on trend; in the remaining three, on two occasions one was correct, in the other one, two were.

It wasn't until December 1985 that the majority of forecasters who had chanced their fundamental skills one year previously finally got the trend right.

Technical analysts took no part in these surveys; we know better: a trend is a trend is a trend, and while some last several years, they don't necessarily last for one. Our job is to call a change in trend after it has taken place, riding it until a change of direction. Despite this, in November 1985, I forecast that by June 1986 $/DM would be significantly below the then 2.5100. In June 1986, it was 2.2000.

Was I breaking the rules?

No, following a five year advance, $ had peaked in Q1 1985. Once the up trend had changed direction, calling it down for two years or more was a no-brainer. That particular down trend lasted until end-1987.

Treasurers walk where angels fear to tread

Corporate treasurers had been so ill-served by the banks that, following Stephen Goodman's survey, and unlike investment managers, they were only too willing to listen to technicians. Accordingly, it wasn't difficult to get major U.S. corporations to subscribe to services that had more than a 50% chance of keeping them on the right side of the trend. UK companies were a harder nut to crack however.

Trying to get business from Tesco in the 1980s – I knew the chairman – I was told that they could always call Lord Chatto (who he?), and since the company had two actuaries they had no need for more advice.

Two actuaries?

That's like having been to two good public schools: one is considered enough.

WPP's treasurer told me that when he wanted an opinion, he called a friend who worked in a bank. Evidently he didn't know that on the sell desk they are there to get customers to deal, not to give advice.

The chairman of Binatone told me that he didn't like my £/$ forecast. I told him that if he wanted an opinion he would like, he should call Lloyd's Bank: they were thinking the opposite to me on £/$.

Sainsbury took my service mainly because the wholesalers of tinned salmon were really FX traders, just as Jaguar were. If Sainsbury got £/$ wrong (£/$Can, to be precise), putting tinned salmon on the shelves at the wrong price, it didn't walk out of the shop, the shoppers did.

With £/$ at 1.3000, the grocery division wanted to know if they should buy $. The rate was in a trading range between 1.3000 and 1.2900, and I told the treasurer that if £ closed above 1.3000 they should do nothing; below 1.2900, they should buy $ immediately.

A close below 1.2900 was posted several days later. £ held there for three more days, and then fell rapidly to 1.2000. What should they do now, was the question. I said that, provided they had done what I'd advised in the previous call, they should smile, and be able to sell lots of tinned salmon.

They hadn't bought $ at just below 1.2900 however. Why? Because "the directors had been hoping that £ would go above 1.3200".

Health warning

Writing about the Topix/FTSE ratio earlier in this chapter I told you that the chart's message was, buy Topix, sell FTSE. The message from the second chart was, sell the S&P and buy FTSE. In other words, my view of the likely relative performance of these three indices was, (1) Topix (2) FTSE (3) S&P. That was then; now (September 2006) the S&P has changed places with FTSE.

When the charts change, I change my mind. What do you do, sir?

Then, and now, I was not giving you an invitation to buy any Japanese shares or to sell any UK ones, any more than it was an invitation to sell U.S. shares and buy UK ones: the ratios tell you about the indices relative to each other, not about any of their constituents' actual performance.

The message now is that Topix is likely to out-perform both the S&P, and FTSE, while the second-named is likely to out-perform the third.

How long is that relative performance likely to last?

Until the relative charts reverse their current long-term trends, as FTSE/S&P appears to have done recently, recorded elsewhere in these pages.

Ratio charts

Chart 8-9: ratio chart

> **NOTE** Ratio charts tell you what the ratio is likely to do – that is the only thing the charts of ratios do.

If the Topix/FTSE ratio (see preceding chart) does continue rising, it can do so for any one of the following reasons:

1. Topix and FTSE both rise, but the former rises more than the latter.
2. Topix rises, FTSE moves sideways.
3. Topix rises, FTSE falls.
4. Topix moves sideways, FTSE falls.
5. Topix and FTSE both fall, but the latter falls more than the former.

> **NOTE** Never infer what the absolute price of one of the ratio's components will do

No matter how strong the message being given by the ratio may be, apart from anything else your reading of the ratio might turn out to be wrong.

The nonsense talked about ratios by some experts and brokers

DJIA/gold

The *Financial Times* reported recently that according to a French broker the Dow Jones Industrial Index/gold ratio averaged 12.5 since 1971's collapse of the Bretton Woods Agreement.

Chart 8-10: DJIA/gold

The charts disagree with the unnamed *agent de change*. Monsieur was wrong: since the collapse of Bretton Woods, the ratio has never averaged 12.5, or anything near it, except very briefly. As the chart above shows, the ratio did average 1.8 for one week in 1980.

But brokers being wrong should never surprise you: I was a broker for 27 years, and I was wrong all the time until I became a technician eight years into my sentence.

Broking is like playing golf foursomes: always having to say you're sorry.

Chart 8-11: DJIA/gold

Source: CQG, Inc. © 2006 All rights reserved worldwide.
www.cqg.com

According to the same broker, at its 2000 peak the Dow was 40 times the gold price. As you can see from the chart above, *M. Agent de Change* boobs again! It was 43.84. He continues, "when gold was $850, the ratio was 12.5 again". No, it wasn't. As the first of the two charts shows, when gold was $850 in January 1980 the Dow/gold ratio was 1; the one year average at the peak, approximately 1.9.

Now here comes the kicker: supposing the broker had been right about 12.5, with the Dow now trading at around 17.5 times the price of gold, if it were to fall to the post-1971 average, gold would rise to nearly $900 an ounce. But he wasn't right.

As far as I can work out, and my maths might be suspect, using the ratio's 10-year average, and calculating its level at all years ending in 6 (four of them), since Bretton Woods' collapse the average of the ratio has been 35. Accordingly, for it to go to its average level of the past 35 years, gold would have to fall to $317. Given my negative reading of gold, nothing would please me more or surprise me less.

But why should this ratio equal its average level of the past 35 years?

There are no "shoulds" in this business, except what the chart says, and what the chart of the ratio says at present is that although the trend is down, the 19-year average, encountered recently, is potential support.

Not only was the Inspector Clouseau of French broking wrong about the ratio's average level since 1971, that's nothing compared with the double whammy that followed his comment concerning gold at nearly $900 an ounce: it would have to go there, assuming (don't you just love that word, "assuming"?) that "the Dow stays where it is now" (26th July, 2006).

Chart 8-12: Dow Jones Industrial Average

Source: CQG, Inc. © 2006 All rights reserved worldwide.
www.cqg.com

The Dow always stays where it is of course, which is why it never goes up or down, or does it? Of course it does. If markets didn't go up and down, how would brokers make a living?

Oil/gold ratio

M. Clouseau has also been looking at the gold/oil ratio. Apparently, its long-term average is around 16. Currently, it's 8.4. Ah! A return to the long-term average would take gold past $1,000. But shouldn't that statement include an "assuming"? Something like "assuming oil stays the same as it is now". Like the Dow Jones Index staying the same as it is now, that is quite an assumption.

Chart 8-13: oil/gold

What is the ratio's chart saying now?

1. The double top between the two red lines implied 7.17, an objective already achieved.

2. The one year average is rising, implying that the ratio might find support at current levels: rising averages are potential supports.

3. There is potential resistance at 10, not only because it was the recent high but also because the three year average is at that level, and falling (a falling average is potential resistance).

Gold/silver

Chart 8-14: gold/silver

At the start of the 1970s, gold was $35.00 and experts said that the historical gold/silver ratio average was 15 and couldn't go any higher because, if it did, the arbitrageurs would sell gold and buy silver, in which case the ratio wouldn't alter. But you already know what I think about experts and their opinions.

Why the experts were saying the historic average ratio was 15 in view of the evidence provided by the chart, I don't know, but my database only goes back to 1971, and maybe it was 15 in the 1960s, although I doubt it. In any case, at the beginning of 1971 the ratio had already risen to 25 (see the LHS of the chart), so what had happened to the arbitrageurs and long-term *averageurs*, I wonder?

I suppose no one had told the ratio it couldn't or "shouldn't" be able to go above 15, or, if he did, it didn't listen. Since the days it couldn't stray too far from the long-term average of 15 (it did go down to that level once between 1971 and 1986, at gold's 1980 high), the ratio has been as high as 102.2 (1991), as low as 45.48 (1998), compared with the current 56.16. Its current long-term tend is down.

Brokers' outpourings and economic forecasts too, are always full of "assumings": give me two assumings and I can beat Tiger Woods any time I like.

To be a broker it helps to be articulate (also if you're a lorry). Robert Bernstein, former CEO of Random House put it this way,

> *Only intuition can protect you against the most dangerous individual of all, the articulate incompetent.*

The yield gap

Did you ever hear of the yield gap, the ratio between the yields on equities and on gilts? Equities always had to yield more than gilts; they always would yield more than gilts in order to reflect the greater risk in holding them. Then something called inflation appeared, closely followed, in 1963, by the Trustee Investment Act. The yield gap ratio became the reverse yield gap ratio. Which leads us on to…

What lessons should be learned about ratios?

1. Never pay attention to experts; be your own.
2. Ratios do what they have to do.
3. The chart will tell you what ratios have to, or might be about to do.
4. Historic levels are interesting, but irrelevant.

The expression "they're as different as chalk and cheese" applies: if you're trading chalk, don't look at the chart of cheese.

Case History 1 – Anglo American relative to FTSE100 index

Chart 8-15: Anglo American/FTSE100; weekly chart

Source: CQG, Inc. © 2006 All rights reserved worldwide.
www.cqg.com

Between 2003 and 2005 I was running a ghost portfolio for a European hedge fund. The chief trader was addicted to relative strength, and at the beginning of March 2004 was naturally very pleased with the relative performance of Anglo American. Why not? Since 2000's relative low at 100, Anglo American had out-performed the market by 200%.

As for the relative chart (the averages are one and three months), if you can see anything wrong with it, I can't nor could I then.

If you look at the upper red lines (potential resistances), you can see that the weekly price was in contact with neither of them. True, at 1st March's high it had got close to both, but close wins no cigar.

The longer red line was the return line drawn parallel to the major up trend line (lower blue line), the shorter was the internal upper return line. Both were potential resistances, of course.

I sold short at March 4th's 1370 close

The following charts explain why I made that short sale, at least I hope they do...

Chart 8-16: Anglo American, daily

My main reason was that on March 2nd price had made two terminal blow-offs, the first was above the internal return line, while the second, far more important, was above the diverging upper trend line of the whole bull market. If that isn't a reason to look for a fall, what is?

Chart 8-17: Anglo American, daily

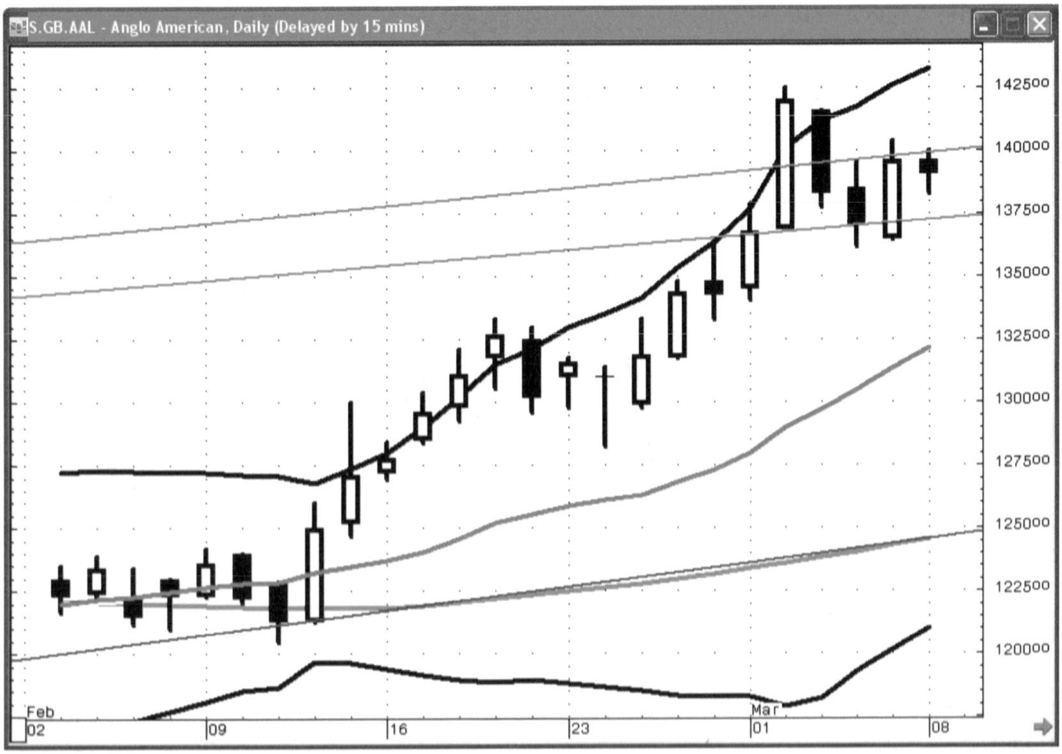

S.GB.AAL - Anglo American, Daily (Delayed by 15 mins)

That being so, why didn't I sell on 2nd? Because there was no way of telling if the blow-off would continue or reverse. 3rd saw Anglo choose the latter. Why didn't I sell then? There were two reasons:

1. 3rd's black candle was still in contact with the upper Bollinger Band, i.e. no trend reversal yet.

2. That candle confirmed the rally had stopped (Harami), but not necessarily reversed. A white candle on 4th would imply that the rally had decided to continue, a black one that it had reversed.

Fourth's candle was not only black but also separated from the upper Bollinger Band, confirming that the Harami had been a top reversal, the separation being a second. Given the now confirmed blow-off, and the further evidence provided by my reading of the candle chart, a *sale was mandatory*.

I made the sale at 4th's close. On 5th, I received a phone call from the hedge fund's chief trader. "Why did you sell Anglo when price relative is at a peak?" "Have a look at the absolute price", I replied.

Take a look at what followed…

Chart 8-18: Anglo American, daily

The chart below is the daily price relative chart, which came along on the same ride as the absolute.

Chart 8-19: Anglo American/FTSE100, daily

This case history was no fantasy; every word is true.

Case History 2 – 1972-74 bear market

This one relates to the great bear market, 1st May1972-13th December 1974, when the All-Share Index (there was no FTSE100 Index in those days) fell 74%, the largest bear market since the 1929/1932 disaster on Wall Street.

I was there; during the former, not the latter, but having started in the City in 1952, I had read all about it; specifically in J.K. Galbraith's *The Great Crash*.

The value of history

Young men out to make their fortune no longer seem to read anything. In the 1960s, for example, Bernie Cornfeld revolutionised the whole investment industry, yet ask most people in their fifties (if you can find anyone that old in the investment industry) who Bernie was, and what it was he did, and very few, if any, will have heard of him.

Young men in the business now (oldies call it the City) don't seem to have any feeling for or understanding of market history. How many chart services (Datastream apart) have chart data going back to 1945 for example?

The longer you can look back, the farther you can look forward
Winston Churchill

Just after the Baring disaster, Evelyn de Rothschild told me that when young people with any experience were applying for a job, they didn't even bother to tell the bank their CVs, only how much they were earning. I doubt that things have improved since then.

In the aftermath of 1929-32, a whole generation didn't go into Wall Street, partly because "it was finished", partly because of World War II. They were saying the same about the London market when I went into it in 1952, and they didn't appear to be wrong: bargains averaged 7,000/day, a very small number. Nowadays the number of bargains has been superseded by actual volume.

Accordingly, The Great Crash haunted us, and was to return, in stock market terms, even if not in economic consequences, although we had to wait until 1973 for it to start.

Back to Case History 2, although I've never left it despite the above.

During the early stages of the 1970s crash, I took the view that the market would be like the trade unions (remember them?). What do I mean by that?

One out, they're all out!

In stock market terms this meant, I thought, said and wrote, like the baby washed out with the bath water, everything would go down. On hearing this, I was told scathingly by one investment manager (he's still around, so I won't name him):

> *...the market can't go down because it's on a P/E of 19, and prospectively 17, and banks, especially, can't fall because their P/E is 16, and prospectively 14, therefore they're cheap, absolutely and relatively. As for Discount Houses, no one will sell them.*

Discount Houses were *the* market favourite at the time, but another bad absolute chart, although their chart, relative to the market, was still good. If you're wondering where the charts are, the answer is that they no longer exist. You're just going to have to believe me.

Banks did fall apart. So did Discount Houses. In a big bear market there comes a time when the only things that it doesn't hurt too badly to sell are the sectors and shares that have held up the best.

What about the market's P/E ratio?

That fell apart as well, going to 3 before the bear market ended. Yes, I did write 3; it was not a typo. Why not 3? After all, it was "the end of capitalism as we know it" according to one expert.

Burmah Oil, a market icon, had gone bust, and Natwest was rumoured as being likely to follow.

As for the property sector, it was totally bankrupt, we were told. The shares of British Land, led at the time, as it still was until recently, by John Ritblat, had fallen from 390 pence (if my memory is correct) to 6.

But even while the most terrible stories were circulating, in the final weeks of the bear market several leading property shares, British Land being one of them, made double bottoms on their absolute charts, while Land Securities made an up trend. Since the All-Share Index didn't complete its double bottom until January 1975, the price relative charts of British Land and Land Securities were superb.

Lessons to be learned

1. Price isn't always led by price relative.

2. Unless you are managing a tracker fund, you are dealing in price, not in price relative.

3. If you are not managing a tracker fund, what is the point of losing money, even if you are doing so at a slower rate than the market?

Case History 3

In the most recent bear market, someone described as a City expert advised investors to buy shares in water companies, giving as his reason "people aren't going to give up drinking water". Of course they weren't, but that didn't mean that people were going to buy water shares in sufficient quantities to keep their share prices going up.

A bear market is a bear market because in a bear market investors decide not to value shares as highly as they had in the preceding bull market. Accordingly, price/earnings ratios go down. Before earnings. Then earnings go down, then price.

A cautionary tale

A consultant came into the terminal ward on the tenth floor of a hospital. He opened a window and jumped out. On the way down, the consultant felt well, relatively speaking, compared with how he would feel when he hit the ground.

One of the patients, already confirmed as a terminal case, watching his fall, felt relatively better than the surgeon. A few days later, the patient died.

Moral: relative strength is all very well, but you can die of it.

Stops

Since chartists aren't fishing for bottoms
And mustn't go shooting for tops,
To avoid self-delusion
And end all confusion
Their only solution is stops.

Everyone who's ever looked at a chart on a screen thinks he's a bit of a chartist – you might as well be a bit of a surgeon. Technical analysis isn't for amateurs: the battle of Waterloo may have been won on the playing-fields of Eton, but the battle of beating the market can't be fought by part-timers.

Nor is it a part-time occupation played by fundamental analysts. I have never seen the point of second-guessing the chart by looking at the fundamentals, having nothing but contempt for technicians who think they need to up-grade what they do, at least in the opinion of doubters, by mixing technical and fundamental analysis.

When I first became a technician I asked myself what I should do if my technical and fundamental views contradicted each other. The answer was simple: if I thought I was a chartist, I had to believe the chart. Accordingly, why pay any attention to the apparent fundamentals, since it is undeniable that shares frequently lead a life totally at variance with the fortunes of the companies they supposedly represent?

Why put pig on pork? And if you mix champagne with Guinness, it diminishes both.

In any case, technical analysis without fundamental analysis does far less harm than fundamental analysis does without technical analysis; technical analysis being by itself a valid discipline, and discipline is the name of the game.

Technicians should initiate positions only for technical reasons, and the same discipline applies equally to closing them. If you buy because of the confirmation of an inverted head & shoulders that subsequently aborts, you should sell, there being no point in thinking of another reason for holding. The same applies in respect of positions initiated by the confirmation of any other pattern.

Supposing you buy (or sell) because of a pattern, and there is subsequently a trend reversal or reversal at an average, an adverse crossing of averages, the non-appearance of expected support or resistance etc, but the pattern is still valid; what do you do then? You exercise judgment, I'm afraid; under these circumstances you are not making a technically-driven decision but managing your P&L account.

What about placing a stop to minimise losses, even if any of the events mentioned above haven't taken place? That's a perfectly reasonable thing to do, but it isn't a technical stop, it's a trading one. Occasionally I do impose a trading-stop in the foreign exchange market, but only if there is a large profit that I want to protect and there is no valid technically justifiable one nearby.

But do remember that I am an adviser and clients pay me to give technical opinions and only technical opinions. It isn't my business to try to get out at the top or in at the bottom but to maximise profits and minimise losses for purely technical reasons. As an investor, you can do what you like.

I never stop any position except at a close, whether it is daily, weekly or monthly. If you are using either of the two last-named however, when you read the daily chart it might lead you to seek a better dealing opportunity, and you might get one as a consequence of dealers' remorse qv.

As you will see in many of the reports appearing in the next chapter, I often advise a position without including a stop in the recommendation. Chartist speaking with forked tongue, since I believe that a forecast without a stop isn't worth the paper it's written on? Not at all: I manage the stops daily. At the close of every day I review all open positions and advise clients what to do as a result of my reading of the latest technical situation.

If you are reading this as personal investors, when opening positions you should always know at what level you ought to close them. If you don't know, don't deal at all; there are countless numbers of shares and technical conditions, and you'll soon find other opportunities.

A stop is a stop is a stop…..stopping profits, losses and pain.

He who stops and steps aside
Can always book another ride.

I promised this would be the shortest chapter and it is.

10

The Nitty-Gritty

OED definition:

The realities or basic facts of a situation, subject, etc; the heart of the matter.

his chapter was going to be "Putting It All Together", but then I discovered that at this stage of most books on technical analysis there is a chapter called that, and this book's aim is not to be like other books. Voila! (The computer refuses to give me a grave accent; a grave error, but it is an American computer, and since they are now calling *pommes frites* freedom fries, I suppose it's not surprising).

There's only one way of dealing with the nitty-gritty; showing you what I wrote about various markets at various times; not one report showing you a particular call, but a sequence of them. I have chosen three markets that particularly interest me, FTSE, gold and the $ index.

If I've done what I set out to do in this book, you will find it very easy to follow the technical arguments in the reports, because although most of those for whom I write are only interested in conclusions rather than reasons, some are interested in both, while I have always been concerned to explain the reasons why I arrive at my conclusions: I am not a black box merchant.

Although I frequently refer to the previous report when writing a new one, and often repeat sections of it where necessary, I actually approach each issue as though I had never written before. When writing for newspapers or journals I am often criticised for not doing what journalists want me to do, which is to start with the conclusion and then show why I came to it. I don't know what conclusion I will reach until my arguments have convinced me.

Report #1

5th November, 2005

FTSE 5423.6 (5213.4 last time)

A week ago, with FTSE at 5213.4, I concluded that in view of the (rate-of-change's) down trend and an unfavourable momentum background, I would be surprised if the reaction low were posted before the week ending 11th. I was wrong.

When FTSE crossed above the Three Month Average on 1st, the latter was about to start rising, and when it did, became potential support, prompting 2nd's update that a test of the highs was possible unless a 5315.5 close was posted. 5344.3 at the time, FTSE could still make further progress.

The Coppock Indicator started rising again five weeks ago, and markets don't peak until after it has started falling. But even when Coppock's indicator does turn down, that isn't a sell signal because the delay between that downturn and a market peak is of variable duration. cont...

...cont

Accordingly, the indicator's current message is that the bull market high hasn't yet been posted. October's peak is likely to be bettered, but (as ever) FTSE must first exceed that peak by 2% in order to create the possibility of making significant progress above it.

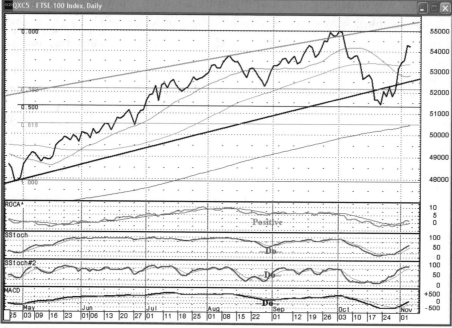

The conundrum is this: has the recent advance pre-empted a Christmas rally. There is a greater incidence of year-end rallies when November has seen a largely weak market.

With the indicators, including the high/low ratio, positive, there is no reason to call off the rally.

The reports (usually sent weekly) continued calling the market up.

Report #2

8th January, 2006

FTSE 5731.8 (5531.6 last time)

Having started in March 2003, by historical standards the bull market is mature.

Wall Street's, dating from October 2002, is more so.

But until there has been a deterioration in the long-term indicators, calling that the end is nigh would be premature.

The technician's job is not to call the peak in advance but to say when the trend has reversed.

Although, with more than 80% of shares above their long-term average, FTSE is overbought, until this long-term indicator falls below 70%, the market is unlikely to prove significantly vulnerable.

As for the short-term, while the rising One Month Average continues to provide support, as it has been doing since late October, downside risk is limited to around 5560. Meanwhile, as a consequence of last week's upside break by ROCA, the outlook remains good until end-January.

There were reports between 8th January's and 29th April. But they all said the same thing: the market was going to rise.

Report #3

29th April, 2006

FTSE 6023.1 (6029.4 last time)

Bull/bear? The technician's job is not to call the market names but its direction; not to call the peak in advance but to say when the trend has reversed.

FTSE is overbought with 90% of shares above their long-term average. Although there is no sell signal until the total is below 70%, with the percentage above their three month average down to 74, from over 90 since the beginning of January, buyers need to be even more selective than usual.

COPPOCK INDICATOR:

Although the indicator doesn't give sell signals, since 1985 there have been eight Coppock downturns. On two occasions FTSE turned down simultaneously with the indicator, signalling a bear market. On three, FTSE turned down one month before. On the remaining three occasions, the delay between the Coppock Indicator's downturn and FTSE's has been three, 23 and the current 21 months. At end-April, the indicator is still rising.

The momentum background is unfriendly for many weeks; this is significant only when the rate-of-change indicator is in a down trend. Last week, it started one.

No excuse for repeating what I have written nearly every week since last October: as long as it keeps rising, the one month, like any other average, is potential support. It is now 6043.7 and FTSE closed beneath it yesterday, the eighth time it has done so during the past seven months. A close at/beneath 6024 next Friday would make the average start falling.

cont...

...cont

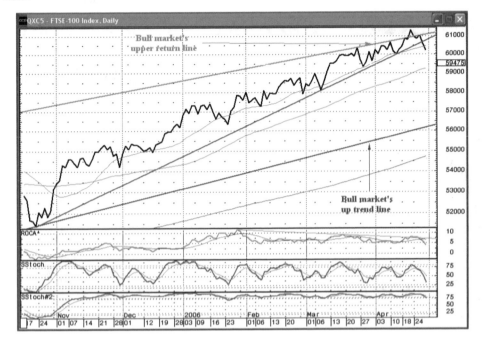

FTSE would have to close at/beneath 5947.4 to break the up trend line from October's low,

Sell in May?

Given the significant advance since late October's low (Halloween/end-April is habitually a better period for shares than May/October), a reaction, though not yet on the charts, may not be too long in coming. Nevertheless, 31st May won't arrive until another 24 trading days have passed. In markets, a great deal can happen in 24 days.

But that's not all: if sell in May is interpreted as the start of the last week in April and/or the first in May (dependent on what day of the week 30th April occurs), since December 1983 there have been 22 Aprils.

On 11 occasions, selling at end-April has been right, but on one of them, only for three weeks. On three more occasions you needed to buy again in mid to late June, on the seven remaining ones you could have afforded to wait until late July. On 11 occasions selling at end-April has been wrong.

cont...

...cont

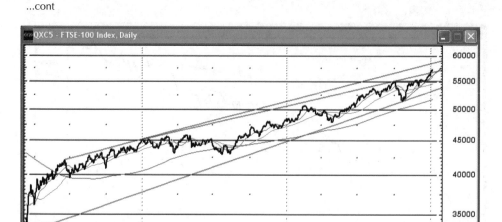

On the upside, there is potential resistance from the upper trend line illustrated, crossed last week. This resistance extends to 5778, but if that level were to be posted, the inference would become a no time limit advance to the bull market's upper trend line, now 5855.

Report #4

23rd May, 2006

FTSE 5600.5 intraday

COPPOCK INDICATOR

In the All-Share Index (it has a longer history than the FTSE100) the indicator has made eight downturns since 1985. Twice, the market turned down simultaneously; three times, the All-Share's downturn preceded the indicator's downturn by one month.

On the three remaining the delay between the Indicator's downturn and the start of an All-Share Index' bear market has been three, 23 and the current 22 months. An end-May close below 3024.86 would cause a downturn, implying that a bear market had started.

The previous report said:

> Nearly every week since October I have written that as long as it kept rising, the one month, like any other average was potential support. It is now 6057 and falling: potential resistance. Unless the three month average, now 5965, provides support, the bull market up trend line at 5660 will be tested.

It was tested; it was broken; it is now potential resistance.

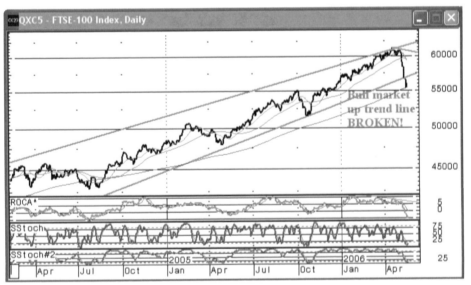

Source: CQG, Inc. © 2006 All rights reserved worldwide.
www.cqg.com

cont...

...cont

The one year average was 5330.8 at yesterday's 5532.7 FTSE close. I prefer one or more closes below the average, followed by a renewed close above it, when considering that a successful test has been made, so I am open-minded on whether there has been a test or not.

Given the oversold condition of Stochastics and the ROC, the latter more oversold now than at any time since July 2004's low, FTSE may rally, especially since the one month has just crossed below the three month: a rally to/towards the crossing-point frequently follows such events.

None of my three criteria for calling the major trend down has yet been met. One of them is the crossing by the three month below the one year average, not likely for some time, while the latter is unlikely to start falling for several months. The market needs to rally to create a sustainable down trend line for the next bear market, but although it might be tested, it is now looking likely that the bull market has peaked.

Note: Although there were three ROC top reversals between October's low and May, the one month average kept on rising: using this as a second filter kept me long during this period.

Report #5

5th June, 2006

FTSE 5764.6 intraday (5600.5 last time)

Last time's forecast at 5600.5 (23rd May)

Given the oversold condition of Stochastics and the ROC, the latter more oversold now than at any time since July 2004's low, FTSE may rally, especially since the one month has just crossed below the three month: a rally to/towards the crossing-point frequently follows such events.

So far, the market has obliged. But the one and three month averages and their crossing-point are potential resistances at 5805, 5938 and 5955. So are all red trend lines. To overcome the broken major up trend line, a close at 5802 is needed.

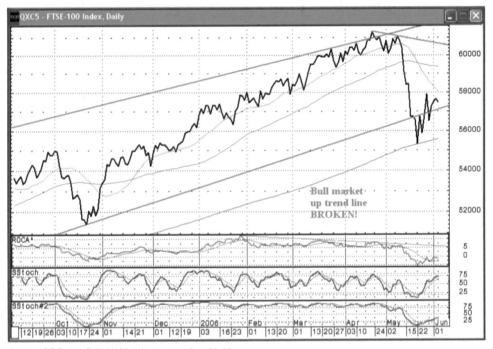

Source: CQG, Inc. © 2006 All rights reserved worldwide.
www.cqg.com

Given the indicators' positive condition however, it would be premature to call off the rally unless it is reversed by either of the averages (a renewed close beneath one following one or more above it).

Coppock Indicator

The Coppock Indicator which appeared likely to start falling at end-May, did so. What does end-May's downturn imply? According to Edwin Coppock, who devised it, nothing. Predicated on the 11-14 months required by the human psyche to recover from bereavement, divorce, illness, losing a job or money, it can't ever be a sell signal.

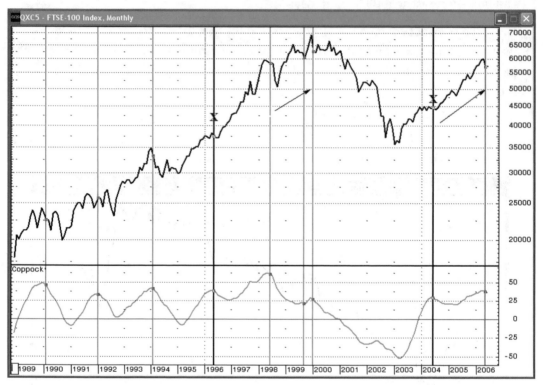

But technical analysis is about empirical observation, and except for 1996 and 2004, both marked with an X, in the period covered by the chart whenever the indicator has started falling it has been in the region of highs. In 1998-99 there were three downturns, the first far too soon, but the second and third (separated by many months from the first) found the top.

2004 saw one of the two occasions when the signal was completely wrong. It could also be argued that 1998's was a wrong signal. But look what happened 15 & 19 months later: two very good signals bracketed the bull market high.

May 2006's downturn was 23 months after June 2004's wrong one, raising the possibility that that period was a re-run of 1998-99. If it was, May 2006's downturn could indicate that the indicator has found the top, or thereabouts, again.

Report #6

8th June, 2006

FTSE 5594.7 intraday intraday (5764.6 last time)

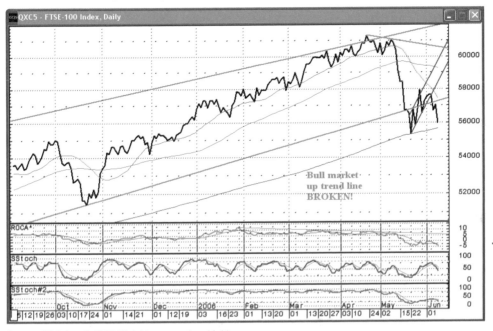

Source: CQG, Inc. © 2006 All rights reserved worldwide.
www.cqg.com

Given the indicators' positive condition last Friday, I concluded that it would be premature to call off the rally unless it was reversed by either of the averages. Since then there may have been a reversal without either being reached: if the recent 5532.7 low is broken at any close within the next few days, a flag would be confirmed.

The inference would be a further decline to 5330. The abort: three successive up-days or a close 2% above the lowest.

I have seen few flags work in recent years, but my job is not to guess whether any particular technical development will work or fail but to let you know when there is one, and set the appropriate stop.

Flags are limited by time, and those mentioned throughout this report will be stopped if the objectives have not been reached by 23rd June.

Previously stated view: "The market still needs to rally to create a sustainable down trend line for the next bear market, but although it might be tested, it is now looking likely that the bull market has peaked". I haven't changed that view.

Report #7

5th July, 2006

FTSE 5826.7

INDEX TO TAKE A BREATHER

Resistance works; Hanging Man and Belt-hold line both bearish.

A falling average is potential resistance if a renewed close below it follows one or more above. The average here is the three month. FTSE closed above it on Monday and Tuesday, beneath it today.

The hanging man is a top reversal: Tuesday's was one. It also formed tweezers, a minor top reversal with Monday's candle. Today's candle was a belt-hold line, a bearish candle.

Source: CQG, Inc. © 2006 All rights reserved worldwide.
www.cqg.com

Following a narrowing of the Bollinger trend channel such as 13th/ 28th June's, the *obbligato* is that that channel becomes tram-lines going east. The first white candle that closes above the upper Bollinger Band or beneath the lower one determines the new trend, 12th June's providing an example of the latter, 30th June's, of the former.   cont...

...cont

But that trend can end following the first "wrong" candle, wrong being a white candle separation from the lower Bollinger band in a down trend (25th June), a black candle separation in an up trend. We saw the latter today.

CONCLUSION: FTSE appears likely to take a breather.

NB: Candles signal a reversal, not *the* reversal. Provided the potential supports indicated become actual ones, a test of the highs is still on the chart once the forecast breather has exhaled.

The inference of the failure to overcome the three month average is a return to the lows unless the one month or one year average provide support, just as the inference when the one year average did provide support at June's low was a test of the highs unless the one or three month averages acted as resistance.

The latter has acted as resistance, and the only thing that could abort the fall and reinstate the recent advance is a new rally high within days.

Report #8

25th July, 2006

BREATHER OVER.....FTSE BREATHES AGAIN

Yesterday's rise provided the proof.

At 5870 on 11th, I concluded that FTSE, then 5876, was going to take a breather, the one month and one year averages being nominated as the potential supports. At its low on 17th, FTSE hit 5654.6.

Yesterday's advance put the index more than 2% above the recent low (proof that support had been found) and also above the rising one month average (proof that it too had provided support).

The grey line is the neckline of a potential inverted head & shoulders; confirmation, a 6080 close.

Source: CQG, Inc. © 2006 All rights reserved worldwide.
www.cqg.com

cont...

...cont

At present FTSE is range-bound between the neckline and recent lows, yesterday's close increasing the likelihood of the upper end being tested.

Once the one year average had provided support in June, the inference became a test of the highs unless the one or three month averages acted as resistance. The latter is potential resistance despite yesterday's advance above it, and will remain so until it starts rising, unlikely before 10th August.

If the inverted head & shoulders is confirmed, the inference would be a return to the highs, and maybe above them. All indicators are positive except the ROC, which is likely to make a bottom reversal around 10th August unless the head & shoulders is confirmed beforehand.

Report #9

5th August, 2006

FTSE 5889.4 (5851.2 last time)

FAILURE AT RESISTANCE

Last time's forecast – test of the range's high – came good.

Index range bound. Direction of breakout depends on S&P

Report #10

13th May, 2006

GOLD $725.75 PM fix (625.00 20th April)

The advance since 1999 is nearly seven years old, the longest since Bretton Woods' failure. Having gained 187% at Friday's new high, it is the third largest bull market since then.

Huntin', shootin' & fishin': Technicians shouldn't fish for a bottom or shoot for a top, just hunt for a trend. Since I haven't yet called a top, my mistake has been to look for one instead of waiting for the one month average to start falling, as I have been doing in stock market indices. The reason, unjustified so far, is the blow-off currently underway, which has separated price from average by a substantial amount. The average is now $650, higher than price was on 20th April when I last wrote.

WEEKLY CHART

cont...

DAILY CHART

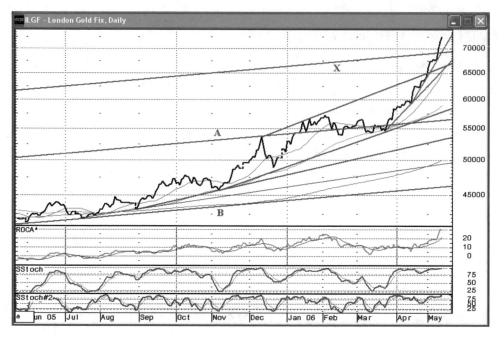

This chart and that on the previouse page both show terminal blow-offs. X is parallel to and equidistant from A & B. It was overcome last week.

The ROC is at its highest level, so far, of this bull market, extremely rare, but not unprecedented: the ROC's high is usually reached in the opening stages of a bull market, the only other exception having been 1980. The ROC was above 100 on 21st January 1980, and if that record were matched this time, and the high is between now and the end of June, gold will be $1085 or higher.

When I last wrote on 20th April, gold was $625.00. What was the ROC's state then? My answer was:

> Good. At 19th's PM fix, without showing any overbought condition, this indicator reached its highest level since mid-February, while its average (blue line) started rising. Where the ROC points, price tends to follow: gold could rise further.

cont...

...cont

I was concerned however about two potential resistances. But both have since been overcome. I have been in this business since 1955 and seen the following bull markets that were going to last forever, Canadian Natural Gas (1953/1956); Gold (1970/1974); Gold (1976/1980); Nickel (two, the Western Mining one and Poseidon's); dot.com; Oil (1970s); Commodities (1980s), Tokyo (1982/1990).

Greyhounds (post-WWII); Bakelite Gramophone Records (pre-WWII) were both before I went into the City, as was Wall Street (1929). So was the Dutch Tulip Mania (C17).

Most of those listed, I've experienced. The ones before my time, I've read about.

In the end, price takes care of everything; it also takes away the Emperor's clothes. And we have been here before. In the 1976-80 bull market, another one that was going to last forever, substitute Kuwait, Saudi-Arabia, Japan and several others at that time for China today and it's an old story.

In any case, what's so amazing about Central Banks buying (and selling) gold. The bottom of the last bear market in the yellow one was in 1999. Have we all forgotten that the UK wasn't the only country where the central bank (our Chancellor, Mr Brown, to be precise) was selling?

Central Bank selling didn't extend the bear market then. Why should Central Bank buying extend the bull market now?

Am I calling the end now? No. But this one will not last forever. They never do. Bull markets end when the news is good. Only bear markets end when it's bad.

Report #11

29th May, 2006

GOLD $642.25 PM fix

Contrary to popular misconception I haven't called the top in gold. But people believe what they want to believe, and having never joined the "going to $900-$1,000" brigade, only calling gold up on one occasion this year, evidently a myth has arisen that I have been calling it down throughout 2006.

Between 16th January and 27th February, with gold never above $569.75 or below $539.70 at the time of writing, every report concluded:

> While not having the slightest idea where Gold will be tomorrow (charts don't tell you that), I am not bullish, even though it might rise further in the short-term. If my general posture is right however, and Gold does fall significantly from around current levels or even from somewhat higher ones, in the long-term it could easily go much lower.

> Even if I am wrong about the long-term, since the last two times it was as overbought as it is now Gold fell 13% & 8%, shouldn't we expect a similar fall in the next three months?

I did over-estimate the fall: at its worst, gold was only 5.44% down from the Q1 high.

7th March's report ($565.25) concluded:

> I would have to change my mind if February's $572.15 PM fix were to be exceeded by one at least 3% higher, i.e. at $589.03. Given that all bear markets since the failure of the Bretton Woods agreement started between December and February, would it mean that the bull market had to go on for another 10-13 months? Not necessarily.

5th April, "if a $589.38 PM fix is made, the bull market continues". The first PM fix at/above $589.30 was 6th April's $592.50. 12th's concluded, "The bull market continues", 20th's (gold, $625.00), "gold could rise further", adding that that day's 3.06% fall between the two fixes had been the fourth largest since 1970 and that large differentials between AM & PM fixes had always been associated with major peaks, even though on one occasion the peak had been delayed 39 days.

cont...

...cont

LGF - London Gold Fix, Daily

One year average

On 12th May gold fixed at $725.75. On 13th I concluded:

> Am I calling the end? No. But this (bull market) won't last forever. They never do. PS: bull markets end when the news is good[9]. Only bear markets end when the news is bad.

That may have been my biggest mistake in gold this year. The peak in all gold bull markets is the highest PM fix, and that is looking increasingly likely to have been 12th May's $725.75.

The weekly charts have been drawn to the same semi-log scale. Between August 1975 (lower chart) and January 1980 (upper), gold rose 415%; in the same 4½ year period between December 2001 and May 2006, gold rose 165%: the former was 1.515 times greater than the latter.

The bull market peaked in January 1980 and gold fell 20% in the first two weeks. In the two weeks between 12th May's $725.75 and 26th's $642.25, gold fell 13%. But if the second fall is adjusted for the difference in size of the preceding 4½ year advances, the initial falls have been identical.

cont...

---

[9] The "good news" was the Chinese were rumoured to be buying.

...cont

But the similarity doesn't end there: in the weeks immediately preceding the 1980 and 2006 peaks on both charts there were breakouts above the bull market's upper return line. When the advance becomes almost vertical, it usually signals the end of a bull market, and certainly did in 1980.

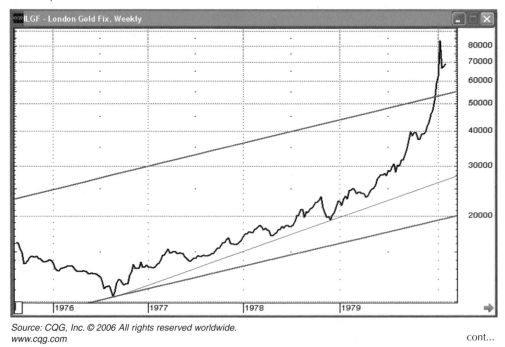

cont...

...cont

In 1980 the one month average didn't start falling until 18 trading days after the January peak.

I am not suggesting that it is has to be 18 days before the average starts falling this time, but having resisted the temptation of calling the FTSE100, FTSE250, S&P and Eurotop 300 indices down throughout 2006 until their one month average started falling, and having missed very little compared with the falls that followed, I am not about to innovate with gold.

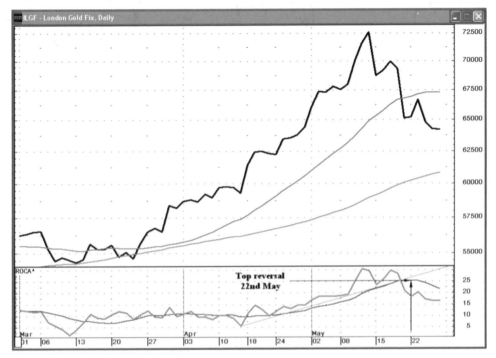

But the one month average will start falling if the PM fix is below $661.00 on Tuesday, $673.60 on Wednesday, $673.50 on Thursday or $678.00 on Friday. But look at the three month rate-of-change.

It made a top reversal on 22nd May, four trading days ago. In 1980 the top reversal in the ROC was on 28th January, 13 trading days before the one month average started falling. When calling a top, I consider the ROC to be an even more important indicator than the one month average.

cont...

...cont

ILGF - London Gold Fix, Daily ...Working...

One month average starts falling

Top reversal
28th January

ROCA*

Feb 80 Mar Apr May Jun Jul Aug Sep Oct Nov Dec Jan 81

A combination of the two is what I need to call the end of the bull market, not just for those two reasons but also because of the bull market's length (two months short of seven years, the longest ever), its shape – similar to the 1976/1980 bull market – the spike top/blow-off, the recent overbought condition (greater than any other apart from 1980's), the talk that this time it's different, indeed, all the things I've been writing about since January except one.

The chart shows seven up trends, the same as in 1980. I have never seen more. 1, 3 & 7 have been numbered (the grey line is the parallel to line 3, the effective trend channel of the bull market: look at the blow-off since end-March). cont...

...cont

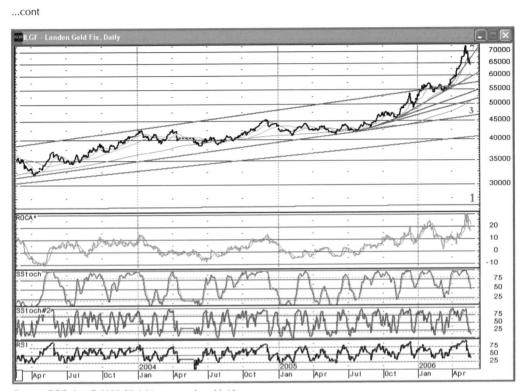

According to my definition of a bull market, and it hasn't changed for over 40 years, gold is still in one of course, because the one year average is rising. The trouble with this average however is that it doesn't start falling until a bear market has been going on for several months.

In 1980 for example (see previous chart) the one year average didn't start falling until a year later, by which time gold was $550.00, having been as low as $481.50 (a 43.35% decline) less than two months after January 1980's peak.

Do you want to wait for $518.11 before I make the call ($518.11 being the possible fall this time, making the same adjustment as that already made earlier in this report)?

If the one month average starts falling, I'm calling a bear market.

Supposing the facts change. As JM Keynes said,

If the facts change, I change my mind. What do you do, sir?

For "facts" read charts. If the charts change, I'll change my mind. I've done it before.

I called the bear market on 1st June when the PM fix was below $661.00.

Report #12

1st May, 2006

$ INDEX 86.11 intraday (87.23 last time).

$'s major trend is up and likely to stay up until 2007-08.

Major up trend.

The interval between two major down trends, starting at the preceding one's low. It ends at the high on the eve of the next one's birth.

For most of the up trend's duration, the one year average goes up, only reversing after the high.

The major down trend from July 2001's high ended in December 2004 after 42 months; the longest since 1985-87's 34 months (decline: 48.15%). 2001-04's decline: 33.40%.

The longer and larger the down trend, the longer and larger the succeeding up trend tends to be.

After 1985-87's major down trend, the succeeding major up-trend lasted 17 months, $ rising 23.40%. The highest point, so far, of this major up-trend (13.84% above the low) was posted after 11 months.

If the present advance did end last November, it was the smallest and second shortest of all, having followed the second longest and second largest decline in over thirty years.

cont...

...cont

Source: CQG, Inc. © 2006 All rights reserved worldwide.
www.cqg.com

Is it likely that the seventh up trend since 1979 ended after the smallest advance since 1975?

Between 1978 and 1981 $ was in a base area. It entered the current one more than 28 months ago. After 1978's low $ spent 27 months before emerging from the base area entered 33 months earlier; it then gained 64% in the next four years.

If $ behaves as it did in the base area ending June 1977, current $ bulls must remain patient for a further 4-5 months at somewhere between 2004's low and last November's peak.

Unlike the following daily chart, the major up trend line on the weekly chart above, now 84.90, remains unbroken; indeed, it hasn't even been tested.

The inference of the downside break from the red triangle is a further decline to the down trend line drawn from September's low, currently 83.30.

The main problems facing $ during the next four weeks are (1) the ROC's trend is down; (2) the momentum background unfriendly until 25th May. To cause an upturn in this indicator, and maintain any subsequent up trend, $ would have to rise faster between now and 25th than it did between end-January and late February; difficult, but not impossible.

...cont

In considering the possibility of a rally, it is important to note the proximity of potential support (the blue horizontal, hit on Friday, is the nearest, the grey line at 85.62, the second) and the condition of the three oscillators beneath the ROC. All are showing an extremely oversold condition. But their trend remains down, and until a reversal has taken place, it would be naive, technically speaking, to call a rally: oversold conditions in oscillators can continue for a long time.

Source: CQG, Inc. © 2006 All rights reserved worldwide.
www.cqg.com

Whereas the ROC (and Stochastics) are calculated on 63 & 34 day movements, the RSI and Stochastics 2 are calculated on movements of only 5 & 9 days. Accordingly, they are highly sensitive; even a one/two day advance can cause a bottom reversal in both of them.

Unlike the weekly chart's major up trend line, the major up trend line from 2004's low was broken at Friday's close. Can a major up trend continue once that trend line has failed? There are many examples of it doing so, especially when a rate is making the right shoulder of an inverted head & shoulders. While there is never a head & shoulders until it has been confirmed (a 0.50% break of the relevant neckline in the present case), look at the grey parallel lines on the following chart.

cont...

...cont

The upper line, at 92.35, is the hypothesised neckline, the lower, at 85.62, the approximate level of the point where the hypothesised right shoulder would be likely to start from, provided the market decides that it is going to make an attempt to form the pattern.

If the hypothesis sounds fanciful, I don't make comments unless I have made the necessary empirical observations, and I have frequently seen the appearance of inverted head & shoulder patterns similar to this potential one; and when the major up trend line has been broken.

What about $'s fundamental outlook in view of recent comments that the present cycle of rising interest rates will stop sooner rather than later? The market factors in all new developments very efficiently and extremely quickly, hence the recent heavy fall in $: the recent news is already "in the market". What isn't in is the un-stated possibility that the cycle isn't going to stop sooner, but later.

But I'm not a fundamentalist. From many years of experience as a technician however, I know that at this stage of a major up trend the apparent fundamentals appear to make nonsense of what the chart might be saying: when I was much younger, and less experienced, far too many times I was faked out of young bull markets, even if only temporarily, when, as it is today, the chart was suspect.

When the chart has gone wrong, I will tell you: it hasn't gone wrong yet.

Report #13

10th May, 2006

$ INDEX 84.63 intraday (86.11 last time).

The previously broken blue down trend line, still potential support, has been cut. But this is a weekly chart, and a Friday close at 84.98 is needed to confirm that that support has failed.

The major up trend line would be broken by a Friday close at 84.53.

The main problems facing $ during the next two weeks are (1) the ROC's trend is down; (2) the momentum background unfriendly until at least 25th May. To cause an upturn in this indicator, and maintain any subsequent up trend, $ would have to rise faster between now and 25th than it did between early January and late February; difficult, but not impossible.

As I wrote on 1st, the oscillators show an extremely oversold condition. But their trend remains down, and until a reversal has taken place, from a technical point of view it would be naïve to call a rally: oversold conditions in oscillators can continue for a long time.

cont...

...cont

The ROC and Stochastics are calculated on 63 & 34 day movements in price, the RSI and Stochastics 2 on movements of only 9 & 5. Accordingly, the two last-named are highly sensitive; even a one/two day advance can cause a bottom reversal in either or both.

On the daily chart on the next page, the major up trend line from 2004's low was broken on 26th April. While there are many examples of a major up trend continuing after its up trend line has been broken, especially when there is the possibility of an inverted head & shoulders being formed, the possibility of one forming here will disappear in the present case if any close is below 84.59.

The index broke the grey line at yesterday's close (see 1st May report for the significance), and one at 84.59 would break February 2004's 85.02. If so, there would no longer be any justification for expecting the point of the right shoulder of any inverted head & shoulders to appear at current levels.

The inference of the red triangle on the chart on page 298 remains a decline to approximately 83.00.

The most damning point of all however is the likely appearance today of a Dead Cross. Having already been crossed from above by the three month average, the one year average on the daily chart will start falling today if the index closes below 84.94. If the close is higher than that, the average will still turn down tomorrow unless the close is 86.11 or higher.

As for the weekly chart, it is Friday's close that counts, and unless Friday's is 86.64 or higher, the one year average will start falling then.

Two of the three criteria needed to confirm that the major trend has turned down have already been met; a downturn by the one year average being the third.   cont...

...cont

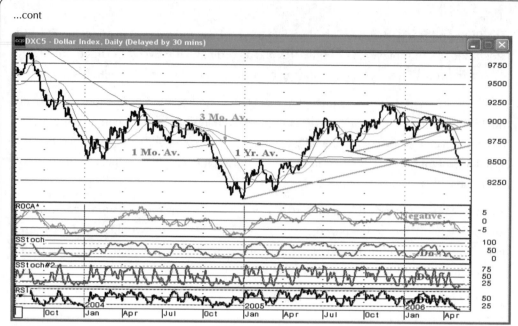

I don't fight the major trend's direction, and while there have been examples of long-lasting lows being posted within days of a Dead Cross' appearance, unless the news from the Fed later on today provides reasons for one, if the one year average does turn down, long $ positions should be covered.

Of course, if $ does continue falling, it might reverse at the 2004 low. But October/December's decline was 8.48% in just under two months. A five day rally followed, with $ rising 1.96%. That was the only rally on the way down. Then $ fell a further 2.45% before grounding.

The present rally started one month ago, and $ has lost 5.86% so far. A similar decline to that experienced at end-2004 would see it at 82.11 in four weeks, 81.65 in eight.

Report #14

18th August, 2006

$ INDEX: The long-term.

Between June 1976 and October1978, $ index fell nearly 23%. After the low it spent 27 months before 1981's upside breakout from a 33 month wide base area (double bottom). $ index then went up for four years, gaining 69.64% from the breakout-point, 100% from 1978's low.

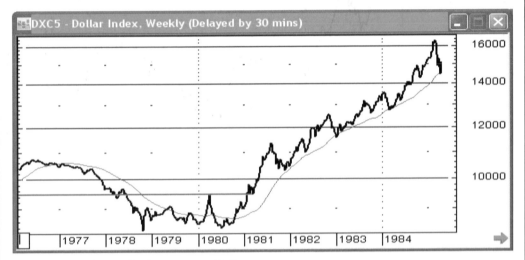

Between 2002 and 2004 the $ index fell 33%. During the 20 months since the 2004 low the index has been tracing out what will become a base area provided that low isn't broken.

cont...

...cont

Since 2002-04's decline was nearly 50% greater than 1976-78's, and the base area thereafter took 33 months to be completed, why shouldn't the current base area, now 33 months wide, last rather longer? There is no reason at all, especially if you consider the period 1985-02.

Between 1985 and 1992 $ index fell more than 50%. The base area (inverted head & shoulders) took 90 months to be formed. The advance from 1992's low lasted 56 months; $ gained 51%.

cont...

...cont

DXC5 - Dollar Index, Weekly (Delayed by 30 mins)

Source: CQG, Inc. © 2006 All rights reserved worldwide.
www.cqg.com

The point I am making is that since the inception of the $ index in 1971 there have been only two completed base areas, 1978-81's and1989-97's. The advances that followed, measured from the low, were 100% and 51%.

If, and I admit it may be a big if, $ index does complete the current base area, and only matches 1992-02's advance, it will reach 121.50, 43% above current levels.

My thesis that the index might have made the right shoulder of a potential inverted head & shoulders remains valid. It would cease to be however if the hypothesised right shoulder, 12th May's 83.96 close, were to be broken by 0.50%, any close at/beneath, 83.54. Were one to be posted, the inference would be a further decline to/towards the 2004/2005 lows.

cont...

...cont

Source: CQG, Inc. © 2006 All rights reserved worldwide.
www.cqg.com

Provided there is no close at 83.54 however, and, line NL is eventually overcome (a close at 93.50 being needed), the pattern would be confirmed no matter how long it takes, the inference being a no time limit advance to at least 102, though the advance from such patterns is frequently more than the minimum expectation.

I realise, of course, that none of the foregoing is of any use to a short-term trader, but there is obviously more to life than the short-term, and hence for the market.

Report #15

10th September, 2006

$ INDEX 85.95 (84.75 on 4th).

An 86.04 close would break March/July's down trend line, while one at 86.07 would confirm the range between the parallel lines as a double bottom, inference, 86.72. The indicators speak for themselves: short-term, positive; longer-term (ROC), negative.

The momentum background is $-unfriendly for two more weeks. As I wrote on 4th September, "if $ is going to break below 84.57, the most likely time for it to do so is between now and 25th. Since then $ has done very well, but 25th has neither come nor gone".

At the close of any trading day it is impossible to know price's direction on the next one; charts can't tell you that, which is why day-to-day analysis is best left to fools. Nevertheless, after four successive up-days, and a strong Friday, the following week frequently disappoints short-term bulls. Not always however; runs of 8 to 10 being neither abnormal nor rare.

cont...

...cont

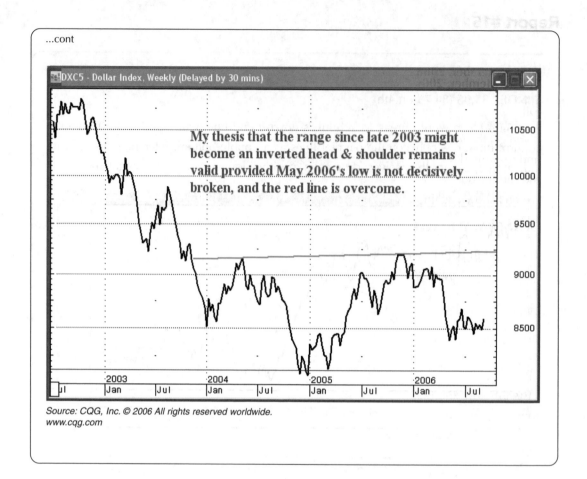

DXC5 - Dollar Index, Weekly (Delayed by 30 mins)

My thesis that the range since late 2003 might become an inverted head & shoulder remains valid provided May 2006's low is not decisively broken, and the red line is overcome.

Source: CQG, Inc. © 2006 All rights reserved worldwide.
www.cqg.com

Report #16

10th September, 2006

Oil

If you get the feeling you've seen this page before, you're right: it was 29th August's report, and re-printed on 31st. No apologies. To look into the future, you have to know the past: the further out you look, the further back you have to go. In any case, if what follows weren't shown again, I would have no option but to paraphrase myself.

DON'T SAY YOU WEREN'T WARNED

The tower of Babel was forecast to reach the sky.

It never made it. Nor has any bull market.

What price Oil $100 now?

Brent, Dec '06 $71.58 intraday

Last time's conclusion (Brent, $75.45)

"The July low and the three month average at 74.55 and 74.23 are potential supports. If they fail however, and a 72.31 close were posted, the inference would be 70.38. If achieved, that objective would break the up trend line from end-2004.

It is important to note that August's high was posted with the ROC far below its own July high: the stuff of which double tops are often made."

The double top was confirmed today.   cont...

...cont

QOZ6 - ICE Brent Crude, Dec 06, Daily (Delayed by 10 mins)

From Jan 2005 low

Now look at the grey triangle on the RHS of the chart. It has just been confirmed as a Flag. The inference is a further decline to $68.00 by no later than 8th September. The abort is three successive up-days or a close 3% above the lowest, whichever is first.

There is potential support at $70.00 and $67.50.

8th's September's close was $67.64.

cont...

...cont

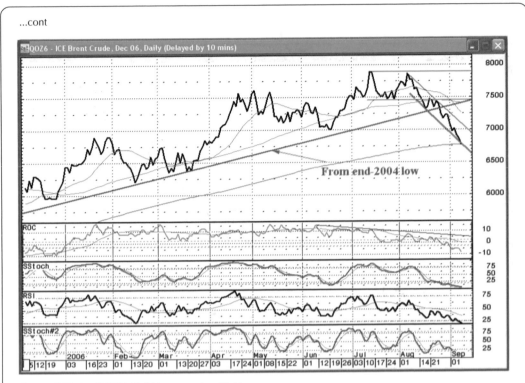

The flag's $68.00 objective was achieved that day. On the way down, the up trend line from 2004's low was broken and the $70.38 objective resulting from the double top was reached and exceeded.

How important is the breaking of that trend line from 2004? All trend lines matter, and the weekly chart over the page shows that 2004's trend line is one of many. The bull market trend line is now $39.00, but what good does it do to know that when, according to the standard definition, the bull market continues until it has been broken?

cont...

...cont

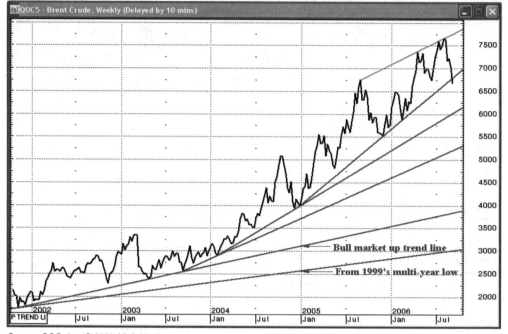

QOC5 - Brent Crude, Weekly (Delayed by 10 mins)

Bull market up trend line

From 1999's multi-year low

Source: CQG, Inc. © 2006 All rights reserved worldwide.
www.cqg.com

Do you want to lose another $29 to find out? The technician's job is not to call the market names but its direction, and if you've been following me, you haven't lost because at $71.58 on 29th August I told you that the double top and flag that had just been confirmed implied $70.38 and $67.50. Your paper profit is now 5% on sales made that day when the trend incontrovertibly turned down.

Dealing against the trend sometimes makes money, and no doubt makes you feel clever, but does it make sense? Not to a technician, it doesn't. The trend is your friend; why fall out with a friend?

What about this bull market? Mature; having gained 450% between that 2001's low and 2006's high, it is certainly no calf. When a double top sits on a big old bull, it can be the final straw that breaks not only the camel but also that bull's back; and what about sentiment, to say nothing about extrapolation? In 2001 who was talking Brent up to $100? No one, but they have been doing recently. Who is talking bearishly now apart from chartists? And everyone knows they're mad, of course.   cont...

...cont

Source: CQG, Inc. © 2006 All rights reserved worldwide.
www.cqg.com

The technical condition is bad, and although the three shorter indicators (34-day stochastic, 9-day RSI and 5-day stochastic) are oversold, which might spark a rally, especially since two supports, the lower trend line and the one year average (Brent closed beneath it on Friday), were hit on Friday.

To confirm that a rally has begun, Brent must close above the average. Were it to do so, the nearest potential resistance is the red trend line, now $71.50, but falling.

But the red arrow shows where Brent was trading three months ago. One week from now, June's advance will start to exert downward pressure on the ROC, the three month rate-of-change, for my money the indicator that matters most. That pressure will exist for four weeks. If it works, and the ROC, in no way oversold, continues to fall, the prospects for an extended rally, apart from next week, are dim.

One week up followed by four weeks down is not my idea of good odds for going long. I prefer to wait for any rally to take place, and then sell short. But if you are short at $71.58 on my advice, now is the time, if you're a short-term trader, to take your profit, and stand aside.

Report #17

13th September, 2006

Commodities

HEAD & SHOULDERS CONFIRMED

Objective: 364

Provided the objective is achieved, on the way down the up trend line illustrated, already cut, will be decisively broken. That line is the effective up trend of the bull market; there is another one at 360, but who wants to wait for that to be broken before taking action.

If the objective is hit the index would be at the same level as June's low and the one year average. If/when the former breaks, a double top will be confirmed: inference, 330.

By definition, the index is still in a bull market, but the technician's job is not to call the market names but its direction. I would be surprised if we haven't already seen the bull market's peak.

If you want to know where you're going, you need to know where you've been, so I am repeating the report written on 14th August.   cont...

...cont

14th August's report

Nothing wrong with this bull market; or is there?

On 9th August, more than 4¾ years after 22nd October 2001's bear market low, the CRB Commodity Index made a new bull market high at 398.87, having gained 117.34% during that period.

How does that compare with the length of other bull markets? It is already far longer than any of its predecessors. The longest bull market before the present one was 1977-80's, lasting a mere three years, four months. 1993-96's lasted three years, two months; 1971-74's, a paltry two years, four months.

Given that the last-named was a calf compared with the present bull market, why mention it at all? Because it produced a gain of 134%, the largest since my records began in 1971. At last week's high the current bull market's 117.34% gain had made it the second largest so far.

Source: CQG, Inc. © 2006 All rights reserved worldwide.
www.cqg.com

I say "so far" because, apart from its age, there is little technical reason for thinking that this bull market has peaked, apart from the undeniable truth that if any market falls even one point from a high, that fall might be the birth of the mother of all bear markets.

cont...

...cont

Nevertheless, the age of a bull market, and its size, are major determinants when considering the possibility that it might have ended.

Having noted that there was little technical reason apart from that already stated for considering that the bull market might have ended, "little" doesn't mean "no".

Source: CQG, Inc. © 2006 All rights reserved worldwide.
www.cqg.com

If everything in the bull market-garden were lovely...

The grey triangle, confirmed in favour of the bulls when July's high was overcome, and implying 435, would not have failed, as it did, not when price was reversed at May's high, that's par for the course, but when the horizontal line from the triangle's apex was broken during last week's fall.

Price would not have failed to overcome May's high: failure is a test of a high followed by a fall of 2% or more from that high.

When the test occurred, the rate-of-change (red indicator below price chart) would not have been at zero; should not have been at zero: the June/August advance in price took place to the accompaniment of a decline in the indicator, and such divergences are indicative of a potentially weak market.

cont...

...cont

While the recent fall might be short-lived, and it has already reached potential support at the one month average (green line), with the three month (red) not far beneath it, it is also possible that those supports will fail. If they do, June's low will be tested, and if it is broken by 2%, the resulting double top would suffice to end the bull market.

What do I think will happen? I don't think, I interpret the chart, and when a previous high is tested and the rate-of-change is negative, a double top frequently follows. Given the age of this bull market, the chances of one being formed are correspondingly greater.

11

I Remember

I remember, soon after joining N.M. Rothschild & Sons, asking a financial journalist, "Do you know Jacob and Evelyn?". "Love him, hate her", was his reply.

I remember giving up economics and switching to law. But since I didn't want to be a solicitor, what was I going to do when I came down? I was introduced to a stockbroker. Having no idea what being a broker entailed, I asked this excessively smooth young man what he did. "Buy and sell stocks and shares for a commission on behalf of other people". What a stupid way to make a living, I thought. I became a broker, but never changed my mind.

I remember reading about Jesse Livermore, known as the Great Speculator; made and lost fortunes. He committed suicide in a seedy hotel room, having lost all his money.....again! Call that a great speculator? Great speculators live in up-market hotels; they don't die in down-market ones.

They may shoot their mouths off, but not their heads. Jesse Livermore was nothing more than a bad speculator, putting great piles of money at risk; winning sometimes, then losing all of it again, frequently and, eventually, terminally.

I remember a manager telling me that his job was not to make money for clients but to keep the trustees happy. When I was at NMR I adopted his methods with one outside director who habitually made stupid recommendations. At one meeting he suggested we buy shares in some small and totally unsuitable garage company. "Certainly", I said, "shall we put in 5% of the fund (the maximum allowed at the time)?" Terrified, he said that 1% would be enough.

I bought the holding (1% wasn't going to make any difference either way) and ever afterwards, if it had performed well, I praised his perspicacity outrageously, if it hadn't, I said nothing. So did the director, about that share or anything else

I remember going to a broking house; the senior partner showed me an office. Like the City, it was devoid of humanity but full of green leather-topped desks with gold tooling. "What's this" I asked; my worst question ever. "It's where the attachés sit". I already had an attaché case, given by my mother to encourage me to become a barrister. Kismet! An attaché was what I was destined to be. I had been caught by the attachés. I was to do life (27 years without parole).

An attaché was paid nothing; he was there to schlepp business, receiving a third of the commission on what he introduced; the firm pocketing the rest.

I remember being in Abu Dhabi, teaching the young men of The Investment Authority the essential elements of technical analysis . Approached by a trader who told me it was his job to make £5,000 a week, and finding it hard to do, he asked if there was some easy way of doing it. I told him not to try; it was easier to try and make £20,000 a month, far easier.

I remember being shown one of the doors of the Stock Exchange. It had a white enamelled sign on which, printed in blue, was this, "SUBSCRIBERS ONLY ADMITTED". What on earth did that mean? Having been admitted, did they have to stay forever? Weren't they allowed to do anything once they had been admitted? What was a subscriber?

I remember being made a manager at NM Rothschild & Sons. Not NM Rothschild and Sons Ltd., just NM Rothschild & Sons; a partnership. When I was appointed, my mother went around telling everybody her son was a bank manager, but at NMR a manager was rather grander; just below the partners and associate partners.

Managers at NMR had "per pro": the signatures of two holders binding the bank anywhere in the world. This created a problem: per pro holders were terrified of the responsibility.

That's how I got to be a manager: I advised a Guernsey-based unit trust; orders came from there. My advice went by telex, and because the per pro holders' signatures would be on the authorisation, and therefore the ultimate responsibility was theirs, it was impossible to get any holder to sign one.

I told Evelyn de Rothschild. "You better be made a manager", he said. "I don't want to make problems for you", I said. His reply: "There won't be any; it's my bank".

My becoming a manager did however present problems for the senior partner, Edmund de Rothschild: I was on one year's probation, and as Mr. Edmund explained, "I don't normally shake a probationer's hand". He shook it.

I remember in Economics, Part I, I had to do a paper on the stock market. It was 1952 and I was 18; in those days boys that age had no idea what the stock exchange was; not this one, anyway.

There I was, without a clue what the stock market was, so I went to the college library and looked it up. What I discovered shaped if not my life, at least my business life: the law of supply and demand. It made sense, especially what happens when there are more buyers than sellers.

I became a technical analyst on the spot, although I didn't know what a technical analyst was, of course. But I didn't start working as a technical analyst until 1963, and I've been working at it ever since, trying to become one.

I remember that although Edmund de Rothschild was Senior Partner, he was only a *capo*; the godfather was Evelyn de Rothschild, *capo di tutti capi*. Always known as Mr Evelyn, he owned the whole bang shooting-match. The associate partners were *consiglieri*; the managers, "made men".

I remember a friend at another family-owned merchant bank who, amongst many other clients, was also responsible for the bank's dealing account, and for a non-family board member's. He wasn't enamoured by this director, the task or the broker he was obliged to deal with.

One morning this director told my friend to sell a holding in a share that he, the manager, had bought for him, but on no account to tell anyone. My friend gave his word. Within minutes he was asked to go and see two other directors, one a family-member, who questioned the wisdom of holding shares in this company.

Since they weren't known for their investment expertise, my friend decided to ignore them but, puzzled by the whole affair, went to see the CEO, also a family-member.

My friend said nothing about the sale he had made, merely relating what had happened at the first meeting. The CEO stood up. "This meeting has not taken place", he said, showing my friend out.

Which meeting hadn't taken place, the one with the two other directors or that with the CEO? He never knew, but the next day, the company went into liquidation. Clearly, the director who had told him to sell knew what was going to happen, had betrayed his trust and defrauded his colleagues.

Reflecting that if his word had not been his bond, my friend could (should?) have shopped that director and emerge smelling of roses. As it was, having kept quiet, to this day he thinks that from then on, by those that mattered he was consider no more than an honest fool.

I remember being a regular speaker at the Australian Gold Conference. I had to tell the delegates my qualifications: My first was, I was a pundit: pundits are pundits because we give good quote.

My second qualification to speak to an audience which already knew everything there was to know about gold was this: I knew less than anyone else in the room about it, less than everyone in New South Wales, and probably less than the Princess of Wales too.

It was my ignorance that qualified me. I carried no baggage; I had no agenda. Freed from unreliable intellectual and emotional pre-conceptions, relying solely on my experience of what price tended to do, I was the most qualified person in the room to speak on the question of the day, how the price of gold was likely to behave in the future.

I remember at a meeting with Union Carbide in 1979 the treasurer telling me how impressed he was with my ability to make long-term calls. I asked what he meant. He replied that he and his colleagues had been struck by the accuracy of my calls for periods of up to three months.

Having been criticised frequently by UK treasurers for being too short-term in outlook, naturally I was interested to know what he meant by the long-term. His answer, "in FX markets, three weeks is the long-term".

I remember the lady-client who told Sir Sigmund Warburg, one of the founding uncles (not a misprint for fathers; at SG Warburg the founders were always known as uncles) how disappointed she was with her purchase of one of the in-house funds. "How long have you held it", asked Sir Sigmund. "Five years", she said. "But you bought it for the long-term", he replied.

I remember my brother telephoning me: "Isn't it lucky we didn't inherit £4,000,000 each?" "Why?" "We'd have done it in at Lloyds!"

I remember being approached by a friend, who worked at Rothschild. They were looking for a fund manager. I was lunched at the Savoy by James Joll and Jacob Rothschild. The waiter suggested melon, Charentais or Ogen, explaining that the latter was Israeli; which I knew.

Morton's Fork: was I to appear anti-Zionist (which I'm not) or a creep? I opted for the latter. "Thank you", said Jacob. Immediately I had visions of thousands of hectares in Israel with Ogen melons coming out of the ground already stamped "Rothschild".

I remember Gordon Brown won't wear evening dress when everyone else does: isn't the mark of a gentleman that he doesn't do anything that offends his peers?

I remember the senior partner in one of the firms I worked for in the 1950s going to a dinner at the Guildhall. The invitation said "Evening Dress, Decorations". He wore a dinner jacket, and his medals, a social solecism at the time. Until the end of his life and, as from now apparently, in the thereafter, he was known as dinner-coat.

I remember the late 1970s as though it were yesterday; my problem is I can't remember yesterday. I was a broker at the time, and although by then I had already survived two broking partnerships in other houses, or maybe because I had survived, but only just, I had no desire ever to be a partner again: I didn't want to have to accept personal unlimited liability for the actions of 26 partners, none of whom I knew. How can you trust your life to a load of strangers?

The only good thing that unlimited liability ever did for me was stop me becoming a name at Lloyds. Had I done so, it would have done for me.

I remember, when NMR was considering my bona fides before employing me, I wrote to Evelyn de Rothschild, telling him what I earned. It was so much that I never expected to hear anything. I was wrong. A meeting followed. He tapped my letter, "to get in the ball park I suppose we have to match this". I couldn't believe it; I was home and dry, also sweaty, from nerves.

Evelyn leaned over his vast desk in his vast office and asked if he intimidated me. My glasses were steamed up, I was so nervous. "Of course you do" I replied, "look at my glasses". "You'll do very well here, you've got a good Jewish sense of humour and people will like you". "Not when they learn what you're paying me, they won't". "Why should that be?" "You're a Rothschild, you wouldn't understand; they'll hate me". They did; they got rid of me.

I remember being a consultant to a broking firm when I decided to start a foreign exchange service. Brokerages were and still are renowned for their inability to have anything but a short-term view and the partners were no exception: they offered a 10% increase on what I was earning. I suggested they write the service, which they couldn't, so a deal grossly favourable to them was struck, including their insistence on taking 100% of the fee on the one client already signed.

The partners had been horrified, in any case that I was going to charge any fee at all: brokers give their advice for nothing in the hope of receiving commission on any transaction (hence the expression, advice given for nothing is worth what you pay for it).

After a year I suggested a revision of our agreement. The initial reply was, "I was expensive", the fees from the first client had been insufficient to pay the expenses involved in producing the service. By then I had 57 clients.

I remember Grant Manheim, whose father sold him into bondage at NM Rothschild & Sons. More correctly, he was apprenticed to Evelyn & Jacob Rothschild over lunch or dinner at a smart New York restaurant.

In 1981, at the height of the "names" bubble, Grant did me the most enormous favour. I had asked him if I should sign up for Lloyds. "Don't do it, Brian. It's not for nice Jewish boys: it's an upper class British rip-off! If you want tax losses I'll find you some oil-leases". I asked Grant if he couldn't find me investments that made profits. How unsophisticated can you get?

I remember at NMR you didn't have to be Jewish to get a kosher turkey, but once you had accepted a non-kosher bird you couldn't switch at any succeeding Christmas unless you could prove you'd converted to Judaism in the interim.

Why should you want to? Because kosher turkeys have had their claws and lower legs removed along with the innards: they're oven-ready. Naturally, non-Jewish colleagues saw the advantage of being Jewish, at least at Christmas. But since that's a contradiction in terms, they weren't able to.

I remember, being asked at NMR to price the shares of a meat producer for an IPO managed by NMR It wasn't hard: there were already three similar quoted companies. At 16/- I was prepared to underwrite the issue; at 16/3, 50% of it; at 16/6, 25%. At any level above that, zero.

The offer for sale was priced at 20/-; closed 1½ times oversubscribed; went to a 4/- discount. Months later when it had recovered to the issue price, I was going to buy the last 500,000 shares left in the bank, but changed my mind when they were offered. Discretion is the better part.......etc.

But it didn't do me any good. The executive who had priced the issue so badly switched jobs, becoming my boss. In due course he sacked me.

I remember 1997. The Financial Times World Gold Conference in Istanbul. Everyone in the industry was bullish: they have to be, I suppose – they're in it. The consensus was that gold, $350 at the time, would be $850 by the millennium. How bullish can you get?

I spoiled the party; forecasting a big fall. Gold had just broken down from a 12-year wide triangle, the inference being a further decline to $150.

Source: CQG, Inc. © 2006 All rights reserved worldwide.
www.cqg.com

Gold never got below $250, but I got to change my mind in time. One thing I never got however was another invitation to speak at an FT gold conference. Virtue is not only its own reward but also its only one. People don't want you to be right, just to tell them what they want to hear.

Gold at $850? It didn't get there by the last millennium, or in the 1999-2006 bull market, which most people apparently think is still going on; a very good reason why it ended last May. Maybe they meant by the next millennium.

I remember the senior partner of one of my employers. He was the king of the front-runners.

I remember the senior partner of another firm. He couldn't run because he always drank a bottle of brandy at breakfast. He once got so annoyed with his partner, Bill Citron, who, was making far more money short-term trading than he was, that he instructed his dealer to follow Bill round the House, as the Stock Exchange trading floor was called, and buy and sell everything that he did.

The plan failed. When reconciling the day's bargains, the senior partner discovered he was long ICI, Bill wasn't. He had gone long, but while the dealer was busy replicating the bargain, a process lasting only a few seconds, Bill changed his mind and covered the position. "You've got to be flexible, old man," was Bill's watchword. Later I went into partnership with him, but he was too flexible for my temperament. Nevertheless, he was a brave speculator.

I remember becoming a consultant. A consultant is asked for his expert opinion, but when he gives it, particularly if his expertise is in technical analysis, he might be listened to, but his opinion won't be acted on unless it happens to coincide with that already held by the questioner. Why become a consultant? Because it's indoor work, no heavy lifting, and you can have lunch with your friends.

I remember the broking firm where I was first a consultant. The gold analyst, having chosen the constituents himself, created his own gold share index. But no one, not even its creator, had ever seen it; the index existed only in a large computer.

Purely as an exercise I drew the chart of that gold share index; computers couldn't draw charts in those days, and a chartist's lot was not a happy one, merely a very busy one. Even though no dealer in gold shares, nobody at all, in fact, had ever set eyes on it, the chart showed all the things technicians expect to see; patterns, support & resistance-points etc, while if you had a pencil, you could draw trend lines and channels to your (c)heart's content.

What does that demonstrate? Although they may not know it, people think in parallel lines. Why, who cares? Until I drew it, no one had seen that previously un-drawn chart, yet it still behaved like the chart it had only just become.

I remember the brokerage where I was a consultant jibbing at my expenses for a trip to the USA to market the foreign exchange service: I had claimed £5.00 for "papers to read on the plane" (I flew on a Sunday to cut down on the time I was going to be away). During the working week I was there, I saw 27 potential clients: several became actual ones. I resigned and founded Brian Marber & Co.

I remember as a partner in another broking firm, discovering that one of the major merchant banks we were taking orders from had a crooked dealing-room manager. I told my partners we must tell the directors. They wouldn't. I resigned my partnership.

I remember the day my publishers, Harriman House, contacted me about writing this book. They didn't want another book on the rules of technical analysis, which was good news: I didn't want to write one. They didn't want me to fight the battle of Agincourt over the old territory of technical versus fundamental analysis. It was won long ago; otherwise I wouldn't be a technician.

What Harriman wanted was a plain man's guide to the things I've found useful; the reasons I find them useful; how I use them. This would involve me writing about my attitude to the market; my feelings about the awesome, awful but endlessly fascinating beast that is the market; reminiscing about 51 years in the business with no time off for good behaviour.

I remember the best advice I ever gave. A younger colleague wasn't finding favour with the head of the department: he wasn't grey enough for him. I told this extremely bright young man that the City was a lousy place to make a lot of money and that he should give it up and do something intelligent like become a barrister.

He became a barrister, a Q.C, a High Court judge, and is now a Lord of Appeal. He tells everyone that it was all due to me. I like that; a lot.

I remember wanting to be a stage performer, I like making people laugh more than I like making them money: "Nothing's funnier than Brian Marber trying to make people money", someone said unkindly; yet I must have succeeded from time to time because I've survived.

I wouldn't have minded being a brilliant stock-picker. But you've got to play the hand you're dealt.

I remember wondering if I could write this book. Now that I've finished writing it, I'm still wondering.

Index

A

B

C

Cable 4, 188

Call xx, 4, 9, 23, 39, 73, 76, 98, 128, 138, 140, 152, 162, 170, 185, 190, 241-244, 256-258, 267-270, 275, 277, 290-291, 294, 296, 308, 310, 317

Candlestick chart 42, 58, 199-202, 221-225

Candlesticks xvi, 197-227

Cassandra 4, 15, 74

Chancellor of the Exchequer 23

Charting 3, 4, 162, 199, 218

Churchill, Winston 14, 89, 161, 242, 258

Closing 5-10, 18, 38-39, 42-43, 123, 199-201, 204, 207-208, 211, 225, 242, 263

CNBC xvii, xxv

Coggan, Philip 172

Coppock Indicator 168-169, 267, 270, 273, 276

Coppock Signals 171-172

Coppock, Edwin 168, 170, 276

Cornfeld, Bernie xx, 258

Correlations 5, 161

Cover 6, 60, 182-185, 193, 211, 242

Crowd xiii, xiv, 6, 20, 87, 128

D

Daily Telegraph 91

Dark Cloud Cover 211

Day trading 58

Dead Cross 108-109, 297-298

Dealer 6, 25, 40, 128, 188, 323

Dealers' remorse 6, 109, 264

Descending right angle triangle 147

Diamond, The 129-130

DJIA/gold 247-248

Doji 201, 204-205, 210-217, 220-222, 226-227

Double Tops and Bottoms 131, 135

Dow 2, 6-7, 14-18, 21-23, 34, 42-44, 117, 168, 247-250

Dow Jones Industrial Average 18, 22-23, 168, 249

Dow, Charles 6-7, 16, 21, 42-44, 117

Down market 176

Down-trend lines 62, 63

E

F

G

H

I

J

K

L

M

N

O

P

R

S